SHADES OF GREEN

Shades of Green

Business, Regulation, and Environment

NEIL GUNNINGHAM

ROBERT A. KAGAN

DOROTHY THORNTON

STANFORD LAW AND POLITICS

An imprint of Stanford University Press • Stanford, California

Stanford University Press
Stanford, California
© 2003 by the Board of Trustees of the
Leland Stanford Junior University
Printed in the United States of America

Library of Congress Cataloging-in-Publication Data

Gunningham, Neil.
Shades of green : business, regulation, and environment / Neil Gunningham,
Robert A. Kagan, and Dorothy Thornton.
    p. cm.
Includes bibliographical references and index.
ISBN 0-8047-4806-3 (alk. paper) —
ISBN 0-8047-4852-7 (paper : alk. paper)
    1. Wood-pulp industry—Environmental aspects.   2. Wood-pulp
industry—Law and legislation.   I. Kagan, Robert A.   II. Thornton, Dorothy.
III. Title.

HD9769.W52 G86   2003
338.4'767612—dc21
                                                                        2003011529

Original printing 2003

Last figure below indicates year of this printing:
12   11   10   09   08   07   06   05   04   03

Designed and typeset at Stanford University Press in 10/13 Minion

Acknowledgments

This book was made possible by the generous contributions of a number of people. Most important are the corporate officials who gave of their time and insight to explain their companies' environmental behavior, and the regulators and environmental activists who made themselves (and their records) available to us. We are also grateful to the many corporate and trade association officials, consultants, and financial analysts who provided general insight into the industry as a whole. Our pledge of confidentiality constrains us from naming many of the subjects of our gratitude.

We extend special thanks to Magali Delmas, Cary Coglianese, Michael Hanemann, Kathryn Harrison, Bill Howard, Jessica Landman, Aseem Prakash, Joe Rees, Christine Rosen, Keith Smith, Jeffrey Smoller, and Beth Vaughan, all of whom provided discussion and critique of an early manuscript. Jessica Landman's and Kathryn Harrison's formal notes made the task of revision infinitely easier. David Sonnenfeld's generous sharing of his knowledge of the industry and his comments on early drafts are also much appreciated. We are grateful to Peter May for his review and feedback on an earlier paper in which our research was first reported. We would also like to extend our thanks to four anonymous reviewers who provided valuable insights and suggestions for improving the manuscript.

David Vogel and the California Management Review provided funding for a workshop on Corporate Environmental Management, which provided a forum for discussing the study and its findings. The Center for the Study of Law and Society at the University of California at Berkeley housed the research project. And research help was provided by Biyi Adesina.

Portions of this work first appeared in Law and Society Review, vol. 37, no. 1 (2003) and are reprinted by permission of the Law and Society Association.

Parts of Chapters 3–5 were first published as "Social License and Environmental Protection: Why Businesses Go Beyond Compliance," CARR Discussion Paper, Centre for Analysis of Risk and Regulation, London School of Economics and Political Science, Houghton Street, London WC2A 2AE, United Kingdom.

Contents

Figures and Tables

Abbreviations

AOX	adsorbable organic halides
BAT	best available technology
BC	British Columbia
BOD	biological oxygen demand
CDC	[U.S. Dept. of Health and Human Services] Centers for Disease Control
CEO	corporate executive officer
DJSI	Dow Jones Sustainability Group Index
ECF	elemental chlorine-free
EMS	environmental management system
ENGO	environmental nongovernmental organization
EPA	[U.S.] Environmental Protection Agency
GA	Georgia, state of
IPC	integrated pollution control
ISO	International Organization for Standardization
kg/admt	kilogram per air dried metric ton
kg/day	kilograms per day
kg/ton	kilograms per ton
NGO	nongovernmental organization
NZ	New Zealand
RMA	Resource Management Act
SMEs	small and medium-sized enterprises
TCF	totally chlorine-free

TRI	[U.S.] Toxic Release Inventory
TRS	total reduced sulfur
TSS	total suspended solids
VOC	volatile organic compounds
WA	Washington, state of

The Authors

NEIL GUNNINGHAM specializes in the fields of safety, health, and environmental regulation. He is currently professor in the Regulatory Institutions Network (REGNET) of the Research School of Social Sciences and in the School of Resources, Environment and Society (SRES), both at the Australian National University. His publications include *Smart Regulation: Designing Environmental Policy,* written with Peter Grabosky (Oxford: Oxford University Press, 1998); *Regulating Workplace Safety: Systems and Sanctions,* written with Richard Johnstone (Oxford: Oxford University Press, 1999); and *Leaders and Laggards: Next Generation Environmental Regulation,* written with Darren Sinclair (Sheffield, U.K.: Greenleaf Publishing, 2002).

ROBERT A. KAGAN is professor of political science and law at the University of California, Berkeley, and director of the university's Center for the Study of Law and Society. He has written extensively on regulation in the United States and on comparative legal and regulatory processes. His publications include *Regulatory Justice: Implementing a Wage-Price Freeze* (New York: Russell Sage Foundation, 1978); *Going by the Book: The Problem of Regulatory Unreasonableness,* written with Eugene Bardach (Philadelphia: Temple University Press, 1982; new ed., New Brunswick, N.J.: Transaction Publishers, 2002); *Patterns of Port Development: Government, Intermodal Transportation, and Innovation in the United States, China, and Hong Kong* (Berkeley: Institute of Transportation Studies, University of California at Berkeley, 1990); *Regulatory Encounters: Multinational Corporations and American Adversarial Legalism,* co-edited with Lee Axelrad (Berkeley: University of California Press, 2000); and *Adversarial Legalism: The American Way of Law* (Cambridge, Mass.: Harvard University Press, 2001).

DOROTHY THORNTON is a research associate at the Center for the Study of Law and Society, University of California, Berkeley, studying mechanisms of deterrence in environmental regulation. She obtained her Ph.D. in health services and policy analysis from the University of California based on her dissertation "The Effect of Management on the Machinery of Environmental Performance."

SHADES OF GREEN

1

Introduction

In humankind's struggle to prevent further deterioration of its natural environment, the capitalist business corporation—typically thought of as a major source of that degradation—holds one of the keys to success. Scientists and environmentalists analyze and publicize environmental problems, and governments promulgate environmental laws and regulations. But it falls to business corporations to develop, finance, and install pollution prevention technologies and practices. The day-to-day effectiveness of such environmental control measures depends on the training and diligence of the corporate employees assigned to maintain equipment, monitor systems, and take appropriate action when malfunctions occur. In terms of point-source pollution,[1] corporations have in fact made very considerable progress in the past thirty years. Nonpoint sources now discharge more pollutants into surface waters than do point sources of pollutants.[2] One might say that almost all business corporations in economically advanced democracies are significantly "greener" than their predecessors were a mere quarter century ago. Indeed, public policy analysts today often call for a "second generation" of environmental regulation that relies less on governmental prescription and more on the imagination and innovativeness of corporate environmental management.[3]

On the other hand, current-day corporations are different shades of green, varying considerably in environmental performance. They range from environmental laggards who fail to meet even minimal standards to environmental leaders who go substantially beyond compliance with legal standards, with the large majority located at some point between these two poles. Understanding the *reasons* for this variability is central to the study and design of environmental regulation. This book is therefore inspired by these basic questions: Why has corporate environmental performance improved over time? Despite this improvement, why are some firms better environmental performers than others? How, and to what extent, can corporations be motivated to go beyond compliance with existing environmental regulations?

These broad questions give rise to a number of more specific ones. For example, has corporate environmental performance improved over time because the march of new technology "automatically" improves environmental performance along with economic performance? Or has increasingly demanding governmental regulation been the primary driver of improved corporate environmental performance? Or has better corporate environmental performance stemmed primarily from the degree to which environmentally concerned communities and customers become better organized and more demanding? Or have social and political expectations concerning corporate behavior induced corporate managers to internalize a duty to make environmental concerns a strong constraint on the pursuit of profit?

Similarly, when one asks why corporations currently *differ* in corporate environmental performance, or why some firms (but not others) have made environmental improvements that go beyond regulatory requirements, one is again confronted with a series of more specific questions, each reflecting a different causal hypothesis. Are those interfirm differences attributable primarily to differences in the *external pressures* that businesses experience—such as (a) the nature of the regulatory regimes they are subject to, or (b) individual firms' economic and financial situations, or (c) the extent to which enterprises are monitored and harangued by environmental advocacy groups? Or are differences in corporate environmental performance more powerfully shaped by *intracorporate* factors, such as the attitudes and commitments of the managers in particular corporations? Or is the answer even more complex, involving various interactions between internal and external variables?

To date, social scientists have not offered satisfactory answers to these questions. The aspiration of this book is to take some steps toward providing them, for we believe that progress in improving the environmental performance of industry generally, or in redesigning environmental regulation, is more likely when policy-makers have a detailed understanding of how and why firms go about addressing environmental issues. At present, there is considerable uncertainty as to whether environmental regulation is successfully motivating enterprises or targeting the key environmental decision-making "pressure points" within them. And there is even less certainty as to how such pressure points might vary as between environmental leaders and laggards.[4] The empirical research and analysis in this book is therefore an effort to help fill the considerable gap in our understanding of the pathways to better corporate environmental performance.

Empirical Focus: The Pulp and Paper Industry in Four Countries

Any effort to answer the questions raised above immediately encounters a formidable obstacle. Adequate statistical data on the environmental performance of individual corporate facilities, particularly time-series data, exist only for a very limited range of environmental problems and in relation to a very small number of industries. It is even more difficult to obtain data that enable one to compare and explain variations in environmental performance among *technologically comparable* industrial facilities. For that reason, studies of regulatory implementation and corporate environmental decision-making have rarely been able to compare the actual environmental performance of different firms.[5] Our quest in designing the study discussed in this book was to overcome those obstacles to the extent possible, using a combination of quantitative and qualitative data.

Industrial point-source pollution, which has been regulated for over three decades, was an obvious focus for our research. Point-source regulations often require firms to monitor, record, and report their emissions of specific pollutants. We also opted for a sector-specific approach in preference to examining a selection of firms in a variety of industries, because the environmental challenges confronting enterprises and the actions of regulators are likely to be highly dependent upon the characteristics of each particular industry sector.

In deciding *which* industrial sector to study, the pulp and paper industry was an attractive option for a number of reasons. In every nation, pulp and paper mills, which historically have been sources of extremely serious water pollution and offensive fumes, have been at or near the top of the environmental agenda. Consequently, many firms have been compelled or induced to develop complex systems of internal regulation, facilitating our studying intercompany differences in environmental management and their relationship to environmental performance. Because pulp and paper manufacturers are closely regulated in many countries and jurisdictions, it was also possible to explore differences among different regulatory regimes and examine whether such differences elicited different corporate-level responses. Because the industry is carefully scrutinized by environmental advocacy organizations and local communities, we were able to examine the influence of these bodies on corporate environmental performance. Because pulp mills have been obliged to develop complex systems of regulation, firms seemed likely to have (and report to government) relatively detailed data concerning their control technologies and emissions. Because the industry's production technologies and environmental problems are relatively similar across firms and jurisdictions, we were able to explore both convergence and divergence in corporate environmental performance. In addition, the characteristics of being highly polluting, closely watched, and capital-intensive are not unique to the pulp and paper sector. To at least some extent, they are mirrored by other mature heavy industries, such as manufacture of metals, chemicals, and other commodities, and it would therefore be reasonable to assume that findings from research in this sector might generalize well to other similar sectors.

Within the pulp and paper industry, we chose to focus on one particular type of facility—plants that manufacture bleached pulp through a similar chemical process. Concentrating on a single technology enabled us to be sure we were comparing apples with apples.

We studied the environmental performance of a sample of fourteen pulp mills (see below) located in four countries, the United States, Canada, Australia, and New Zealand. Since Canada, New Zealand, and Australia generally are regarded as employing less adversarial, detailed, and legalistic methods of regulation than the United States,[6] the comparative focus enabled us to determine the extent to which U.S. regulatory methods provide greater incentives for (or impediments to) corporate decisions to go "beyond compliance" with regulatory requirements. We were also able to explore how community or environmental groups' pressure was facilitated or inhibited by different types of regulatory regime.

Our choice of four historically common law nations on the Pacific Rim was in part pragmatic, reflecting the researchers' particular contacts, linguistic limitations, and prospects for access and cooperation. Beyond that, however, although the modes of government and regulation of Canada, New Zealand, and Australia provided a valuable contrast with the generally more adversarial and legalistic U.S. regulatory style, the countries are not so different as to make comparison meaningless. All four countries have substantial timber, pulp, and paper industries. Each has a form of government whereby environmental regulation is divided (and contested) between the central and subnational governments, and this enabled us to compare regulation and pulp mill environmental performance in different subnational jurisdictions, at least in the United States, where we looked at two states, Washington and Georgia.[7] Each country has regulatory agencies that are generally knowledgeable and honest. The overall levels of economic development and political culture in the four countries are sufficiently similar for each to derive useful lessons from the others' experience.

Selecting Our Sample

Most studies of variation in corporate environmental policies and performance have relied either on (a) structured questionnaires mailed to large numbers of companies in various lines of commerce,[8] or (b) in-depth case studies of one or two companies, often selected because of their reputation for innovative environmental management.[9] The survey methodology often suffers from low response rates (which makes the data less representative),[10] from the researchers' inability to probe general responses for concrete details and reliability, and from variance in the industrial processes and environmental contexts of the respondents. The in-depth case studies rank higher in reliability but are weak in external validity (representativeness) and explanatory power.

In this study, we have charted a middle course, conducting interview-based studies of fourteen firms (manufacturers of bleached paper pulp) that use a single production technology. Thus we have sought to hold constant (more or less) the nature of the environmental challenges and the economic and technical constraints our respondents face, while varying their regulatory environments, broadly defined.[11] The sample is small enough that we were able to conduct lengthy interviews in person, followed in many cases by telephone conversations.

In determining the size of our sample (i.e., the number of firms selected for study) there were inevitably trade-offs to be made between breadth and depth. We were mindful that we wanted a sample size large enough to explore the main variables, but small enough that, given resource constraints, we could examine each of our selected firms in sufficient detail to explore adequately the key research questions identified earlier. We chose fifteen firms in all: seven in the United States, four in Canada, and four in Australia/New Zealand. One of the Australian/New Zealand mills subsequently closed before it was possible to obtain adequate data, leaving a total sample size of fourteen.

The total number of mills that met our study criteria (the same technology) in each jurisdiction were: British Columbia (BC) = fourteen, Georgia (GA) = five, Washington (WA) = four, New Zealand (NZ) = two, and Australia = one. We then chose all the available mills in WA, NZ and Australia. In GA, two mills were excluded for logistical reasons. In BC we deliberately chose one mill that was operated by the same parent corporation as two other mills already chosen in other jurisdictions, enabling us to compare the relative impact of corporate management and regulatory jurisdiction. We then chose one mill in BC that had a reputation for environmental excellence (as did one mill in each of WA and GA), and two mills in BC that had a reputation for being average or below average. Although we chose only four out of fourteen mills in BC, our sample appears to be representative. For example, in 1999, discharges of adsorbable organic halides (AOX)[12] among the fourteen British Columbia facilities ranged from 0.2 to 0.72 kg/admt. Among our sample of four facilities, AOX emissions ranged from 0.31 to 0.53, and the four facilities ranked third, sixth, eighth, and eleventh out of fourteen. While the worst-performing facilities in our BC sample are not generally among the three poorest performers in the province, by 1999, the range of AOX emissions across mills was small.[13]

Data

No single data-gathering methodology, we recognized from the outset, would be wholly satisfactory for addressing the research questions described earlier. For example, qualitative interviews of corporate officials depend upon information supplied by parties who, on occasion, may be reticent about telling the full story, and interviews at one point in time may not be reliable for assessing the effects of corporate environmental initiatives taken some years earlier. On the other hand, quantitative data concerning pollution levels are often incomplete, flawed, or difficult to interpret or compare across firms. Recognizing these limitations, we used a combination of soft and hard data sources.

In terms of *qualitative* data on corporate environmental performance, we conducted lengthy on-site, semi-structured interviews with environmental managers at each sampled facility and in most cases with mill managers as well. Our discussions were designed to elicit information about each facility's environmental management and pollution-control history, control systems, general approach to environmental problems, and relations with regulators and environmental activists. We probed for specific examples, collecting detailed stories of particular environmental, regulatory, and economic problems, current or past, that illustrated the firm's characteristic response to challenges. More specifically, in our interviews with pulp mill personnel, we asked, inter alia,

1. What environmental protection actions company personnel were proudest of and why they had taken them;

2. What actions they believed still needed to be taken and why these actions had not yet been taken;

3. The extent to which production and environmental management decisions were integrated;

4. How the company evaluated its environmental performance;

5. What specific environmental technology was currently in use at the facility, and when and why it had been installed;

6. What their experience had been with environmental regulators and inspectors;

7. What their experience had been in relations with host communities and environmental activists concerning environmental issues.

In most cases, we also interviewed officials in corporate headquarters, regulators, and environmental activists familiar with the mills in question.

We sought additional perspective on each facility through interviews with industry association officials, environmental consultants, financial analysts, corporate lawyers, other commercial third parties, and, on occasion, mill employees.[14] We achieved a high response rate, partly (we assume) because we provided guarantees of anonymity to our respondents and partly (we assume) because of the nonconfidential nature of most of the information being sought. In total, we conducted approximately seventy interviews. In a small minority of cases, where direct contact was not practicable, we conducted telephone interviews.

Drawing on our qualitative data, we were able to construct a typology of corporate environmental management styles, based on (a) managers' "expressed attitudes" toward environmental problems, (b) their actions and implementation efforts to meet specific economic, regulatory, and community challenges, and (c) their explanations for those actions. Based on these data, we constructed five ideal types—*Environmental Laggards, Reluctant Compliers, Committed Compliers, Environmental Strategists,* and *True Believers.* Each successive managerial "type" displays incrementally greater commitment to *compliance* (or "overcompliance") with regulatory requirements, *scanning* for environmental information and opportunities, *responsiveness* to regulators and environmental activists, and development of reliable *implementing routines* for their environmental policies. Chapter 5 contains a more extensive description of each type and our scoring methods.

In terms of *quantitative* environmental performance data, our task was particularly challenging. Because good environmental performance requires progress on so many dimensions, measuring relative success, even within an industry with comparable processes, is far from simple. The first difficulty is obtaining useful measures of progress on all relevant dimensions. It was possible to obtain only certain kinds of environmental performance data for some firms in our sample, partly because of differences across jurisdictions in reporting requirements. Secondly, it was difficult to *rank* facilities on degree of environmental success, since mill A that has made unusual progress on one dimension (e.g., reducing use of chlorine) may be only average in avoiding inadvertent leaks and spills that contaminate its effluent, while mill B, demonstrably a leader in reliability and better than average in reducing chlorine use, may have done a weaker than average job in controlling odorous fugitive emissions.

With those difficulties in mind, we obtained a variety of quantitative and qualitative environmental performance indicators, albeit not as many as we would ideally have liked. For a number of reasons, we focused primarily on measures of water pollutants. Reducing water pollution generally has been regarded as one of the most important aspects of environmental performance for pulp and paper mills. Uniquely among measures of environmental performance, comparable parameters are measured for water pollutants in different jurisdictions. Measurements of the primary water pollutants are based on verified methodologies, not estimates or self-reports or (as in the case of the U.S. Toxic Release Inventory) reported in relation to an arbitrary baseline. The same water pollution parameters have been measured often, over long periods of time. Finally, because most facilities only have one or two discharge points for effluent, total pollutant loads can be calculated for water pollution from each mill. (For discharges into the air, in contrast, each facility typically has a great many emissions sources, and not every jurisdiction requires the same pollutant sources at a facility to be monitored, so variation between facilities is sometimes attributable to the suite of equipment being monitored rather than the quantity of pollutant discharged.)

Although we were not able to obtain precisely the same environmental measures for all mills in our sample over the same time periods (largely because governmental reporting and record-keeping demands vary somewhat across jurisdictions), we were able to obtain data for most mills in our sample (especially for much of the 1990s) on the following principal measures:

1. *Biological oxygen demand (BOD)*, measured in *kg/day*, is a standard measure of organic pollutant content of water and a universally important measure of effluent quality. We were able to obtain 1998 and/or 1999 BOD data for twelve mills in the United States, Canada, and New Zealand (but not in Australia).[15]

2. *Total suspended solids (TSS)*, measured in *kg/day*, is the standard measure of particulate content of water, and is another universally important

measure of effluent quality. We were able to obtain 1998 and/or 1999 TSS data for twelve mills in the United States, Canada, and New Zealand (but not in Australia).

3. *AOX*, measured in *kg/ton of pulp produced*, measures the level of adsorbable organic halides (including chlorinated organics such as dioxin) in mills' effluent waters. AOX is used as a proxy measure for dioxins and furans, a family of persistent chlorinated organic compounds that accumulate in the food chain and have been associated with the poisoning of aquatic life, ecosystem damage, and possible human health effects. We were able to obtain comparable 1998 and/or 1999 AOX data for nine mills in the United States, Canada, and New Zealand (but not Australia).

4. *Chemical spills.* For seven mills in the United States, we were able to obtain data on the incidence of accidental spills of chemicals used in the pulping and bleaching process. Such spills can result in toxic water pollution and overwhelm a mill's wastewater treatment system, and they also are an indicator of the relative quality of a mill's environmental management program.

The Pulp and Paper Industry and Its Environmental Impacts

To provide the context for our empirical analysis, we provide here a brief overview of the pulp and paper manufacturing process itself, its environmental impacts (primarily on water), and the main regulatory mechanisms governing water discharges.[16]

To make paper pulp, mills take a fiber source, typically wood chips, and cook that material in a potent chemical soup, at high temperature and pressure, inside a huge vat called a digester. The cooking chemicals are sulfur compounds, and hence any releases to the atmosphere from these processes are highly obnoxious. The cooking process separates the cellulose fibers in the chips from the lignin and other naturally occurring "glues" that hold the fibers together. Once the chips have been cooked, the pulp is washed so that clean pulp, consisting only of cellulose fibers, can be bleached[17] and turned into paper products. The dirty wash water, which contains cooking chemicals and dissolved lignins, is sent to a recovery boiler or furnace, from which the cooking chemicals are recovered for reuse; heat from the recovery boiler is also used for power. Wastewater finally discharged from the facility contains organic matter washed from chips and pulp and the organic matter released by the cooking process. It also contains chlorinated organic compounds from the reaction of chlorine-based bleaching chemicals with waste organic compounds. There is also a risk that spills of chemicals that occur during the manufacturing process, if not properly contained, will escape directly into the environment or overload wastewater treatment facilities, causing them to malfunction.

Historically, pulp and paper facilities have generated large and very adverse environmental impacts. In the United States, analyses of all-industry toxic release inventory data identified the pulp and paper industry as the third most serious polluter. In the 1960s, the discharge of pulp mill wastes into surrounding waters "created severely anoxic conditions in the sediments and in the overlying water column."[18] As dissolved oxygen levels decrease, species diversity decreases:

> Low oxygen levels threaten the survival of desirable fish species such as trout, salmon, and bass, which may be replaced by populations of catfish and carp. If the oxygen level drops low enough, even catfish and carp cannot survive. In the worst case, when the oxygen concentration reaches zero for extended periods, no higher organisms can survive, and the only life remaining in the water consists of anaerobic bacteria.[19]

In the 1950s and 1960s, pollutant discharges from pulp mills (BOD and TSS) into water were sufficient to kill all species of fish downstream of the mill, leaving an impoverished ecosystem consisting only of worms able to tolerate extremely low dissolved oxygen levels. By the 1980s, however, all oxygen breathing life was no longer under threat downstream of pulp mill discharges. At one pulp mill in North Carolina, for example, dissolved oxygen concentrations in the mill effluent improved 91 percent between 1987 and 1995, resulting in an 81 percent improvement in species richness.[20]

In the 1980s, elemental chlorine bleaching agents were linked to the subsequent formation of dioxin compounds, which were believed to be highly carcinogenic.[21] In Germany, dioxins were discovered in disposable paper coffee filters, which led to a huge public outcry. Further concern was directed at tampons and disposable diapers. In the United States, concerns about dioxin contamination of fish downstream of pulp mills due to the use of elemental chlorine in the bleaching process led the Environmental Protection Agency (EPA) to publish fish advisories warning people not to eat fish caught down-stream of certain mills. In the past decade, however, changes in production processes—primarily the substitution of chlorine dioxide for elemental chlorine as a bleaching agent—have led to dramatic reductions in dioxin loads.[22]

Nevertheless, pulp mills today vary in the extent to which they have sub-stituted chlorine dioxide for elemental chlorine as a bleaching agent. A mill that has achieved 100 percent substitution (as some have in fact done) is said to be elemental chlorine-free (ECF). A further goal, recommended by some environmental advocates, is totally chlorine-free (TCF) bleaching. To that end, some mills have adopted alternatives such as oxygen, hydrogen perox-ide, ozone, or enzyme bleaching. All these methods depend on much higher levels of prior "delignification," achieved by technologies that reduce the amount of lignin still in the pulp by the time it reaches the bleaching stage. On the other hand, because differences between the environmental effects of ECF and TCF mills appear to be negligible, and because TCF processes are highly economically inefficient, many firms argue that investment in them is unnecessary.[23] Some environmentalists, however, continue to advocate uni-versal TCF pulp production, arguing that it is a necessary step in achieving the further goal of effluent-free "closed loop" production that will eliminate effluents altogether.[24] In the interim, environmentalists would also prefer to see development of pulping via wholly organic (and hence more benign) chemicals or solvents. At this point, however, those more ambitious goals remain controversial, both technologically and economically, and have not been incorporated into either general industry practice or governmental regulations.[25]

In any case, pulp mills still generate significant adverse environmental ef-fects. Even as environmental performance at mills has improved, our under-standing of more subtle environmental impacts has improved in tandem. Modern-day levels of BOD discharges are not nearly as oxygen-depleting as they were thirty years ago. But they still decrease dissolved oxygen levels and therefore still decrease species diversity.[26] Similarly, although modern pro-duction processes and secondary treatment of pulp mill effluent generally prevent acute toxicity in fish and invertebrates, field and laboratory research still shows adverse environmental effects due to exposure to pulp mill wastes. These include, in a variety of fish species, problems with enzymes involved in normal growth and development (including changes in the blood levels of reproductive hormones),[27] changes in secondary sex characteristics,[28] and changes in population structure (such as age at maturity and ratio of males to females).[29] In addition, changes in community structure, particularly declines in species diversity, have also been observed.[30]

Environmental Regulation and the Pulp and Paper Industry

By the 1970s, the environment had become a major political issue in many advanced industrialized states. Governments in North America and, subsequently, Australia responded with the introduction of environmental legislation and the establishment of more potent agencies to implement it. The pulp and paper industry, as one of the most visible and egregious water polluters, was an obvious and early target. In the United States, regulation was based primarily on the federal Clean Water Act of 1972[31] and on implementing regulations promulgated by the U.S. EPA and by state agencies responsible for translating the federal legislation into concrete results. In Canada, regulation was based on the 1971 federal pulp and paper regulations.[32] Australia and New Zealand imposed pollution-control conditions on individual mills through each facility's license or consent to operate, but regulations relating specifically to pulp mills did not emerge until the discovery of dioxins in pulp mill effluent in the mid to late 1980s.[33]

In all of these countries, the principal statutory approach was some variation on the requirement to introduce the "best available technology" (often qualified by economic considerations). The U.S. Clean Water Act, for example, required the achievement of "best available technology economically achievable" by 1983. As implemented, however, direct governmental regulation of the point-source pollutant emitted by pulp mills depended in large measure on the terms of the permits (consent or license), which generally established emission standards for each pollutant, perhaps based on notions of what was technologically achievable, but without mandating the use of particular technologies.[34] Permits are generally negotiated individually for each facility, often taking their particular production technologies, financial constraints, investment cycles, and environmental niches into account. Besides specifying permitted emission limits for particular contaminants, regulatory permits often required the pulp mill to monitor the quality of receiving waters and to undertake toxicity-testing programs. In many cases, the regulatory permits also include provisions requiring the pulp mill to conduct studies concerning its environmental impact or abatement possibilities and to develop internal control procedures and mechanisms for particular environmental concerns. Some permits require the firms to survey local communities regarding the facility's environmental performance. And most prohibit any significant modification of equipment or operations without first obtaining clearance from the regulatory agency.

In all the countries in this study, the principal burden of negotiating individual mill permits and enforcing their provisions falls on subnational units of government, while the central government generally dominates (without totally monopolizing) the formulation of basic environmental goals and policies. In Australia, for example, a very substantial majority of environmental regulation, particularly concerning point-source pollution, is undertaken at state level. In Canada[35] and the United States, substantial regulation of point-source pollution and related issues occurs at both provincial/state and federal levels, while in New Zealand, the administration of nationally promulgated legislation is devolved to regional councils. In Australia, Canada, and New Zealand, the political and administrative process for the development of environmental regulations has generally been more informal and consensual than in the United States, where the administrative rule-making process is more formal, adversarial, and subject to judicial review than in other democracies, leading to more detailed and prescriptive legal rules and permits (Kagan and Axelrad 2000). However, it is not clear, as will be discussed in later chapters, that those general differences in "regulatory style" emerge in all aspects of regulation within each country, or that they result in significant substantive differences in individual mill permits or in corporate environmental performance.

For the most part, the "first phase" of environmental regulation aimed to achieve end-of-pipe solutions (that is, the treatment and removal of pollutants from various waste streams after those pollutants had already been created). Thus, in order to meet performance limits, pulp mills were required to construct primary treatment facilities to settle out suspended solids in wastewater,[36] and in the United States, secondary treatment plants as well. While these (particularly secondary treatment) were expensive for firms, no major change in pulp-production technology was required. And the regulatory requirements varied significantly in stringency, especially for older mills. Thus while regulation in the United States was quite demanding, typically requiring 90 percent declines in pollutant loads from all pulp mills by the early 1980s, Canadian regulators established a much less stringent target for older mills and those that discharged effluent into coastal waters, so that even as of 1990, the activities of some 90 percent of mills were not substantially affected by the regulations.[37] In Australia, weak regulatory standards were coupled with outright exemptions in response to political pressure.[38] Moreover, the different jurisdictions developed generally different regulatory enforcement styles, with the EPA and some state regulators in the United States having a reputation for a more legalistic and adversarial approach to detected violations, while regulatory officials in other American states, Australia, Canada, and New Zealand adopted a more conciliatory and cooperative style.[39] Again, whether those differences in regulatory style (which in any event may be overstated) were so different as to generate significant differences in environmental performance among pulp mills, at least as of the end of the 1990s, is an empirical question, addressed in some detail in Chapter 4 of this book.

The discovery of carcinogenic dioxins and furans in pulp mill effluent in the mid-to-late 1980s led to growing environmental activism and political pressures, and then in the early 1990s to a second wave of regulation. In Canada, the federal government responded by promulgating new regulations in 1992 that provided for maximum permissible rates of release, not only for furans and dioxins (measured by AOX), but also for BOD and TSS, requiring coastal mills to undertake secondary treatment of effluent.[40] In Australia, in 1989, in the wake of environmental protests that successfully blocked the building of a new mill in Tasmania,[41] the federal government introduced comprehensive (and more stringent) environmental guidelines for future pulp mills and put increased pressure on existing mills to improve their environmental performance.[42] Similarly, in New Zealand, the Resource Management Act (RMA) of 1991 comprehensively restructured and integrated environmental regulation and imposed a number of specific requirements on effluent discharges (although only much later was a specific organochlorines program developed).[43] In the United States, the federal EPA in 1989 required state governments to address dioxin issues in any new permits issued to pulp mills and began the regulatory process of establishing a new rule for water emissions from pulp mills. The EPA issued the proposed "cluster rule" (covering dioxin as well as other pulp mill emissions) in 1993 and its final rule in April 1998, establishing emissions limits for AOX and dioxins based on the "best economically achievable technology" (which takes account of factors such as the age and size of equipment; the process used and potential process changes; and non-water-quality environmental impact). The EPA's cluster rule also offers pulp manufacturers some economic incentives, regulatory relief, and public relations benefits if they agree to go beyond compliance and commit to "higher tiers" of environmental performance.[44]

This second phase of regulation of the pulp and paper industry represents a convergence in all the jurisdictions under study toward quite demanding environmental standards.[45] Most strikingly, it has compelled not only the installation of more sophisticated (and expensive) end-of-pipe treatment systems for organic and suspended-solid water wastes, but also a major shift in bleaching technology toward sequences that no longer use any elemental chlorine. At the same time, in the past decade or so, the relationship between regulators and regulated firms has become more complex, as regulators have sought more consciously to encourage corporate environmental innovation,[46] drawing on innovations by environmental leaders and regulators in other jurisdictions in developing domestic performance standards.[47]

The Structure of This Book

The book is divided into three sections. Chapter 2 provides an overview of the existing literature on corporate greening and the trend to moving "beyond compliance" with environmental regulation. It shows that while there are studies that have documented how some corporate *environmental leaders* have instituted beyond-compliance environmental measures, there is a paucity of empirical evidence documenting or explaining how common that practice is, under what circumstances it tends to occur, or why, even in the same industry, there may be substantial variation in corporate shades of green. Chapter 2 goes on to outline a provisional model of corporate environmental behavior based on a combination of "external" and "internal" variables. Corporations are envisioned as subjected first of all to the demands of a socially constructed "license to operate," whose terms include economic and social demands as well as the demands of government regulators, but which are also subject to negotiation at the individual corporation or facility level. However, we contend that those license terms are interactive, often negotiable, and subject to varying degrees of uncertainty. Consequently, the attitudes and commitments of corporate environmental *management* operate as an important "intervening variable." Managers reinterpret and operationalize external license pressures in different ways, resulting in differences in environmental performance even among facilities subject to ostensibly similar external license terms. This interactive model is used to structure the book's subsequent empirical analysis.

Subsequent chapters report the *results of our empirical study* of corporate environmental performance in the pulp and paper industry. Chapter 3 shows how the environmental performance of pulp mills has both improved and converged in the past thirty years. Both improvement and convergence, we show, are closely related to the gradually tightening terms of the mills' regulatory and social licenses to operate. Governmental regulation has been primarily responsible for the large improvements associated with the installation of costly pollution-reduction technologies. And the expectation of periodic tightening of regulatory standards has been responsible for beyond-compliance investments taken in anticipation of those governmental requirements. Social pressures have increasingly operated to strengthen the effectiveness of regulatory standards, while pushing many mills to undertake certain beyond-compliance measures. In consequence, we found no real environmental laggards in our four-country sample and meaningful levels of beyond-compliance activity in most firms. At the same time, common economic constraints have kept environmental leaders from leaping very far ahead of the industry norm.

In Chapters 4 and 5, we try to explain the important remaining variations in shades of corporate greening. Chapter 4 demonstrates that differences in the "tightness" of different mills' regulatory, economic, and social licenses help explain some of the variability in environmental performance, but fall well short of explaining all those differences. For example, we found more variation in the environmental performance of mills *within* regulatory juris- dictions than *across* regulatory jurisdictions. And while mills owned by larger or more profitable corporations did better on average in some respects, they did not in others, so that economic variables did not adequately explain en- vironmental performance. Chapter 5 shows that "environmental manage- ment style" does strongly correlate with mill-level variations in environ- mental performance. At the same time, however, regulatory and social li- cense pressures have been sufficient to push even those mills we found to be "reluctant compliers" into compliance, and economic license pressures have deterred the most environmentally committed managements from under- taking costly environmental measures that go vastly beyond the industry av- erage.

We are left with a complex, multivariate explanation of corporate envi- ronmental performance, summarized in Chapter 6, which also addresses some policy implications of our empirical findings. In the pulp and paper industry, we note, governmental regulation has played an important coordi- nating role. Environmental law has focused, as law usually does, on defining minimum standards of behavior, but it has also encouraged beyond- compliance behavior. At least in the realm of control of water pollution, regulatory permits, rather than specifying the use of particular pollution- control technologies, have often encouraged firms to test and devise their own control methods. In specifying performance limits for particular pollut- ants, regulators have generally looked to the achievements of environmental leaders—in any country—that have demonstrated what is actually feasible. Put another way, environmental regulation has focused on the behavior of corporate leaders to define standards for corporate laggards, which it has then compelled the latter to meet. As long as leaders feel assured that regu- lators will compel their competitors to match their expenditures, they can continue to innovate, gaining some economic advantage by meeting com- munity and social environmental expectations, while achieving the efficiency rewards from moving ahead at their own pace. If their technology becomes institutionalized in law, they garner what scholars have labeled a first-mover advantage.

Environmental regulators also have encouraged leaders by speculating openly and formally about what future mills will look like, so this image of the future mill comes up for debate within the industry. No-discharge mills are currently in this category. TCF mills were too, but were rejected by the industry, and eventually by regulators as well. But it was the EPA's speculation about TCF mills and call for data that made the industry examine and support its position.

2

Beyond-Compliance Corporate Environmental Performance

Theory and Evidence

Why do some regulated enterprises achieve better environmental performance than others, going beyond compliance with existing legal requirements? What does it mean for a company to aspire to environmental leadership or "corporate greening"? How far might we expect business corporations to move in that direction? This chapter reviews the existing literature on these issues and outlines the analytical framework that we found helpful for understanding the environmental behavior of the pulp mills we studied.

Compliance and "Beyond Compliance"

The sociolegal and policy literature on regulatory administration has traditionally focused on explaining corporate compliance and noncompliance with existing legal requirements. The tacit assumption has been that legal compliance by targeted groups is the key to adequate environmental performance. And underlying that assumption is another: that regulated business corporations take costly environmental protection measures only when specifically required to do so by law and when they believe that legal noncompliance is likely to be detected and harshly penalized.[1] From the viewpoint of traditional models of business firms as "amoral calculators,"[2] why would a profit-maximizing company want to do more than the law requires, since environmental protection measures are often expensive and usually do not in any obvious way provide the company with any marketplace advan tage?[3] Thus for most environmental activists, law-and-economics-oriented scholars, and politicians, simply pushing firms into legal compliance is a formidable task for any society.

Of course, even in the implicit economic model of the business firm as an "amoral calculator," a firm might invest in environmental measures not required by law if such measures will increase its profits. If a company saves more in reduced waste than the cost of installing pollution-abatement equipment, for example, it makes economic sense to make the investment.[4] Yet until the past decade or so, politicians, environmentalists, and scholars, observing the ongoing degradation of the environment in industrial societies, understandably assumed that the opportunities for such "win-win" investments were few and far between, or at least not prevalent enough. Otherwise, there would have been little political demand for governmental regulation. And hence it has been assumed that legal coercion is necessary to compel the vast majority of corporate environmental measures.

Some empirical studies of regulation, however, have begun to paint a picture in which business firms display more complex motivations concerning environmental protection. Regulatory regimes in western Europe and Japan, which are less legalistic and less punishment-oriented than their counterparts in the United States, have sometimes achieved equal or larger reductions in pollution.[5] When regulators are more flexible in enforcing prescriptive rules, many firms have been willing to devise and invest in nonrequired methods of responding to regulatory values.[6] Sometimes, the firms do so because the nonrequired methods are more cost-efficient than those required by the rules, and sometimes because they feel it is "good business" to develop cooperative and mutually trusting relationships with regulatory officials. Not infrequently, groups of firms have institutionalized voluntary self-regulatory plans more stringent than those required by law in hopes of warding off the possibility of more intrusive and less flexible governmental regulatory initiatives.[7] And quite commonly, firms that are investing in new production facilities or pollution-abatement systems "overcomply" with current regulatory demands so that anticipated future tightening of regulatory requirements will not compel them to make costly retrofits.

In addition, many business firms have been shown to respond to legal and regulatory values for a variety of other motives, such as protecting their reputations and social legitimacy.[8] Hence many corporations take measures that are not legally mandated in order to avoid adverse publicity[9] or to win the support of environmental or social activists in their home communities.[10] Multinational manufacturers, it has been shown, often install and operate pollution-control equipment in their facilities in developing countries that is identical to equipment in their facilities in the United States, western Europe, and Japan, or at least more effective than demanded by regulatory regimes in the developing countries.[11] When a 1986 U.S. statute[12] required industrial firms simply to file public reports that detailed their emissions into the environment of various chemicals, many companies embarked on sharp reductions of their emissions, although not compelled to do so by regulation (Konar and Cohen 1997). To be sure, all these beyond-compliance corporate actions are not necessarily altruistic. More likely, they are based on calculations of what will be good for the company's bottom line in the long run. Yet they involve an economic calculus that is significantly broader and more sensitive to cultural and political values than the narrowly economistic "amoral calculator" model suggests—and they do in fact produce protective measures that go beyond the demands of current law.

Some beyond-compliance activity by corporations, moreover, may be motivated by a more direct managerial responsiveness to environmental values. Corporate officials and employees, after all, are not immune to the sentiments and norms that pervade their social and political environments. The CEO who vacations in the outdoors may come to care deeply about the integrity of ecosystems and seek to use his corporate power as beneficently as possible. A study of nursing-home regulation found that regulated enterprises' *attitude and sense of social responsibility* was a stronger predictor of compliance than their perceptions of the likelihood of legal detection and punishment;[13] one might expect similar results with respect to environmental regulation, at least for some companies. More generally, "new institutionalism" theories of organizational behavior reflect findings, as summarized by Mark Suchman and Lauren Edelman, that

> institutional factors often lead organizations to conform to societal norms even when formal enforcement mechanisms are highly flawed. Frequently cited institutional influences include historical legacies, cultural mores, cognitive scripts,

and structural linkages to the professions and to the state. Each, in its own way, displaces single-minded profit-maximization with a heightened sensitivity to the organization's embeddedness within a larger social environment.[14]

Finally, in the 1990s, the conventional wisdom that corporate spending on environmental protection will almost inevitably impose costs rather than benefits was seriously challenged. A variety of business strategists and environmental commentators, and, ultimately, some corporations themselves, argued that the business community could successfully combine the objectives of environmental protection and economic growth. This might be achieved by preventing pollution and thereby cutting costs and avoiding waste directly, by more effective risk management (including minimizing the risk of accidents, costly cleanups, and environmental liability), by gaining an increasing share of expanding "green markets" or price premiums within them, or by all of the above. In so doing, it was asserted, they could not only ease the pressures imposed by regulators, the public, and the financial community but also increase profits directly and develop the environmental technology to compete effectively in the global environmental market.[15]

Of particular influence were the views of Michael Porter, who argued that in a highly regulated world, innovative companies can acquire competitive advantages or cut costs by developing novel methods of reducing environmental problems.[16] Marketing products produced in a "green" manner might garner new customers in countries with large populations that valued environmentalism. Notwithstanding some differences of emphasis, a common refrain was that going beyond compliance was both good for business and good for the environment.[17] Indeed, one of the central tenets of a recent body of theory, known as ecological modernization,[18] is that economic and environmental imperatives can be reconciled,[19] and that there is considerable potential to increase profits by reducing costs, provided appropriate policy frameworks are established.[20]

In general, therefore, we can specify at least four types of beyond-compliance environmental protection measures by business firms:

1. *Win-win measures* that reduce pollution but are also instituted because financial analyses indicate that they will increase corporate profits (Porter

and van der Linde 1995a, 1995b). Among these measures might be the installation and operation of waste-recycling systems, which often can lower a facility's expenditures on chemicals and on treating and storing wastes (Reinhard 2000). Similarly, a corporation may invest in new production equipment that is simultaneously more efficient and less polluting.[21]

2. *Margin of safety measures* that overcomply with current regulations, much as a motorist might drive 5 mph below the speed limit on a well-policed highway. Thus many firms construct effluent treatment systems that establish limits on pollutants that are more stringent than required by regulations or their permits, or that have a larger-than-required capacity, in order to ensure that irregularities or breakdowns in the normal production and treatment operations do not result in serious violations.

3. *Anticipatory compliance measures* that overcomply with current regulations because a firm anticipates specific increases in stringency in regulatory requirements and it would be more economical to make the anticipated changes today rather than tomorrow.

4. *Good citizenship measures* that go well beyond existing regulatory requirements and are not justified in terms of traditional, quantitative analyses for assessing likely profitability; rather, they are justified on the grounds that enhancing the firm's reputation for good environmental citizenship will in the short or long run be good business.

Assessing the Extent of Beyond-Compliance Corporate Environmentalism: What the Literature Tells Us

What proportion of corporations have actually been persuaded to go beyond compliance with environmental law, to what extent, and in what circumstances? How substantial has the overall shift in corporate attitudes and behavior toward the environment been? Has the new win-win rhetoric permeated corporate boardrooms and produced any substantial change in industry environmental practices? Has any such movement been uniform, or have some corporations and some sectors become much greener than others? How far beyond compliance are firms willing to go? Existing research points to some interesting trends but does not provide any systematic answers.[22]

Certainly, there is now evidence of a widespread shift from resistance toward full compliance with regulation. This does not mean that regulatory violations are no longer common. Business firms are complex and imperfect organizations; pollution prevention and abatement equipment and preventative routines are subject to erosion, complacency, and breakdowns. Subunit managers subject to special pressures may decide to cut corners on maintenance costs or try to cover up environmental failures. Nevertheless, there is a general consensus that firms now try much harder to avoid noncompliance. Some scholars have documented how, since the 1980s, managers of U.S. firms have increasingly endorsed the obligation to comply with environmental regulations fully and at all times (Fischer and Schot 1993). To that end, most large firms with significant environmental impacts have built substantial environmental management staffs, established internal compliance auditing systems, and embraced pollution prevention strategies to help meet regulatory requirements more efficiently.[23] Mehta and Hawkins's study of fifty firms subject to the British "Integrated Pollution Control" (IPC) regulatory regime concluded that "the days of companies consciously polluting the environment for purely financial motives (because it is easier to pay a fine than the costs of compliance) may well be disappearing. Indeed, most managers interviewed agreed with the principle of IPC and with the broad aims of pollution control in general. Many also mentioned a strong sense of moral and legal obligation supporting compliant behavior."[24]

Yet that does not tell us how far beyond compliance environmental leaders have been willing to go, and whether most, rather than just a few firms, are willing to follow. There remains much disagreement as to whether or to what extent it is rational to go beyond compliance, particularly in the good citizenship sense mentioned above. For the view that there is a happy coincidence between private profit and public interest has been strongly challenged by critics who argue that opportunities for win-win investments are, at best, grossly overstated. Like Kermit the Frog, they suggest that "it's not easy being green,"[25] and they go on to challenge the new conventional wisdom as highly unrealistic at a time when "environmental costs are skyrocketing at most companies, with little economic pay-back in sight."[26] Their argument receives empirical support from studies that have found that in some industries, plants with higher pollution-abatement costs experienced lower productivity, or that regulation has diverted economic resources and managerial attention away from productivity-enhancing innovation.[27]

The empirical picture, however, is very unclear. Various indirect indicators of environmental strategy suggest that a sea change in corporate attitudes toward the environment may indeed be taking place. There is increasing evidence of (1) application of "total quality management" and "continuous improvement" strategies to corporate environmental management; (2) voluntary environmental audits and ecological life-cycle analysis of inputs, products, and wastes; (3) environmental cost accounting; and (4) industry-association-led environmental management certification plans. Corporate officials have increasingly adopted the rhetoric of win-win outcomes and competitive advantage.[28] Yet whether or to what extent they are "walking the talk" is not known. Reviewing the limited evidence on the effect of formal environmental management systems, such as ISO 14000 plans, Jennifer Nash concluded, "Firms that see environmental practices as marginal to their strategic and competitive objectives will treat EMSs as tools for external image manipulations and unimportant for internal change. Firms with strong environmental commitments will use EMSs as tools to become even stronger."[29]

Some commentators, particularly those within the "greening of industry" network, have suggested that business strategy commonly evolves through a number of stages as companies become progressively more environmentally conscious, with the leaders positioning themselves substantially beyond compliance with existing regulatory requirements.[30] For example, Newman suggests three stages in corporate development—reactive, proactive, and innovative—each representing a particular attitude to environmental risk and responsibility (e.g., reactive companies focus on risk, innovative ones on opportunity).[31] And Roome, in what is probably the most widely cited of the numerous models so far developed,[32] has postulated a scale of environmental strategies ranging from (a) noncompliance to (b) compliance to (c) compliance plus to (d) leading edge/excellence.[33]

The stage models, however, have simply assumed (or in some cases exhorted) an evolution toward excellence, suggesting that once companies begin to pursue a high level of environmental performance (with attendant

economic gains), this behavior will develop its own momentum,[34] "propel-
ling a company along a continuum toward excellence, albeit by necessity,
over time."[35] But Schaefer and Harvey concluded from a series of case studies
that the "stage model" of corporate greening fitted the facts poorly, and that
"more comprehensive and interpretative explanations of organizational
'greening' are needed."[36] Ghobadian et al. found that "the UK companies in
this sample recognize the importance of developing effective environmental
policies, but . . . the motivation for policy development is primarily reactive
and dependent upon the expected development of environmental legislation.
There appears to be little strong evidence of companies actively seeking environmental leadership."[37] Their overall conclusion is that "although there is
considerable enthusiasm for a proactive environmental stance in the literature, this message appears to have reached just a few large organizations and
even fewer SMEs."

Most of the empirical evidence that does support the proposition that
corporations are now moving "beyond compliance" comes from case studies
of a very few individual firms or multisector studies of environmental leaders. For example, Prakash's (2000) detailed study of environmental policy
decisions at Eli Lilly and Company and Baxter International Inc. found that
on some issues, both companies did indeed make large expenditures on environmental improvement measures that went well beyond compliance.
What's more, Prakash found that Lilly and Baxter instituted some beyond-
compliance environmental policies even though those expenditures did not
meet well-defined criteria for ex ante assessment of their contribution to
firm profits: "[P]olicies on underground tanks, the 33/50 program and Responsible Care were initially opposed by some managers since they do not
meet formal profit criteria. Over time, however, policy supporters succeeded
in convincing policy skeptics that these policies indeed serve the long-term
interests of their firms, although their profit contributions cannot be quantified."[38]

Yet one might legitimately wonder whether those beyond-compliance
efforts by Lilly and Baxter, two very successful multi-billion-dollar companies, are typical. Overall, only 13 percent of eligible American firms, and only
64 percent of the 600 largest corporations, signed up for the EPA's 33/50 pro-

gram (Prakash 2000, p. 135). In a study of over 100 U.S.-based corporations, including intensive study of 30 thought to incorporate "best practices" in their environmental management systems, Marc Epstein (1996, p. 239) found that while many companies often thought to be the worst polluters are progressing rapidly, most firms have a "compliance orientation rather than a planning orientation for environmental impacts" and there is surprisingly little functional cooperation between environmental and other departments.

A survey of corporations in Germany was similarly negative about the extent of corporate greening "on the ground" (Steger 1993), and the consulting company Arthur D. Little noted: "Although some companies are moving ahead with reliable strategic environmental initiatives, still others are backing away ... Why? Because they have hit the Green Wall. ... Early symptoms include ... deferred decisions because of reduced managerial support, and an inability to demonstrate return on investment in environmental programs"(Arthur D. Little, Inc. 1995, p. 2). This conclusion resonates with the argument by Walley and Whitehead (1994) that win-win environmental investments have become harder to find and have been oversold, and that the economic costs of making really significant environmental gains are likely to be quite high.

Clearly (and contrary to the assumptions of much of the business and environment literature),[39] while investment in beyond-compliance corporate environmental measures is a very real phenomenon, it is also variable. The questions thus become: How can that variation be explained? Why do some companies take the beyond-compliance path and others decline to do so? Why do companies do so for some measures and not others? As we shall see, no parsimonious answer emerges from the existing research.

Explaining Beyond-Compliance Environmental Policies

Internal Drivers: Attitudes and Leadership. Some of the literature on corporate environmental management implies that managerial attitudes and leadership are the key factors in determining the level of a corporation's investment in beyond-compliance measures (Hirschhorn and Oldenburg 1991), although much of this is speculative.[40] An empirical analysis of the greening of accounting concludes, for example, that "at an intuitive level, our inference is that the degree of response of the company depends upon the attitudes of the senior management, their responsiveness to employee, community and peer/business opinion and the extent of the pressure they experience from their holding company or the stock market ... typical factors like size, industry, country of operations or ownership or consumer orientation appeared to have little or no effect in attempting to distinguish between level of response by companies."[41]

Similarly, it has been suggested that management may play a crucial role in influencing how various environmental management tools will be deployed and how effective they will be. For example, while the adoption of environmental codes of practice and environmental management systems might serve to embed various environmental practices[42] and "lock in" cultural change and continuous improvement, it is by no means clear that they can do so in the absence of committed environmental management. Jennifer Nash's study of sixteen firms participating in the chemical industry's Responsible Care program lends substance to such speculations.[43] She found that participation in Responsible Care dramatically changed the way of thinking of three of the firms and was a useful and important safety health and environment tool in another three. But in ten of the firms, Responsible Care did not significantly change internal behavior. This suggests that corporate managerial commitment may play a key role in determining whether environmental management systems or codes of practice have a real impact on performance.

What is it about management that may either facilitate or impede corporate greening? According to the literature on corporate management, a crucial variable in this regard is whether senior corporate managers perceive environmental protection issues as a potential opportunity or as a threat.[44] There seems to be no right answer: advocates of the opportunity viewpoint argue that companies in jurisdictions with higher performance standards reap a competitive advantage, or are at least at no competitive disadvantage,[45] while others hold that plants in more stringently regulated jurisdictions will be at a competitive disadvantage.[46] Hence management attitudes in this regard clearly matter. But what is never adequately answered by this literature is *why* some managers adopt the first perspective while others adopt the second.

In any event, some theorists argue that the key to corporate greening is individual environmental leadership at the top executive level. For example, Thomas Gladwin argues that in view of "inertial forces impeding adaptation toward greening," it takes "charismatic green leadership" (defined as including a force of personality capable of inducing a high degree of loyalty, commitment, and devotion to the leader) to bring about proactive corporate environmental greening.[47] For Richard Daft, too, significant corporate greening depends on "transformational leadership" whereby management teams are motivated by inspired leaders to "believe in the vision of corporate transformation, to recognize the need for revitalization, to sign on for the new vision, and to help institutionalize a new organizational process" (Daft 1992, p. 468). But while such leadership may be important, it is not obvious why it emerges in some situations and not in others, or whether leadership alone could bring about far-reaching change in corporate policy. Accordingly, others have looked outside the corporation for satisfactory explanations of why some corporations, but not others, have moved beyond compliance.

The Corporation's External Environment. Many scholars have emphasized the explanatory power of factors in the business corporation's external political, legal, and economic environment.[48] In his study of environmental policies in German corporations, Steger (1993) concluded that the extent to which a company was aggressive and innovative in adopting proactive environmental policies is determined by two "external" variables—(1) the intensity of the *environmental risks* inherent in the company's operations (which are assumed to correlate with *the level of regulatory and public scrutiny*) and (2) *market opportunities* the firm can derive from innovations in environmental protection.

The implication is that when (1) a corporation's current environmental performance does not pose significant legal and reputational risks, and (2) improvements, perhaps because they are very costly, do not appear to offer a win-win economic advantage of the "green-gold" type discussed by Porter and van der Linde (1995a, 1995b), then one would not expect to see the firm investing in innovative measures or even taking a strongly aggressive stance toward maintaining legal compliance.[49] Conversely, in Steger's model, one would expect innovative corporate policies when the environmental risks a firm's operations generate (and hence the legal and/or reputational risks it faces) are great, or when the firm clearly can make money by going beyond compliance in certain ways. But that theory does not tell us how far a firm is likely to go in reducing external risks when risk-reducing environmental measures will be very costly and unprofitable. And it assumes that both risks and opportunities are self-evident, so that different corporate managements presumably would respond in the same way to a particular external environment.

Prakash found that external variables were indeed important in shaping Eli Lilly's and Baxter International's incentives to invest in expensive beyond-compliance measures (Prakash 2000, p. 150). One such variable is *local community concern and pressure.* Companies respond to such pressures partly because managers and employees who live in the community commonly are sensitive to their families' and neighbors' concerns, and partly because local dissatisfaction might trigger tighter political and legal constraints on company operations. A study of pollution control in twenty-six pulp and paper mills in Bangladesh, India, Indonesia, and Thailand (Hartman et al. 1997) also emphasizes the importance of community pressure: the nine facilities (mostly in rural communities) that experienced complaints and pressure from local communities were found to undertake significantly more thoroughgoing abatement activities, even when formal regulatory requirements or enforcement were not significant factors. The intensity of local community pressure, as a driving factor, might be assimilated to Steger's emphasis on the intensity of environmental risks or the level of public scrutiny that the facility generates. But community pressure does not always relate to objective risk, for economically dependent or less-educated communities sometimes fail to take effective action against serious environmental risks (Foster 1998; Morag-Levine 1995).

Scholars also have pointed to another external variable: the intensity of the individual firm's *economic stake in maintaining a reputation for good environmental citizenship.* Different authors, however, have emphasized different facets of corporate concern for their reputation. According to Prakash (2000), managers in Baxter and Lilly pushed for participation in the 33/50 program on grounds that it would help their firms' reputation with the EPA, whose adversarial approach to enforcement they had come to regard as threatening; here, the firms' reputation with *regulators* was important, and hence the "driver," to use Steger's term, was the level (or character) of regulatory scrutiny. Yet one suspects that Baxter and Lilly, highly visible manufacturers of health care products, were also concerned about their reputation for reliability and integrity with their customers—health care providers and ultimate consumers. Companies with widely recognized consumer brand names often seem especially concerned about their reputation for good environmental citizenship. Thus some authors have theorized that companies are more likely to pursue environmental leadership strategies when they are particularly vulnerable to campaigns that seek to organize consumer boycotts of environmentally damaging products, or when consumers have displayed a market preference for those perceived to be environmentally benign. Similarly, some scholars have focused on environmental visibility as a trigger for corporate reputational sensitivity and a predictor of green organizational response.[50] (In these studies, the corporate economic stake in maintaining a reputation for good environmental citizenship is simply a more specific aspect of Steger's emphasis on environmental risk and level of public scrutiny as an external driver of corporate environmental performance). Reinhardt, in exploring whether or to what extent "it pays to be green," emphasizes Steger's market opportunity variable, highlighting the importance of industry structure, a firm's competitive position, and the opportunities that a firm has to differentiate its products on environmental grounds (for which its general environmental reputation will be crucial).[51]

Corporations also are influenced, according to scholars who advance "new institutionalist" models of organizational behavior, by what other, perhaps more successful, firms are doing on the environmental front. In many ways, corporations model themselves on others so as to enhance their social, political, and economic legitimacy.[52] As a consequence of institutional isomorphism, "organizations adopt many practices and structures not for efficiency reasons but because the cultural environment constructs adoption as being the proper, legitimate or natural thing to do."[53] Thus if successful competitors are adopting widely publicized environmental management plans or technologies, that increases the pressure for all firms in the same industry or community to follow suit (Cashore and Vertinsky 2000; Hoffman 1997). The widespread adoption of ISO 14000 formal environmental management plans by large western European and Japanese manufacturers provides one example; American firms, operating in a different corporate and regulatory culture, have been much more reluctant to do so (Delmas 2001). Finally, a more pessimistic body of literature holds that firms may be prevented from moving ahead of the pack on environmental matters by a powerful industry association. For example, an industry association may seek to maintain a common industry position—such as that totally chlorine free pulp has no environmental advantages—and then impose this view on firms that would prefer to take a different position.[54] In this view, if any industry member seeks to claw its way toward environmental leadership, or to market its "green" credentials, the others will yank it back down to the lowest common denominator position.[55]

Intra-Organizational Factors. Prakash argues, quite plausibly, that external factors are a necessary but not a sufficient determinant of corporate environmental investment decisions. Risks and opportunities, he found, were interpreted differently by different managers within the same firm. The relative skill of project proponents and skeptics in building supportive coalitions, as well as the attitudes of top management, were crucial in molding each company's responses to various issues. He found that another important variable was the *extent of change* a proposed environmental measure would impose on existing organizational routines and power relationships, making it easier for proponents to push for incremental rather than revolutionary shifts. And R. Gray et al. note that the most commonly given reasons for adopting a green strategy related to enhancing, developing, or protecting the core of the organization as a continuing conventional business.

Many other studies have shown a strong correlation between corporate size and responses to environmental and other regulatory challenges, suggesting that *intracorporate resources (both financial and human)* and concern about external reputational sanctions are important factors in producing beyond-compliance investments (Haines 1997 and references therein; Hartman et al. 1997). Most notably, Florida et al. have produced empirical evidence suggesting that organizational resources and *organizational monitoring sys-*

tems are particularly important in the adoption of environmental innovations.[56]

Other scholars have emphasized such internal factors as an organization's capacity to learn, its general operational control, its organizational structure, and the amount of spare management capacity, arguing that these factors may limit the strategies and tactics that are available. "[S]uch internal factors can explain a large proportion of the differences we found in the details of environmental management in the companies studied," Schaefer and Harvey write. "Companies with the greatest learning capacity and that are most aware of the emergent, processual aspect of environmental strategy may have greater success in adapting to the external pressure for greater environmental sensitivity" (Schaefer and Harvey 1988, p. 119). In their view, future research should look at the way in which organizations acquire knowledge, how it is distributed through the organization, how it is interpreted by organizational actors, and how it passes into organizational memory.

Interaction of Internal and External Factors. In a widely cited paper on environmental management strategies, Roome (1992) argues that the extent of a company's commitment to beyond-compliance measures will be influenced by a combination of external pressures and internal variables. Paramount among the former are regulatory demands and liability risks, market opportunities and constraints, and broader stakeholder pressures. But Roome argues that managerial attitudes also play an independent mediating role. Managerial inertia can lead to noncompliance. A reactive managerial stance will focus the facility's efforts on legal compliance alone, while it takes a forward-thinking approach to turn those external factors into "compliance-plus" and a truly strong orientation to quality and commitment to innovation to produce environmental excellence.

For Ghobadian et al. (1998), in addition to external pressures/opportunities and managerial attitudes, an enterprise's environmental policies are also likely to be shaped by "moderating" (i.e., constraining) factors relating to a company's *ability* (human skills, financial resources, flexibility) to pursue a more ambitious environmental direction. They argue that such factors "intervene between the external pressures and the capability of the company to address the activities necessary to develop successful environmental poli-

cies. The mediating factors fundamentally establish the interpretative framework that informs the decision-making process."[57] Based on a case study of
waste management and reduction in a large U.S. chemical company, Peter
Cebon (1993, p. 169) found that the extent of proactive (that is, "savings-
oriented," rather than legally required) waste-reduction efforts depended on
the skill and determination of in-house waste-reduction managers, who had
to find ways of making their proposals attractive to production managers,
shop-floor operators, or both.

Toward an Interactive Model of Corporate Environmental Performance: The Notion of "License to Operate"

Whereas the scholarly literature on corporate environmental performance
has revolved around the effort to specify various external "drivers" of corporate behavior—such as closeness of regulatory or community scrutiny,
threats to corporate reputation, and various market-based factors—in the
course of our field research, we came to regard the concept of "drivers" as
somewhat impoverished. It implies the existence of independent, unidirec-
tional, and unambiguous pressures, whether from regulation, communities,
or markets, which impact upon corporations with sufficient force that they
react to them. Yet we found that these external factors, rather than being independent, often gain their force through mutual interaction; that far from
being unambiguous, the responses they demand are often unclear; and hence
that they do not operate unidirectionally, for their thrust and content often
are determined by the way regulated enterprises interpret, confront, and
counter them.

The external pressures that push enterprises toward improved environmental performance can be divided into three broad categories: economic,
legal, and social. These categories are a convenient means of classifying the
expectations of various stakeholders. Economic stakeholders include shareholders (including institutional investors), banks, and customers. Legal
stakeholders include regulators, legislators, and citizens (including environmental organizations) seeking to enforce regulations. Social stakeholders include neighbors (the local community), environmental activist organiza-

tions, and the general voting public. We can usefully think of (and indeed industry itself increasingly thinks of) each of these expectations or requirements as terms or conditions of a "license to operate."

The concept of a license to operate, we came to feel, captures the complexity of the relationship between the regulated enterprise and key stakeholders in a way that the concept of "drivers" does not. First, the concept of a license encapsulates the extent to which various stakeholders can bestow or withdraw privileges from a company. It emphasizes that business is dependent upon, and has a direct relationship with, the various economic, regulatory, and social stakeholders who define, measure, and enforce the terms of the license. Second, the relationship between companies and stakeholders, as between many regulated firms and licensing authorities, is an interactive one, with many of the terms of the license open to negotiation. Third, the notion of an overall "license to operate" encompasses our empirical observation that there is considerable interaction among its three different components, which we label the regulatory license, the economic license, and the social license.

Traditionally, the notion of a business's "license to operate" referred only to the company's legal obligations. For example, in order to operate legally, a pulp mill manufacturer had to obtain land use and construction permits before building a new facility. It had to introduce particular pollution-control technology. Once operating the facility, it had to maintain certain process and performance standards (for example, concerning hazardous waste disposal and workplace safety). Together, these regulatory obligations and permits might be referred to as a facility's legal or regulatory license. Today, however, the concept of "license to operate" must include "economic reality" requirements such as the need to meet debt obligations, show growth in earnings, and maximize shareholder return on investment (or at least to provide a reasonable rate of return). The terms of this *economic license*—what is an adequate rate of return on investment or level of profitability—are not written down in detail like a regulatory permit, of course; they may vary over time, "tightening" and "loosening" with market conditions and each firm's economic performance. The economic license to operate is particularly relevant to the study of corporate environmental performance, insofar as it operates as a brake on beyond-compliance investments and expenditures.

In addition, the "license to operate" concept has been extended to include the demands of social actors. Neighbors may complain about odor, international environmental groups may demand the use of less hazardous bleaching chemicals, and both groups may threaten a variety of informal sanctions if industry fails to respond. An extremely serious violation of community expectations—such as a death-dealing explosion in a mill or a chlorine leak that results in severe threats to human health or to severe ecological damage, can trigger political demands to close the plant down. Even short of that, while the terms of the social license are not precisely delineated and may be subject to negotiation and manipulation, a company's failure to meet social expectations concerning environmental performance can impair the firm's reputation, adversely affect recruiting, and trigger demands for more stringent and intrusive legal controls. Indeed, in some instances, the conditions demanded by "social licensors" may be tougher than those imposed by the current legal license, resulting in beyond-compliance corporate environmental measures.

The regulatory, economic, and social licenses are monitored and enforced by a variety of stakeholders, who commonly seek leverage via the other licenses as well. Environmental groups not only enforce the terms of the social license directly (e.g., through shaming and adverse publicity) but also seek to influence the terms of the economic license (e.g., generating consumer boycotts of environmentally damaging products) and of the regulatory license (e.g., through citizen suits or political pressure for regulatory initiatives). Thus the *interaction* of the different types of license often exceeds the effect of each acting alone. The terms of some legal license provisions extend the reach and impact of the social license by directly empowering social activists or by giving them access to information that they can use to pressure target enterprises.[58] Conversely, a company that fails to respond appropriately to social license obligations risks a tightening of its regulatory license, as frustrated community activists turn for help to politicians and regulators.[59] At the same time, the interaction between a firm's economic license and the demands of social stakeholders helps determine how far a firm will go beyond legal compliance.

As noted, the terms of each strand of the license to operate—including the regulatory license—are often far from clear. Different corporate managers, we learned, may interpret similar regulatory, economic, or social demands differently. Moreover, skillful corporate officials can often reshape some license terms—by providing information to and negotiating with regulators or environmental activists, by engaging in community outreach and education, and by scanning for technologies and procedures that simultaneously cut costs and improve the firm's environmental performance.

While the license-to-operate concept captures the reality of this interaction between corporate environmental managers and the enforcers of the external license demands, it further frustrates efforts to find objective measures of the relative stringency of one firm's license to operate as compared with another's. At the same time, the license-to-operate concept provides a language for talking about both the convergence and the variation in corporate environmental performance that emerged from our research.

Empirical Next Steps

As the explanatory model becomes more complicated, it becomes more difficult to assign the appropriate weight to each external and internal factor, and the interaction among them becomes harder to model and to measure. Just as significantly, the variables themselves need further specification and investigation. What kinds of external threats matter most, and in which contexts? Since neither external pressures nor opportunities usually come in well-marked boxes, with clear dimensions and potencies, what determines how they are perceived by corporate managers? How do companies vary in *scanning* for win-win opportunities? To what extent can external factors, such as regulatory agency behavior and community pressures, be influenced by corporate managers? How do companies that do decide to go beyond compliance determine where the Green Wall lies in limiting the extent of those investments? How important are variations in specific legal provisions and in relationships with regulatory officials in determining firm responses? How important are formal environmental management systems in shaping firms' responses?

The answers to these and related questions do not emerge clearly from the existing literature, which is lacking in solid empirical evidence. As Gladwin points out: "[T]he collective track record of academic scholarship on the greening of industry has not been very impressive. We are dealing with a great paradox here—with one of the most important processes or transformations of our time being woefully underdeveloped in terms of theory and under-researched from the standpoint of rigorous empirical testing."[60] If we wish to understand the opportunities for and limits of corporate environmental leadership, therefore, we are still at the stage at which detailed empirical studies of variations and trends in corporate environmental performance are essential.

This book seeks to contribute to that empirical research agenda. As a single study of one industry, it cannot, of course, fully answer the difficult questions listed above. Our strategy, as discussed in the introductory chapter, has been to hold some of the "external drivers" mentioned in the literature relatively constant. Pulp mills' chemical-intensive processes generate visible and serious environmental risks, close regulatory scrutiny, considerable concern from local communities, and, particularly with respect to emissions of dioxin from chlorine-based bleaching process, attention from environmental activists. Organizations such as Greenpeace have attempted to generate consumer pressure for chlorine-free paper. At the same time, pulp manufacturing is capital-intensive and highly competitive, generating powerful pressures for cost-cutting by all mills—and hence providing a good test of whether innovation in environmental protection provides a competitive advantage.

In recent years, pulp mills have had a good record of legal compliance. For the most part, the facilities in our sample comply with the law, as specified in their regulatory permits. Thus the industry provides fertile ground for examining whether and how far firms are willing to go *beyond* compliance, and for determining what intra-organizational and external factors explain difference among firms in that regard.

In the next chapter, we examine change over time in environmental performance in the pulp and paper industry, analyzing the impact of the regulatory, economic, and social strands of the industry's implicit license to op-

erate, which together have both improved pulp mill performance and produced a substantial degree of convergence among mills in that regard. In the
succeeding chapters, we examine the extent to which license provisions and
corporate environmental management style can explain variation in mill-
level environmental performance, particularly in the realm of beyond-
compliance measures.

3

The License to Operate and Corporate
Environmental Performance

Over the past few decades, as noted earlier, the pulp and paper industry has gradually reduced many important categories of environmentally harmful emissions. For the industry as a whole, biological oxygen demand (BOD) in effluent per ton of pulp produced decreased 90 percent between 1959 and 1988, and total suspended solids (TSS) decreased by 80 percent between 1979 and 1988.[1] Between 1990 and 1999, British Columbia regulators report, the twenty-two pulp mills in that province reduced BOD emissions (measured in kg per ton of production) by 91 percent, TSS emissions by 50 percent, and AOX emissions by 83 percent.[2]

Mill-level data from our sample facilities reflect that industrywide trend in improved environmental performance.[3] Figure 3.1 displays BOD emissions per day (as opposed to BOD per unit of pulp produced) and production levels for the two mills for which we obtained the longest time-series data. In the late 1990s, a period for which we have good comparative data, WA2 was among the worst environmental performers in our sample, while WA4 was among the best, so Figure 3.1 can be taken as an indicator of the trend over time for our whole sample. Our sample also reflects the industrywide sharp reductions in AOX emissions in the 1990s. Even WA2, a relative laggard in controlling AOX, had 20 percent lower emissions, on average, in the second half of the 1990s than it did in the first half of the decade.

In 1998–99, none of the mills we visited in the United States, Canada, Australia, and New Zealand were regulatory laggards in the sense of being ignorant of, or systematic evaders of, their "regulatory licenses." All were generally in full compliance with their regulatory permits—which is consonant with the findings of other studies of the pulp and paper industry.[4]

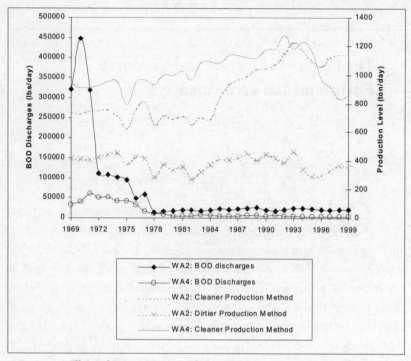

FIG. 3.1. Mill-Level Improvement and Convergence at Two U.S. Facilities: Annual Average BOD Discharges and Production Levels for WA2 and WA4, 1969–99.

What's more, in 1998–99, most of the mills in our sample were not merely in compliance with current environmental regulations and permits concerning the effluents in question; they also pointed out that they over-complied with a margin of error.[5] This can be seen in Table 3.1, which compares each mill's permit limits with its actual emissions of BOD and TSS in 1998–99. For BOD emissions, the nine-facility mean emissions of BOD were only 38 percent of the permit limits, and for TSS, the mean was 36 percent. Many mills also achieved levels of AOX control more stringent than current law required, and many told us of other specific beyond-compliance environmental protection measures their firms had taken.

Nevertheless, there is much that has not been done. While the above-mentioned reductions in major pollutants have had positive and meaningful effects on the environment, the remaining effluent, even from the best-performing pulp mills, continues to have negative environmental impacts.[6]

TABLE 3.1

*Discharges as a Percentage of BOD and TSS Limits
in Mills' Regulatory Permits, 1998–99*

	BOD		TSS
Facility	Performance as % of Limit	Facility	Performance as % of Limit
BC2	25	BC2	31
BC3	13	BC3	21
BC4	16	BC4	39
GA1	34	GA1	14
GA3	85	GA3	66
WA1	55	WA1	42
WA2	72	WA2	57
WA3	14	WA3	14
WA4	32	WA4	40

NOTE: The first two letters of a facility's name indicate its jurisdiction. Data are sorted by jurisdiction. BOD = biological oxygen demand; TSS = total suspended solids.

In their wastewater, all the mills pump tons of organic matter into surrounding waterways. All emit particulate matter and VOCs through their stacks and complex systems of vents. Even if odors have been reduced, all pulp mills (we can attest) continue to make their neighborhoods smell pretty bad. As of 1998–99, none in our sample ran a commercially viable totally chlorine-free (TCF) operation of the kind that many environmentalists had long advocated. None had done the innovative engineering or had made the very costly investments that would be necessary to operate a "zero discharge" mill. None, despite the hopes of some environmental advocates, had switched to source materials other than wood for making pulp or developed a consumer market for unbleached writing and copy paper.[7]

How can we explain this set of developments? What are the factors that have driven pulp mills in all the jurisdictions we studied to converge on improved environmental performance? And what are the factors that have imposed a ceiling on how far in the direction of environmental leadership the firms have been willing to go, so that none, despite significant differences among them in environmental performance, had leapt notably ahead of the others in terms of environmentally innovative process or product changes? The answers, this chapter contends, can be culled by examining common developments in the mills' "license to operate."[8]

To summarize our findings briefly, in the pulp and paper industry, there has been growing convergence across the countries and the firms we studied in terms of the regulatory, economic, and social strands of their licenses to operate. Multinational pulp manufacturers did not regard their *regulatory* license as being materially different in different jurisdictions. Certainly, they referred to differences of enforcement style and philosophy, but they also observed that when the regulatory license ratcheted more tightly in one jurisdiction, other jurisdictions commonly followed that lead. For example, by the end of 1999, regulatory licenses in all jurisdictions, by establishing demanding performance standards, had compelled pulp mills to install secondary treatment plants for wastewater, sharply reducing BOD emissions. The mills also had been induced by current or forthcoming regulations to substantially reduce use of elemental chlorine as a bleaching agent, greatly reducing dioxin emissions. Indeed, the expectation of gradually tightening standards and scrutiny has led most firms to a posture of overcompliance, adopting what we have labeled *margin of safety* and *anticipatory* beyond-compliance measures.

At the same time, *social license* pressures have intensified. While many mills reported that in an earlier era, social pressures concerning environmental issues were minimal, all mills experience some such pressures today. This has led many firms to engage in some beyond-compliance measures of the good citizenship variety, that is, environmental improvements that are not clearly justified by economic and legal calculations, but that appear to be good business decisions in terms of a broader concept of risk management that recognizes the potency of firms' social licenses.

But just as the regulatory and social licenses have demanded tighter controls on emissions, the *economic license* of firms in the pulp and paper industry has become more demanding, pushing all firms to concentrate on cutting costs and improving profits. Globalization and an extremely competitive world pulp market have diminished *variability* in the economic licenses of pulp mills. Institutional investors and financial analysts today are likely to judge all firms by common criteria, constraining how far firms can go in a "green" direction. Explicit regulatory license requirements have trumped economic demands, partially through the implicit promise that all competitors would be obliged to make the same investment. But the net result of accommodating to the demands of the three different types of license is that firms can afford neither to drop too low nor to aim too high: hence the considerable convergence in performance revealed by our statistics.

The Regulatory License: Driving Control Technology and Establishing Minimum Standards

To some scholars, government regulation is largely symbolic, enacted to mollify certain strands of public opinion, but a paper tiger in practice. Regulation fails, they argue, because of systematic underfunding of regulatory enforcement agencies and because of the subtle or not so subtle capture of regulatory officials by politically influential or economically important businesses, both of which lead to inadequate detection, punishment and deterrence of self-seeking regulated enterprises (Edelman 1964; Bernstein 1955). Even less cynical observers note that regulatory compliance policies announced by corporate CEOs are constantly subject to erosion in practice, as short-term production and financial pressures lead managers to cut corners on regulatory routines or lead employees to violate rules through simple neglect.

Drawing on the theories of still other scholars (Hannan and Freeman 1977; Aldrich 1979), one might argue that even if total pollution per unit in the pulp industry has declined, as indicated by the statistics cited at the outset of this chapter, it may be because the number of pulp mills has declined (due to mergers and closures), leaving only those operations that were already cleaner. Or one might argue that declines in total pollution discharged per day have occurred because daily production levels have declined. Or perhaps the decline has been due, not to national regulatory rules and sanctions, but to the development (for wholly economic reasons) of more efficient, less-polluting production or recycling technologies, or to social and political pressures by the communities in which pulp mills are located.

However, we believe that regulation does matter—and matters a lot. Surveys of environmental and corporate managers suggest that regulation is the single most important driver of improved environmental performance.[9] As in other studies,[10] our own data confirm that the regulatory license is indeed an important influence on corporate decision-making, and that pollution-reduction technologies induced by regulatory demands have been responsible for the bulk of the large reductions in pulp mill pollution reflected in Figure 3.1. At the very least, the regulatory license has established the basic floor beneath which mill managers do not want their mill's environmental performance to fall. Beyond this, the relationship between regulation and improved environmental outcomes is complex. This section describes more fully the relationship *over time* between regulation and the environmental performance of the pulp mills in our sample, taken as a whole. (The relationship between the regulatory license and *interfirm variation* in environmental performance is examined in the next chapter.)

The Tightening Regulatory License

For pulp mills in the United States, Canada, Australia, and New Zealand, formal environmental permits are complex and demanding. Although U.S. regulatory permits generally tend to be more detailed than those in other countries,[11] in recent years, pulp mill permits in all jurisdictions have come to establish similar principal obligations; they focus on the same pollutants, and for the water pollutants we studied, they result in the use of similar control technologies.

The growing intensity of regulatory license demands is suggested by a brief review of the permits for WA4 and WA2, two mills in the state of Washington whose emissions are traced in Figure 3.1 above. Over time, government has regulated an ever-broadening range of the mills' activities, and in considerably greater detail. Thus while the two mills' 1973 permits (the earliest we examined) contained eight pages of requirements, by 1991, the permits for both mills were twenty-eight pages in length. Both mills' 1973 permits established numerical limits for BOD and TSS in wastewater, required separate disposal of sanitary and industrial wastes, and established temperature limits for wastewater discharges. The permits also required the mills to file discharge-monitoring reports and a plan for control of slime in receiving waters, and to report any change in facilities or operations that would result in new or increased discharges.

By the time of the mills' 1980 permits, there were additional permit requirements concerning the disposal of solid waste, limits on foam in effluent waters, and periodic testing of toxicity of receiving waters. The 1991 permits added, among other things, mandatory parameter limits for AOX and periodic bioaccumulation tests for organisms in receiving waters. The mills were also required to prepare and file (for public review) corporate plans for dealing with a variety of problems, from the prevention and containment of accidental chemical spills to the reliable operation of treatment systems, the monitoring of particulate emissions, and chemical analysis of influent and effluent.

As this (incomplete) list suggests, from the start, but increasingly in the 1990s, the Washington permits emphasized the creation of mandatory self-regulatory, mill-specific standards and preventative methods, and the provision of environmentally relevant data and other information to regulators and the public. Moreover, the growing list of issues covered in the permits reflects a regulatory pattern of progressive tightening, beginning with the most obvious pollution problems (such as organic matter in effluent at levels that drive fish from receiving waters) and then proceeding toward control of environmental impacts or threats that are somewhat less obvious, more remote, or more complex to deal with. For example, until the 1980s, people were unaware of the high emissions from some pulp mills of the highly toxic and persistent organochlorine dioxin. By the end of the decade, the first regulatory steps to deal with dioxin and organochlorine contamination in pulp mill wastewater had been taken.[12] This progressive tightening of the regulatory license has been associated with significant improvements in environmental performance.[13]

The Impact of the Regulatory License

As we saw in Figure 3.1, two mills, WA4 and WA2, reduced discharges of BOD by over 90 percent between the late 1960s and the late 1990s. For both mills, however, the most dramatic improvement, accounting for the bulk of the reduction, was concentrated between 1970 and 1978—the period immediately preceding and following the enactment of the landmark U.S. Clean Water Act Amendments of 1972. Those reductions were achieved primarily via the installation of new recovery furnaces and secondary treatment facilities for mill wastewater.[14] A tightening of their regulatory licenses appears to be the primary reason that the firms installed costly secondary treatment systems. For example, in 1971, according to WA4's file in the state environmental agency, a regulatory official expressed concern that WA4's average and maximum figures for BOD were increasing, while dissolved oxygen near the facility outfall was declining. By 1973, WA4's new permit required it to "provide treatment and/or equivalent to all mill wastes to reduce the Biochemical Oxygen Demand of mill effluents." In February 1975, WA4 submitted a preliminary engineering report for the installation of a secondary treatment plant designed to remove 90 percent of the BOD load at the facility. Just six months later, however, WA4 expressed considerable concern that the projected cost of such a plant had escalated from $8 million to $17 million (the equivalent of $61 million in 2001). According the regulatory official's memo:

> They [WA4] indicated that their present primary treated effluent is not adversely affecting the water quality . . . and therefore secondary treatment should not be a requirement. . . .
>
> The major point emphasized by . . . [WA4] was the fact that the [regulators'] attitude on water quality seems to be one of simply citing the 1972 law [the U.S. Clean Water Act], rather than whether there is a demonstrated need for the treatment.

Notwithstanding WA4's concerns, the regulatory license had clearly shaped the debate. The issue had become, not what WA4 could afford, but what kind of treatment was necessary to maintain water quality pursuant to Clean Water Act requirements. Indeed, only one month later, WA4 officials acknowledged that there were no possible alternatives to secondary treatment if the mill was to reliably meet its BOD permit limits. Two years later, a new secondary treatment plant was in operation at the mill, and BOD discharges had declined precipitously from their 1975 levels (Figure 3.1).

The link between regulatory license changes, the installation of costly environmental technologies, and improved environmental performance is also evident with respect to reduction of discharges of chlorinated organics in the 1990s. In the wake of the 1985 discovery of dioxin in fish downstream from paper mills and considerable pressure on the U.S. EPA by environmental groups (including a lawsuit), the EPA announced in 1989 that states had to set dioxin levels in pulp mill permits (Norberg-Bohm and Rossi 1998, pp. 231–32). By 1993—just four years after the EPA called on states to establish permit limits for AOX—a majority of U.S. mills were substituting chlorine dioxide for elementary chlorine at a 50–70 percent rate, a degree of substitution that produced levels of dioxin below the analytic detection limits of the time (ibid., p. 233).[15] Thus announcements by regulators of the shape of forthcoming regulations have triggered what we have called *anticipatory* beyond-compliance investments.

When regulatory requirements clearly differed, companies responded differently. For example, the final U.S. EPA regulations on AOX were published in April 1998, establishing a limit of 0.625 kg/ton, to become mandatory for a facility only when it is incorporated into the facility's state agency permit. In British Columbia, on the other hand, a 1990 final regulation required facilities to meet a discharge limit of 1.5 kg/ton of AOX on or before December 1995, and to eliminate AOX by December 2002.[16] Consider the response by two facilities. WA2, a U.S. firm burdened with a particularly "dirty" pulp technology for part of its production, reduced its AOX emissions by 15 percent between 1992 and 1999. A Canadian facility, not in our sample, used the same "dirty" technology, but facing the more stringent BC standard, decreased its AOX emissions by 88 percent between 1991 and 1999, with the largest drop occurring at the first regulatory deadline (1995 = 5.37 kg/ton; 1996 = 1.1 kg/ton). By 1999, all the Canadian facilities in our sample were at 100 percent substitution, and all but one had installed oxygen delignification systems, whereas in the United States, fewer than half the facilities were at 100 percent substitution (one facility operated at only 40 percent substitution), and only two of seven facilities had installed oxygen delignification systems.

In 1992, New Zealand mills were using manual methods to determine TRS (odor) levels. The mills claimed that continuous TRS monitors were unreliable. However, on an overseas study tour, both NZ mill personnel and NZ regulators were shown other mills at which continuous monitors were operating beautifully and where "mill people were singing their praises." The NZ mills, having been told that the continuous monitors would be required in their next consent (permit), put them in ahead of that time.

In addition to inducing dramatic "step" changes in environmental performance through encouraging or requiring the installation of new technologies, the regulatory license, our interviews indicated, has acted as a strong influence on environmental decision-making at both corporate and plant levels in a variety of ways. As one corporate manager put it, "Regulation is the ultimate. You comply with the law." One reason, not surprisingly, is the infrequent but nevertheless looming threat of governmental legal action against the company. In the period January 1, 1975 to July 1, 1985, the U.S. EPA brought sixty-four legal actions in the pulp and paper industry, resulting in fines that varied from $1,500 to $750,000, with an average of $89,437 (Magat and Viscusi 1990, p. 339). In addition, some of our respondents cited the *personal* legal responsibilities of senior officers or managers, who in most jurisdictions are also liable to penalties as individuals (e.g., for failing to meet the standard of "due diligence" in the conduct of their responsibilities).[17] As one Canadian respondent put it: "[T]here is both board and executive liability, and the rules are fairly clear. They are just not willing to be liable. They make sure they stay within the rules."

Others were influenced not only by the threat of government legal action but also by their firm's vulnerability to individual or class actions by citizens and advocacy groups, particularly in the United States.[18] According to one company official: "In the 1980s and early 1990s, class actions claiming property damage and cancer risks were prevalent [in the United States] against pulp mills. In one case, a jury awarded $1 million. This prompted copycat lawsuits. . . . These lawsuits impacted on corporate thinking. We settled one because the cost of fighting it was horrendous."

Many of our corporate respondents also expressed concern about the informal punishments that might accompany breach of regulations or a lawsuit, not the least of these being negative publicity and shaming. "Compliance is the floor—it's not even a question for us," one senior corporate manager said, expressing a common sentiment. In his view, the damage that breach of the regulatory license and consequent adverse publicity might do to the firm's economic and the social licenses (described below) was so serious that extensive steps had to be taken to stay in compliance.

Finally, maintaining the integrity of the regulatory license was seen as important not merely to avoid enforcement action but also to maintain the trust of the regulators. The consequence of a breakdown of trust, one said, might be to have "regulators crawling over you like a rash," along with an inability to avoid regulators' insistence upon "strict" compliance or to negotiate "reasonable" resolutions to technical breaches of regulation. For enterprises did not regard the terms of the regulatory license as immutable, but rather as something to be negotiated. Building up "regulatory capital" (for example, by developing trust with the regulator and the community) was seen—at least by some—as something that might potentially pay considerable dividends in terms of regulatory flexibility. Thus one company official said:

> We take the lead with the [regulator] and we get the benefit of the doubt from them, which is worth megabucks. . . . If we want to try something out, they let us, We were able to get a bubble license[19]—no stack tests! We were able to take all the production limits off the equipment, and that enabled us to speed up because there were no artificial capacity limits. It was getting [the] trust of the regulators that got us the bubble.

Similarly, a good reputation with regulators, some firms believed, gave them greater credibility in negotiating with regulatory officials about the terms of forthcoming regulations.

The Social License: Supporting the Regulatory License and Inducing Beyond-Compliance Measures.

Pressure from social stakeholders affected pulp mills' environmental performance in three major ways. First, they acted as auxiliary and sometimes potent enforcers of the mill's regulatory licenses, pushing managers to comply fully with permits and sometimes to invest in beyond-compliance measures of the "margin of safety" variety. Second, on occasion, environmental activists helped bring about a "tightening" of regulatory licenses, either by generating political pressure for more stringent laws and regulations or by pushing for more stringent conditions in individual mill permits. Third, the social license was the primary source of beyond-compliance measures of the good citizenship variety.

The Salience of the Social License

The concept of a social license is of quite recent origin. It derives from several decades of growing social consciousness about environmental risks and concerns; from the large increases in information about corporate environmental performance generated by regulatory requirements for self-

monitoring and reporting; from the rising number of environmental advocacy organizations; from attention to environmental degradation by the
news media; and from rising community living standards and people's expectations about the quality of their local environment.

The social license is particularly salient for pulp mills, whose very tangible
environmental impact has made them an object of pressure by environmental activists at local, national, and international levels. They are large and
ill-smelling. They emit plumes of smoke and discharge effluent that can dis-
color local waterways. Industrial elephants, they have nowhere to hide. Social
concerns about pulp mills were intensified by a highly visible worldwide
campaign led by Greenpeace in the late 1980s and early 1990s, emphasizing
the threats to aquatic life and human health from the dioxin-laden effluent
generated by the use of chlorine as a pulp-bleaching agent (Sonnenfeld
2000). Local groups in many, but not all, communities have been very vocal
in their opposition to the pollution caused by pulp mills. The most pervasive
complaints involve the mills' pungent odor, but sometimes the threat to local fisheries is the issue, or the broader concerns of consumers about the ac-
cumulation of dioxins in the food chain.

Virtually every pulp mill we visited reported significant environmental
pressures from its host community. With a constantly diversifying economy
and a more mobile workforce, many mills that were once the only major
employer in an isolated "company town" are now surrounded by more informed and more sophisticated communities, in which they are not necessarily the dominant employer. Many pulp mill officials, accordingly, spoke
to us of having to meet the terms not only of their regulatory license but of
their "social license." As one mill-level environmental manager put it: "It's
very important how the community sees the plant—how they are thinking is
our license to operate." A mill manager at another facility said, "We have to
continuously convince the public we have a right to exist." In 1999, managers
at yet another mill told us that the sanctions they feared most for breaching
regulations were not legal but informal sanctions imposed by the public and
the media, and hence they were motivated less by avoiding regulatory violations per se than by avoiding "anything that could give you a bad name." In
the words of one environmental manager: "If you are going to run the mill
in the community, you have got to live with them." For example, he told us,

the mill chose not to appeal its permit conditions (a routine step) because managers feared this would send out the wrong message to the community.[20] The social license, then, is based not on compliance with legal requirements (although breach of these requirements may jeopardize the social license) but rather upon the degree to which a corporation and its activities are accepted by local communities, the wider society, and various constituent groups.

The concept of social license is closely related to the notion of "reputation capital." "[T]he social license gained at the project level creates value at the corporate level. It also becomes a competitive advantage. Reputation capital represents a communications bridge that predisposes NGOs, communities, and other groups to enter into open discussion rather than hostile opposition. Reputation capital carries with it credibility, such that the up-front costs and risk associated with gaining social acceptability are reduced."[21] Those with reputation capital, it is argued, will most readily gain access to the means by which to make future profits: development approvals; preferred access to prospective areas and products; the ear of government; the trust of regulators; the tolerance of local communities; and the least risk of being targeted by environmental nongovernment organizations (ENGOs).

One pulp mill environmental manager reflected the same idea—that building reputation capital is a good economic investment—when he told us, in the context of a discussion of local community environmental activists, "You have to develop the relationship in times of peace . . . [because] . . . when there are spills, tank failures, dioxin issues, it gets tough." It was in these circumstances, he argued, that the trust and social capital that had been built up earlier became crucially important. Building trust may mean disclosure of environmentally sensitive information, but whatever risks are entailed may be worth it in a challenging legal environment. "Citizen suits are a big issue—but if you keep your information secret, groups go dig through the public records, unearth data, and initiate action—if we are more open with our stakeholders, they are not as likely to put forth those kinds of suits," one manager said. "So the environmental community provides a valuable service to industry by setting the standards and rewarding industry for getting up to the mark." A manager at another mill talked about the pitfalls of failing to build reputation capital: "It works against you when things are behind the community's back. If you have a good relationship with the public, then the goodwill will be there, and when there is trouble, you will get the benefit of the doubt—you will have a positive bank account." Regretfully, he added, "We have a zero bank account, or we're in deficit." (One consequence was strong local opposition to the mill's current plans for future disposal of solid waste, which meant the company faced the prospect of having to barge the waste, at much greater cost, to a distant disposal site.)[22]

The terms of a mill's social license, of course, are unwritten, highly contextual, subject to implicit renegotiation, and fluid. They are influenced by changing events, flows of information, and regulatory encounters. The local community may be persuaded to be more willing to accept continuation of the mill's activities in return for greater inclusiveness and transparency and mitigation of some of its polluting activities. Thus some social license terms are procedural, dealing with modes of interaction rather than specific controls. (Cover-up and deception are the worst violations of this aspect of the social license.) Other terms are substantive, such as demands for odor or effluent control.

Increasingly, some procedural terms in the social license are mandated by law, merging the regulatory and social licenses in ways that bolster the influence of social licensors. Almost all our respondents in New Zealand, for example, emphasized the impact of the 1991 Resource Management Act, which gave individuals and activist organizations the right to make submissions and challenge any change in a factory's "consent" (the basic permit or license to operate). In consequence, as one mill manager described it: "It became a very public process. In 1994–95, there were 169 submissions regarding the mill. We had very strong protests. People were finally able to have their say. We had 32 people speaking at the public hearings." Most important, for any New Zealand mill, failure to listen and respond to community concerns created a risk of lengthy delays in obtaining the consents needed in order to introduce technological and production changes. Similar incentives had been created in Australia, too, where a lawsuit led to a court ruling that compelled a mill in our sample to establish a community consultative committee—which mill managers subsequently called the most important influence on their facility's improved environmental performance. In Canada, administrative and court challenges by a single member of the public had for many years caused one mill in our sample to spend considerable effort in justifying and defending the terms of its regulatory permit.

Similarly, social licensors have gained leverage from laws that increased transparency, such as the U.S. Toxic Release Inventory, which requires firms to disclose emissions and inventories of toxic chemicals, or the environmental improvement plans required by some Australian jurisdictions. In British Columbia, periodic reports published by the province summarize environmental performance indicators for all BC pulp mills and major infringements of regulations. These reports were seen by mill officials as an "environmental report card" and, in the words of one pulp mill official, as "a pretty effective tool. If you have recurring environmental problems, you come up on the list. It keeps you in compliance, because public pressure is more demanding than the regulatory agencies. . . . Agencies are more forgiving."

The Impact of the Social License

Different mills in our sample took very different approaches to the issue of protecting their social license and building reputation capital. One or two seemed oblivious of its existence. Some took a strategic approach, such as "buying off" the local community's objections to particular emissions by offering to supply it with better-quality drinking water or trying to "win hearts and minds" through public relations campaigns and by working in local schools and with local community organizations. Still others saw their social license and their reputation capital as central to their very existence, seeking not only to educate the community but also to work directly with local people, to be transparent, and to respond substantially to their concerns. Some gradually shifted from defensiveness toward responsiveness to community and NGO concerns, as in the case of NZ2, whose environmental manager told us:

> Ten years ago, we were reacting to threats from the public, from the regulator, and from the greens, and we didn't control the process. We built a virtual wall around ourselves and no one on the outside was told anything. Now we are going through a process of turning that around, of opening the gates, of an attitudinal change from inside. We went through enormous changes over the years, but we never told anyone, so the only story out there was the green one, that we were en-

gaged in environmental rape and pillage, and it isn't true. So we took stock of real threats, then took the brave step of talking about them, of saying to the public, this is what we've done and this is what we plan to do . . . once you start that process, people come down heavy on you, but you need the fortitude to keep going and be totally transparent—we'll show anyone anything Why? It's the right way to go. . . . It comes down to individuals and, over time, trust—listen and respond.

How did social license actually affect environmental performance? Attributing particular measures to social license pressures alone is often difficult. Yet references to the potency of social pressures permeated our interviews with pulp mill officials. An environmental manager at a U.S. mill, for example, said:

> The EPA is such a monolith it can't adapt. It takes a decade to get something to happen. The environmental community is really setting the tone. It's done far more to make companies accountable for pollution. It does more to keep me on my toes, to give me an incentive to go to my management and say, we have got to do better, because the community can sue us and also give us the biggest rewards.

As this suggests, the social license can make a difference in two significant ways, first by lending extra enforcement energy and weight to existing regulatory and legal license requirements, pushing regulated enterprises toward full legal compliance (and even to "margin of safety" beyond-compliance measures), and second, by rewarding, in terms of enhanced reputation capital, beyond-compliance measures of the "good citizenship" variety. (In addition, as we shall see, social license pressures can result in a tightening of the regulatory license.)

Social license pressures, our interviews indicated, have been a primary source of pulp mills' progress in reducing both the impact of foul odors from their chemical processes and other adverse esthetic impacts, such as discoloration of receiving waters and emission of plumes of steam. Although regulations limit ill-smelling sulfur emissions,[23] odor control may not in itself be high on a regulator's list, since its environmental impact is minimal (as defined by most regulatory regimes, which emphasize demonstrable adverse effects on human or ecosystem health). But in the case of pulp mills, odor is usually the community's highest priority. In some cases, social pressures drove regulators to use the power of law to demand stronger odor controls. Thus in Australia, one environmental manager described his mill's prosecution experience as follows:

> We have been to court three or four times and pleaded guilty. We have only ar-
> gued over the size of the fine. They were all odor-related issues. For example, we
> had a problem resulting in pulp going into the foul water accumulator and
> stuffing that up, so [that] it couldn't be pumped into the stripping system [and]
> was discharged down the drain. The nearest private residence is two kilometers
> away. The towns are five or six kilometers away. It was one of those still, quiet
> nights, and it stank very badly. It was very apparent what it was. There were lots
> of complaints to EPA. There was a degree of negligence, but was a prosecution
> appropriate? We were in a no-win situation. *If you cause odor in a residential area
> you can't win.* [emphasis added]

Even more often, however, social license pressures acting alone and directly compelled mills to take beyond-compliance odor-control measures.
As one mill manager put it: "We want people to know we are here, but not
through their noses." And so, for many mills, odor control became a major
focus. When officials at BC2 were asked, "What are you proudest of in your
environmental program?" the unequivocal response was odor reduction:

> We used to get 300–350 odor complaints per year, but now its down to about 50
> this year so far. We spent a lot of money to achieve this . . . $13M to put in an
> odor-control system that is not required by law. . . . But if there is sustained pub-
> lic pressure, we are responsive. . . . Our behavior is predicated by the feelings of
> the local community. . . . We have dedicated scrubbers and a noncondensable gas
> incinerator system, and we are running at a fraction of what our license permits.
> The driver is to pacify the community.

We heard very similar stories at a number of other mills: "We didn't have
to put in the stripper, but odor is the key to the community. We had a
problem with a particular source, [and] we couldn't do it any other way. The
only way was to remove it at source, but it wasn't a consent [permit] requirement."

A variety of other aesthetic issues also had the capacity to generate a substantial adverse community reaction. For example, some mills, such as BC4,
were highly visible to broader urban as well as local communities. For BC4,
which could be seen by thousands of motorists daily on a busy highway,
"The big issue isn't the regulator, its appearance, it's the steam coming off
the stack. This is 99.5 percent water, but it's an aesthetic issue. We know that

putting in condensers will cost and provide no economic benefits, but it protects our business license." According to the manager of a pulp mill in a smaller town in Georgia:

> A decision was made not to fight it as a battle but to understand what the community wanted and to spend money wisely to get the support of the community. For example, water color is not regulated and is not included in the permit,[24] so we could have fought about it, but we decided not to. We instilled in ourselves the viewpoint that we wanted to be a good neighbor, [because] it's the local stakeholders that give us the right to operate.

Whereas local communities often have made odor control and other esthetic issues part of pulp mills' social and regulatory licenses, activism by ENGOs has focused primarily on the use of chlorine as a bleaching agent and emissions of dioxin, leading to both tightening regulatory license requirements and beyond-compliance measures to reduce dioxin emissions. In 1998–99, BC3's environmental performance was excellent in all three major measures of effluent quality, BOD, TSS, and AOX. A combination of environmental activism and consumer concerns a decade earlier helps explain why. In November 1988, dioxins were discovered in shellfish near the mill. In highly dramatic public demonstrations, environmental activists targeted BC3's parent company, a forestry company, and BC3 itself. At the same time, environmental activists had been generating political pressures in British Columbia. As noted earlier, in May 1989, the provincial environmental ministry announced tighter BOD and TSS limits and increased fines for violations, and in 1991, it demanded complete elimination of AOX discharge by December 31, 2002. Greenpeace kept up the pressure in the early 1990s; it organized a consumer boycott of chlorine-bleached paper in Germany, generating demands from some BC3 customers for chlorine-free paper. At a European port, Greenpeace members painted a 100-meter-long slogan on the hull of a cargo ship carrying pulp and lumber from Canada. By 1989, BC3 was planning to spend $1 billion on modernization and expansion, including improvements in discharge treatment and chlorine reduction. The mill became the first in North America to complete a full-scale mill trial of completely chlorine-free bleached softwood kraft market pulp.[25]

In the early 1990s, GA1corp, corporate owner of another pulp mill in our sample, was the subject of substantial pressure from environmental activists.

THE LICENSE AND ENVIRONMENTAL PERFORMANCE

In May 1990, Greenpeace members scaled the office tower occupied by GA1corp and draped huge banners and slogans over the front of the building, attracting national TV and newspaper coverage. In December 1990, GA1's Georgia pulp mill reported a very large chemical spill. In December 1992, another ENGO publicly labeled GA1corp the worst environmental performer in its industry and one of the country's ten worst polluters. An article in *Pulp and Paper* referred to GA1's reputation for insensitivity to environmental and community issues. When we talked to them in 1999, GA1 head office personnel characterized the company as not having taken environmental issues seriously until the time of the Greenpeace demonstration, which they believed had been pivotal in getting the environment "in the face" of senior management, generating a commitment to improve environmental performance. As one of them put it: "It was the start of a wake-up. We have to do more than just crank the mills."

Between November 1990 and January 1994, average BOD emissions at GA1 declined gradually but erratically by a third, from about 15,000 lbs/day to about 10,000 lbs/day. In February 1993, GA1corp appointed a high profile ex-government regulatory official as senior vice-president for the environment. In July 1994, the company adopted an ambitious set of corporate "environmental principles," including the establishment of companywide environmental goals, strategies, and time frames to achieve them, as well as systematic environmental training and audit programs. In the two years beginning in October 1994, GA1's average BOD discharges declined almost another 50 percent, to an average of about 5,000 lbs/day (except for an aberrant rise in early 1996). The mill's emissions of TSS followed a similar course and timetable, dropping rapidly *before* a new regulatory permit was issued to the facility in November 1995. Thus, in GA1's case as well, social license pressures appear to have been an important source of beyond-compliance efforts, triggered in the early 1990s by the shock of adverse environmental publicity alone and later, at least in part, by anticipated tightening of the regulatory license as well.

Management at a few mills in our sample, or at their corporate headquarters, were less responsive to social license pressures, as will be discussed more fully in the next chapter. There was risk in this strategy, for a mill could not be sure that environmental activists would not be able to prod regulatory license enforcers into action. In the case of the Louisiana-Pacific Corporation's Samoa, California mill (not in our sample), unresolved complaints by the Surfrider Foundation about the mill's chronic violations of permissible pollution discharges into the ocean resulted in a 1989 lawsuit by that ENGO. The U.S. EPA joined the suit, which resulted in a 1991 consent decree. Louisiana-Pacific agreed to install and operate a totally chlorine-free, peroxide-based bleaching system, the first in the United States—thereby going substantially beyond compliance with current U.S. law, but positioning itself for compliance with regulations that were likely to be promulgated later in the 1990s (Norberg-Bohm and Rossi 1998, pp. 234–35).[26]

In sum, for most mills in our sample, social license pressures appear to have mattered significantly. They gave corporate officials an additional incentive to comply with the terms of their regulatory license, for in the minds of social license enforcers, legal compliance often served as an important benchmark of company cooperativeness or commitment. And social license pressures were responsible in many cases for a measure of *beyond*-compliance company activity, both reducing odors and visual impacts and accelerating chlorine substitution and reduction of AOX emissions.

The Economic License: Putting on the Brakes

In environmentally high-profile industries like contemporary pulp manufacturing, as we have seen, the regulatory and social strands of firms' license to operate, acting separately and in interaction, push them strongly to remain in compliance with environmental law, often with a beyond-compliance margin of safety, and also to deal with social pressures by undertaking certain beyond-compliance measures of the good citizenship variety. But business firms' license to operate also includes a powerful "economic license" dimension, which complicates the story considerably. In some respects, firms' economic licenses reinforce the pressure for legal compliance, at least for closely watched facilities in contemporary industrially advanced democracies, in which noncompliance can easily generate adverse publicity. In addition, interacting with the regulatory and social licenses, the economic license generates incentives for managers to search for win-win investments and procedures that both reduce operating costs or generate competitive advantages *and* improve environmental performance in ways not dictated by governmental regulation.

At the same time, however, our pulp industry research suggests that the economic license imposes limits on *how much* firms can spend on innovative beyond-compliance measures of the good citizenship variety that do not pay off in reduced costs or enhanced income. As interpreted by its enforcers— investors, lenders, and financial analysts—the economic license does not encourage a firm to invest in expensive environmental measures or technologies that do not improve productivity and profits unless government regulations compel the firm's competitors to make similar expenditures.

If a firm acts contrary to these economic license pressures, the consequences are often severe. For example, as noted earlier, Louisiana-Pacific revamped its Samoa, California, mill in response to social license pressures to be the first TCF facility in the United States. But that increased production costs and reduced the brightness of paper made from its pulp. Its product was unmarketable in the United States and was sold mostly in Europe, but even there the company could not obtain a significant market premium for TCF paper (Norberg-Bohm and Rossi 1998, p. 235). In February 1994, Louisiana-Pacific temporarily shut the mill due to lack of orders, laying off 240 workers (Knickerbocker 1994). In 2001, Louisiana-Pacific sold the Samoa mill, which is still the only such TCF pulp mill in the United States.[27]

The Nature of the Economic License in Pulp Manufacturing

For business firms, it should probably go without saying, the economic license is fundamental. At least in the United States, Canada, and Australasia, the principal legal and economic obligation of publicly owned corporations is to the shareholders that own the company and is essentially to minimize risk, to maximize returns, and to preserve capital. In Milton Friedman's often cited declaration: business owes no social obligations beyond maximizing profit for its shareholders.[28] Not only companies themselves but also financial professionals who manage funds for others have a legal duty "to maximize returns on investments without reference to the morality of environmental damage or social justice."[29] Public companies that are not seen to be meeting these expectations will be punished in the marketplace: their stock will be devalued, they will have difficulty borrowing at competitive rates, and they may be vulnerable to hostile takeover. Senior management within them may face personal penalties: they will forfeit their bonuses, their personal stock holdings will lose value, and they are vulnerable to being dismissed and replaced by others perceived as more likely to achieve the expectations of the market. Thus the broad terms of the economic license are reasonably clear: firms must make decisions that are viewed by financial markets as economically rational in the short as well as the long term and supply a product for which there is a market demand, at a price the market is willing to bear.

These duties are monitored and enforced by major lenders and by investors in equities (stocks or shares), particularly the large institutions who increasingly dominate the market. To the extent that their expectations are not met or that they disapprove of a particular corporate strategy or action, they can express their disapproval by selling their shares; if sufficient numbers of them do so, this may devalue the share price. Lenders may require higher interest payments—the equivalent of a large and ongoing fine for violation of the legal license. In terms of *environmental* decision-making, "If companies cannot convince investors that environmentally sound policies lead to stronger economic performance, then they will be hard pressed to defend them to their shareholders."[30] As a result, profitability and prudence norms operate as a constraint on investment in environment protection.

But who defines exactly what these profitability and prudence norms are, and what the limits of acceptable environmental expenditure might be? While shareholder resolutions might have some bearing on this,[31] the key figures in this regard are institutional investors, pension and mutual funds, and the financial analysts who influence these investors (including firms, such as Moody's, that provide company financial soundness ratings). In doing so, the research suggests, the analysts tend to emphasize short-term over long-term considerations (e.g., the next quarter's earnings rather than long-term trends).[32]

While financial analysts play crucial roles in defining, monitoring, and enforcing the economic license, research to date suggests that they have not been greatly influenced by environmental performance in arriving at their conclusions and making their recommendations about the economic health of individual companies.[33] As one analyst commented: "Most of them have very little familiarity with regional regulation, most have little operating background, and so they don't distinguish between primary and secondary effluent treatment, or understand why a precipitator might be needed. All they are interested in is the earnings outlook."

Another analyst told us: "Most companies have so much at risk [that] they are environmentally compliant. Most analysts take [it] for granted that companies are on-side environmentally. The massive environmental expenditure of 1988–93 made most companies compliant." Hence financial analysts did not make a point of seeking out evidence of poor environmental performance by pulp producers. At the same time, most of the companies in our sample reported a strong pressure to justify environmental spending to the market. As one corporate lawyer working with the industry pointed out:

> Capital investments have to pay back in, say, four years. If you invest a hundred million dollars, it has to pay for itself in that time period. And there will be competition within the company for capital investment dollars, and so not all investments, however worthwhile, will be undertaken. Where will environment fit within this competition? *In the background will lurk the impact on earnings per share. . . . If a company is seen as underperforming, it will be vulnerable to adverse stock market reaction, or to a takeover.* [emphasis added]

Despite some evidence of the "greening" of financial markets in the broader environmental literature,[34] our interviews with financial institutions, industry analysts, corporate lawyers, and company officials in the pulp and paper industry suggest that the willingness of investment analysts and the financial community to take environmental issues into account is changing only very slowly. One analyst who follows the industry reported paying a great deal of attention to fluctuations in the price of market pulp and to the shipment/inventory ratio for each company, for example, but said he paid very little attention to environmental regulatory factors and none whatsoever to whether companies were positioning themselves as environmental leaders. Notwithstanding the high environmental sensitivity of such companies and the fact that environmental investments can cost them many millions of dollars, such issues did not appear to figure significantly in analysts' calculations.[35] The emphasis is on short-term economic measurements (the "tyranny of quarterly returns," as one respondent described it), with long-term environmental benefits being substantially discounted or effectively ignored.[36]

To the extent that environmental issues did get onto investors' radar screens, it was the potential environmental *liabilities* of pulp mills that gained their attention rather than efforts to go beyond compliance or environmental innovations.[37] As one corporate lawyer pointed out:

> The big investors such as pension funds ask: do you have secondary treatment; what's your compliance record like; will you need to spend $120 million to get into compliance? And the big shareholders want a road show before they make a big investment. They don't just want to know what benefits there are, but also what is the environmental status of a project—will you be required to do anything substantial regarding the environment?[38]

Analysts apparently believe "that investors will apply a discount for poor environmental performance, but will not pay a premium for exceptional environmental performance."[39] As one analyst told us, "The market is not looking for leadership in environmental issues. If a firm goes ahead of the curve, the market becomes concerned about the level of expenditure. The market looks for good financial performance while keeping costs down."

During most of the 1990s, the pulp and paper industry labored in the shadow of increased global competition, oversupply, depressed pulp prices and overcapacity. This accentuated the financial marketplace's rather jaundiced view of the industry.[40] After paper companies borrowed very large amounts to invest in new equipment, they hit tough economic times in the pulp market and returns on investment languished.[41] This served to tighten the terms of the economic license for all companies in the industry. Most firms we interviewed were acutely aware that their economic license constrained environmental spending. A generally expressed sentiment within the industry was: "If you spend too much on environment, you don't get recognition from Wall Street." As one corporate executive in the pulp and paper industry put it:

> Everyone speaks the good speak concerning sustainability, but the bottom line is you want a profitable company. . . . [T]here is nothing against (or irrational in) a pulp mill running for cash and winding it out [not maintaining or updating the facility] and closing in ten years. There is no sense in putting capital in pulp and paper in North America. You can't get positioned on the cost curve to justify the investment. It makes no sense, so you run for cash. For investors, depreciation is viewed as irrelevant, it's viewed as a cash machine, and anything that reduces the

profit margin is viewed as a negative. Financial institutions respond by moving capital elsewhere.

Green Markets and the Economic License

Some observers have suggested that the general insensitivity of financial markets to environmental performance might be mitigated by the emergence of specialized, environmentally conscious investment funds,[42] and by the emergence of better indicators of environmental performance (through mechanisms such as the U.S. Toxic Release Inventory), which would provide investment fund managers with an immediately accessible guide to a company's environmental risk to capital.[43] At present, however, the jury is still out as to how much impact new investment funds and performance indicators will have.[44] Neither pulp mill officials nor paper industry financial analysts whom we interviewed referred to these phenomena.

More significant, at least in some cases, was growing public sensitivity to certain environmental issues, as reflected in consumer behavior. Environmental activists have speculated that consumers increasingly will favor the products of manufacturers who have demonstrated concern for the environment, while boycotting manufacturers who have not, punishing environmental laggards in the marketplace.[45] In the related area of forest products, the independent certification of "well-managed forests" through the Forest Stewardship Council, a body whose existence owes far more to the initiative of major environmental groups than to government, gives paper and timber buyers considerable leverage over forest methods and reportedly has had a significant impact on forest-management practices and environmental performance.[46]

We found, however, that there are difficulties in waging effective consumer campaigns in relation to the pulp and paper industry. In North America, the customers of pulp and paper mills, whether they are large publishing houses or commercial stores, seem to care about their suppliers' environmental credentials only to the extent that their customers (i.e., consumers) care. In the United States, consumers have shown only limited interest in demanding "environmentally friendly" products and have been even less interested in where the pulp that goes into the paper they use comes from or how it is produced. There has been no significant demand from consumers or other customers for unbleached or chlorine-free or less bright paper product. As one company official remarked, "Wood chips grow on barges as far as the public is concerned." As a result, the U.S. industry (other than a very limited number of companies making niche products for European markets) has not experienced any significant economic pressure from consumers to change its environmental practices. The same is essentially true of the Australasian companies, which export principally to Asian markets that are even less environmentally sensitive than those in the United States.

In contrast, as noted earlier, some Canadian companies export to European markets that have at times been consumer/customer sensitive to the environmental provenance of pulp and paper. For periods during the 1990s, European consumers, particularly in Germany and the United Kingdom, were very vocal in demanding totally chlorine-free and effluent-free paper. For example, in Germany, environmentalists put pressure on magazine publishers to use chlorine-free paper, thereby threatening a market that accounted for some 25 percent of the sales of one mill in our sample. Notwithstanding efforts to characterize such campaigns as "invisible tariffs" by which Germany, in particular, protected its domestic markets,[47] European customer and consumer sensitivity temporarily added to pulp mills' incentives to phase out use of elemental chlorine.

More recently, corporate adoption of formal environmental management systems, conforming to the International Organization for Standardization's ISO-14000 series (and in particular ISO-14001), has been seen as useful, if not necessary, for competing in environmentally sensitive markets. Increasingly, western European corporations have asked their corporate suppliers in the United States and Japan to certify that their products have been produced by an ISO-14000–approved facility.[48] Most of the Canadian pulp mills we visited in 1998–99—although not those in the United States—had recently achieved ISO-14000 certification.[49] However, ISO-14000 does not specify any environmental performance standard as a condition of certification, and it is far from clear in our data that ISO certification was an important source of differences among facilities in environmental performance.[50]

Banks and insurance companies have been shown to encourage eco-efficiency in a number of markets.[51] However, we encountered no evidence that they exert any significant influence on the environmental behavior of the mills we surveyed.

The Impact of the Economic License

Based on our research, the economic license strand of pulp mills' license to operate has been somewhat complicated. First, notwithstanding financial analysts' emphasis on near-term corporate earnings and their relative indifference to signs of corporate environmental excellence, it is important to note that the economic licenses of the pulp mills we studied in no way "trumped" their regulatory licenses. Compliance with regulation, as noted above, was regarded by company officials as an unalterable constraint, within the bounds of which the competition for profits had to be conducted. And in some ways, contemporary economic licenses have reinforced the pressure for legal compliance. Companies fear that if they are repeatedly prosecuted or sued, they are likely to attract adverse publicity, and financial analysts sometimes (but unpredictably) regard inability to stay out of legal trouble as a sign of inadequate, shortsighted, or lax corporate management. As noted before, all the firms in our sample generally remained in compliance with the law throughout the 1990s, in times of low pulp prices as well as in better times.

Second, because the environmental performance of pulp mills is closely watched by regulators, environmental activists, and local communities, the mills' economic licenses have encouraged most firms to invest in beyond-compliance measures—particularly those of the "margin of safety" variety. That is, a margin of safety beyond compliance is seen as a good investment because it minimizes the risk of legal penalties and adverse publicity that may be triggered by noncompliance. Moreover, economic considerations have led pulp mills to invest in "anticipatory" beyond-compliance measures, in anticipation of forthcoming legal obligations. Because both major production technology and environmental technology changes in pulp mills are extremely costly, and because retrofitting existing technologies after regulations are announced is costlier still, firms quite rationally seek to take into account anticipated regulatory requirements, as well as current ones, when remodeling their mills. Thus by the mid-to-late 1990s, most mills in our sample had achieved a higher degree of chlorine substitution than required by current law. Regulators, for their part, have generally been reasonably sensitive to this aspect of the economic license, recognizing the importance of the mills' investment cycles. Thus they have generally provided substantial lead times when promulgating new, more stringent environmental performance standards in the pulp industry, and administrators often have been willing to "grandfather in" existing suboptimal control levels in some mills' permits as long as the firm credibly commits to installing state-of-the-art controls in the course of a planned remodeling.

Third, for closely regulated industries like pulp manufacturing, the economic license has encouraged firms to search for win-win beyond-compliance measures, that is, those that reduce operating costs as well as improving environmental performance. Finding win-win solutions also gives firms a larger margin of error vis-à-vis regulatory standards and builds reputation capital. The large majority of pulp mills we visited had therefore found it worthwhile to build meaningful environmental management departments and systems; to invest in explicit environmental training for production workers and for employees who operate pollution-control technologies; and to conduct periodic self-audits (often by environmental managers brought in from the corporation's other mills). A majority (but by no means all) had also developed process-based programs to reduce the number of spills and leaks by improving maintenance, training, and reliability. Eight of the fourteen mills in our sample had invested in an expensive, advanced technology known as oxygen delignification, which reduces the need for the use of chlorine or chlorine dioxide as a bleaching agent; those eight had done so primarily because financial analyses had indicated that oxygen delignification was cost-effective for their particular operations, reducing expenditures on chemicals.[52]

Fourth, customer demands had led managers in a few mills to adopt certain beyond-compliance environmental measures as a way of retaining customers or obtaining a competitive advantage. One example, mentioned earlier, was the rapid reduction of elemental chlorine use in the early-to-mid 1990s by Canadian mills in our study whose European customers wanted "chlorine-free" pulp.[53] Similarly, in 1998–99, GA2 had the lowest AOX emissions of all pulp mills in our sample, far exceeding the performance of the other U.S. mills—which are subject to the same general standard for AOX in the EPA "cluster rule." The company's decision to improve AOX performance was made in 1989 in response to European customers' concerns regarding dioxin in the diapers it produced. As a producer of baby products, GA2 officials "[f]elt it's not good business to be in the middle of the [dioxin] controversy."

Fifth, although pulp mills' economic licenses did encourage the specific cost-effective environmental measures mentioned above, markets did not seem to reward superior environmental performance in general. Consider more closely the experience of GA1corp, operator of one of the U.S. mills in our study:

• As noted earlier, in May 1990, Greenpeace environmental activists unfurled critical banners from GA1corp's office building, which attracted national TV and newspaper attention that coincided with coverage of the EPA's announcement that it would intensively regulate pulp and paper mills' dioxin discharges. The stock market didn't blink. GA1corp's stock price edged up steadily in the succeeding month, from $42.50 to $45.

• In November 1990, the GA1 pulp mill in our sample reported a large chemical spill. GA1corp's stock had been declining in the preceding month and continued to slide, but far from taking the spill as a sign of dangerously lax environmental management—and hence of poor management in general—the market for GA1corp's stock by December had reversed course, and GA1corp share prices began a sharp and fairly steady climb, which extended into the mid 1990s.

• In late July 1994, GA1corp announced a new, far-reaching set of environmental principles for all its production facilities. GA1corp's stock went up in the next five days. But it would be rash to interpret this as money managers rewarding green corporate management, because GA1corp's stock had been trending upward since July 1. The trend continued through September. And GA1's stock was not adversely affected by some bad environmental news. In August 1994, the EPA commenced formal enforcement action against GA1corp for failure to comply with permitting requirements for air pollution from its plywood operations. Although two other forest products companies quickly settled similar charges by the EPA (which arose from a long-standing dispute about how to calculate the emissions in question), GA1corp management determined to fight. The stock market did not judge this position harshly.

Sixth, there is some evidence that periodic loosening of an industry's economic license facilitates investment in environmental improvements. At many pulp mills we visited, managers traced major new investments in environmental technologies to the 1989–91 period. The period 1987–February 1991, we later discovered, had been the most extended period of above-average pulp prices in the past twenty years. Some of those new technologies, such as oxygen delignification and chlorine dioxide plants, were crucial to the reduction of elemental chlorine bleaching in the course of the 1990s. And those higher pulp prices also coincided with substantial—and enormously expensive—remodeling of basic *production* facilities that occurred in many mills during the 1989–91 period. This suggests that economic factors, particularly market conditions and the normal investment cycle for modernizing older production equipment, are important triggers for environmental improvements—as firms making large investments in production equipment take the opportunity to build in environmental improvements sufficient to meet regulatory requirements that are anticipated during the ensuing ten or fifteen years. Thus we found a significant statistical relationship between corporate profitability in the first half of the 1990s and the environmental performance of the pulp mills in our sample in 1998–99.[54]

On the other hand, we found no systematic relationship between economic conditions and other aspects of corporate environmental performance.[55] One might imagine that in periods of lower market pulp prices,[56] firms would find it harder to invest in environmental management and technology, and that environmental performance would therefore suffer. But we found negligible support for this hypothesis. A separate analysis of six U.S. facilities over the 1989–99 period showed that they generally maintained the downward trend in BOD emissions during economic "bad times" (pulp prices below the long-term average).[57] Nor was the incidence of chemical spills (an indicator of the relative diligence of environmental management) consistently lower, on average, in periods of lower pulp prices.[58] This suggests that whereas firms' economic licenses may have constrained their environmental efforts in some respects, as discussed below, the pressures stemming from the firms' regulatory and social licenses were sufficiently potent to compel improvements in environmental performance even during an era of industry overcapacity and severe price competition.

Seventh, and most important, the economic licenses of pulp mills have generally served as a brake on highly significant and costly beyond-compliance environmental initiatives beyond those that can be justified in margin-of-error or win-win terms. The lesson is hammered home by the experience of firms that suffered economically from overestimating the stringency of anticipated regulations or the eagerness of customers to buy "greener" products. Forest Reinhardt relates the experience of Champion, a paper products company that in the high-pulp-price era beginning in the late 1980s adopted an "aggressive strategy [including the expenditure of $1 billion on environmental technologies and systems] for managing both regulatory risk and the business risk inherent in antagonistic relations with downstream neighbors" (Reinhardt 2000, pp. 152–54). This included the expenditure of $300 million in its Canton, North Carolina, mill for oxygen delignification and chlorine-substitution systems. Then in the mid 1990s, Champion spent another $30 million in Canton to recycle water from bleaching, on the theory that EPA eventually would require a "closed mill" system. Its AOX emissions went down to 0.1 kg per ton, far lower than EPA's cluster rule eventually required. But by then pulp prices had declined, and Canton had very large capital cost burdens compared to its competitors. In 1999, Champion sold the Canton mill to its employees and managers, plus a New York investment fund.

Consider, too, the experience of the Canadian firm BC3, which, as noted earlier, made an earlier and larger investment in totally chlorine-free (TCF) technology than most of its industry peers. Yet TCF paper was more costly to make and less attractive to many customers. The anticipated demand and price premium did not materialize, and BC3 backed off from TCF operation (as permitted by its regulatory license). Nevertheless, BC3 ended up losing money, and the company came to be perceived by other pulp mill managers as an example of how not to proceed. BC3's managing director was replaced and his successor reintroduced the conventional emphasis on short-term economic targets (although the mill did continue to be a leader in most measures of effluent control).

Understandably, few firms were eager to follow the environmental technology path blazed by the Canton, BC3, and Samoa facilities. As long as customers continued to care more about cost, brightness, and strength of their paper than about the pulp mills' AOX numbers, most mills used regulatory requirements as their chief guide to environmental performance—achieving a high level of chlorine substitution, and doing so in advance of regulatory deadlines, but not going all the way to TCF.[59] Moreover, they treated these economic license constraints as fairly fixed. They did not strive to generate more customer demand for unbleached or less bright paper in order to reduce the environmental impact of unrecycled bleaching chemicals in their effluent.

As Reinhardt (2000, pp. 25, 28) has pointed out, customers in markets for "commodity products" such as pulp usually will pay premiums for environmentally differentiated products (such as TCF pulp) only if the products lower their own overall costs. And even then a marketer of "greener" products will not benefit if its competitors can easily replicate the same innovation. Thus early movers to ECF pulp derived little benefit since most of their competitors, anticipating regulatory tightening, quickly did the same.

Conclusion

In all the governmental jurisdictions we studied, the license to operate of each of the pulp mills in our sample had basic commonalities, compelling all of them to spend large amounts of money on pollution prevention and control and to take day-to-day environmental performance issues very seriously. By establishing demanding performance standards, the firms' regulatory licenses had induced each mill, regardless of jurisdiction, to install secondary treatment plants for wastewater, which caused BOD emissions to plummet, and to substantially reduce use of elemental chlorine as a bleaching agent, which greatly reduced dioxin emissions. All firms were fundamentally in compliance with their environmental permits. And the expectation of gradually tightening standards and scrutiny meant that most firms often overcomplied, investing in margin-of-safety and anticipatory beyond-compliance measures.

Social license pressures, moreover, impelled many firms to engage in some beyond-compliance measures of the good citizenship variety, such as engaging in odor-control efforts that were neither compelled by regulators nor clearly justified by economic and legal calculations. But just as the regulatory and social licenses have demanded tighter controls on emissions, most firms' economic licenses have become more demanding, particularly due to the industry's propensity toward overcapacity and depressed market pulp prices, constraining how far firms can go in a "green" direction, particularly because win-win investments have been far harder to find in the pulp industry than some environmental management theorists have imagined.

Explicit regulatory license requirements, it should be reemphasized, have consistently trumped economic demands, partially through the implicit promise that all competitors will be obliged to make the same investment. Nevertheless, the economic license appears to impose an upper limit on many conceivable beyond-compliance environmental investments by business firms. Financial markets are likely to look askance at large expenditures made simply to protect a company's social license (for example, to maintain credibility with the local community) and that might arguably be characterized as win-win only in a more nebulous and non-measurable sense (e.g., that it will be "good for business" in the long run). A company that undertakes such spending risks having its share price discounted. Whether this in fact happens may depend on how substantial the expenditure is, and how effective the company is in communicating and justifying its decision to the market. Once again, as with the legal license, the terms of the economic license are not immutable, and some companies, at least, are developing skills in reshaping market perceptions of their behavior.

Regulation has the potential to offset this braking function of the economic license. For firms that may be inclined to invest in innovative environmentally friendly technologies, regulations requiring similar changes provide some assurance that their competitors will be required to follow suit. Air pollution rules banning lead from gasoline and requiring catalytic converters in automobiles gave environmental leaders in the petroleum and motor vehicle industry more security in moving forward, notwithstanding the business strategies of their competitors or the reservations of customers who had other preferences. But regulatory regimes in the jurisdictions we studied—with the partial exception of British Columbia, perhaps[60]—have not sought to override economic license-based limitations by mandating TCF operations or by imposing limits on bleaching per se. Regulators have generally been attentive to business needs to coordinate costly environmental investments with the investment cycles for modernizing production facilities, and they have recognized that frequent changes in emission standards or required technologies are economically inefficient. In this regard, as well as in the flexibility built into many facility-level permits,[61] regulators generally have recognized the importance of pulp mills' economic license, refraining from mandating the use of control technologies that have not been proven to be effective and affordable.

4

The License to Operate and
Interfirm Differences

O ver the past few decades, the pulp and paper industry has substantially reduced its environmentally harmful emissions in
most important categories. The mills in our sample were generally in compliance with their regulatory permits. None were regulatory laggards in the
sense of being ignorant or systematic evaders of their "regulatory licenses."
Nevertheless, as of the end of the twentieth century, they differed significantly in environmental performance. For example, consider Table 4.1,
which displays performance data among a sample of mills, averaged over
1998–99,[1] for three important measures of water pollution: BOD emissions
(kg/day); TSS emissions (kg/day); and AOX emissions (kg/ton).[2]

The spread between the best-performing and worst-performing mills was
substantial. With respect to TSS, the three lowest dischargers (BC2, BC3, and
WA4) averaged 2,660 kg/day, only 34 percent as much as the average for the
three largest dischargers (NZ2, NZ1, and WA2). The BOD emissions of the
three lowest dischargers (BC3, BC4, and WA4) averaged only 23 percent as
much as the three laggards (NZ2, GA3, and WA2). And, even setting aside
the WA2 facility, which was a clear laggard in control of AOX effluent, the
three lowest dischargers (GA2, BC3, WA3) pumped out only 36 percent as
much AOX per ton of pulp produced as the three worst performers on that
measure (WA4, BC4, and BC2).

The difference between leaders and laggards, it should be noted, is not
because the "laggards" are larger mills or have higher levels of production
than the leaders or because they have markedly different production
processes.[3] For the sample as a whole, production and environmental
performance are not closely correlated. In 1998–99, the correlation between

TABLE 4.1

Environmental Performance by Pulp Mill, 1998–99

(ordered by performance level)

BOD		TSS		AOX	
Mill	kg/day	Mill	kg/day	Mill	kg/ton
BC3	993	BC2	2,349	GA2	0.10
BC4	1,000	BC3	2,484	BC3	0.31
WA4	1,271	WA4	3,147	WA3	0.34
NZ1	1,600	WA3	3,487	BC1	0.46
WA3	1,996	BC4	3,525	NZ2	0.54
BC2	2,302	GA1	3,637	BC2	0.58
GA1	2,367	BC1	4,282	BC4	0.60
BC1	2,549	WA1	5,846	WA4	0.91
WA1	3,848	GA3	7,178	WA2	3.49
GA3	4,663	WA2	7,212	WA1	—
WA2[a]	4,726	NZ1	7,900	NZ1	—
NZ2	4,917	NZ2	8,070	GA1	—
GA2	—	GA2	—	GA3	—
AUS	—	AUS	—	AUS	—

NOTE: BOD = biological oxygen demand; TSS = total suspended solids; AOX = adsorbable organic halides.
[a]This facility uses two different pulp production technologies on site, one of which is far more polluting than the technology used at all the other facilities in our sample. The numbers shown here (for BOD and TSS) are figures constructed to estimate what pollutant discharges would have been if all production had been by the cleaner process. These are not the actual figures discharged by the facility.

production and BOD, TSS, and AOX is 0.03, –0.12, –0.19 respectively, none of which are statistically significant. The efficacy of primary and secondary effluent treatment systems varies primarily not with the volume of wastewater processed but with the capacity and efficiency of the systems and how well they are maintained and operated. A larger mill may have to build a larger capacity system, but if well designed and operated, it should be able to reduce BOD and TSS to levels comparable to those at smaller mills that have good equipment and good operational control.

The disparities in emissions shown on Table 4.1 are environmentally significant. While the substantial reductions in these major pollutants in the past two decades have had positive effects on the environment, the remaining effluent, even from the best-performing pulp mills, continues to have negative environmental impacts.[4] Thus we are left with an important puzzle. Why have some pulp mills done a better job in reducing pollution than others? How can we explain the spread between the "leaders" and the "laggards" on Table 4.1?

This chapter examines the extent to which contemporary mill-level variation can be explained by differences in the firms' regulatory, economic, and social licenses to operate. While each of these licenses has some influence on corporate environmental performance, it turns out, not surprisingly, that no single "external driver," acting alone, accounts for the observed variation in environmental performance. It is not explained by regulatory regime: neither leaders nor laggards clustered in any of the five jurisdictions studied (Australia, New Zealand, British Columbia, Georgia, and Washington). Some mill-level environmental performance differences are correlated with some measures of corporate economic resources, but not with others.[5] It proved difficult to construct measures of the strictness of firms' social licenses, and hence to analyze quantitatively the relationship between social license and mills' environmental performance. On the other hand, microanalyses of particular mills or pairs of mills indicate that specific features of the firms' regulatory, economic and social licenses do help explain their environmental performance—yet without yielding a crisp formulaic explanation or set of generalizations. Moreover, as discussed in some detail in Chapter 5, it seems clear that corporate environmental management style is a crucial intervening variable, affecting the ways in which external license pressures are translated into firm-level environmental measures.

The Regulatory License and Facility-Level Environmental Performance

Ideally, we would have quantified the regulatory permits for each mill in our sample, or at least ranked them in terms of relative stringency, and then compared those regulatory stringency scores with the facilities' comparative environmental performance in Table 4.1. In practice, it proved impossible to do so. To refer only to discharges into water in one jurisdiction, the typical regulatory permit for each sampled pulp mill in the state of Washington was over twenty-five pages in length, including scores of particular requirements. The permits are tailored to the particular technologies at each mill, taking into account the type and age of the production and abatement equipment, among other factors. Some permit requirements are stated in quantitative terms, but many are stated in qualitative terms. This makes cross-facility comparison difficult even within one regulatory jurisdiction, and much harder still across jurisdictions, for different regulatory regimes employ different indicators and different levels of specificity and formality in establishing firm-level requirements.[6] However, we were able to estimate[7] numerical effluent limitations for BOD and TSS at nine facilities.[8]

Permit Limits and Environmental Performance

Table 4.2 shows the permit limits and actual emissions of BOD and TSS (monthly averages) for nine facilities in our study. These limit figures are the formal limits that facilities were required to meet, not the de facto limits that result from real world enforcement. The data are sorted by ascending permit limit.

The first thing to note is that the ostensible stringency of the regulatory permit is only a weak predictor of actual performance. The correlation between the stipulated limit and actual performance is only .48 for BOD and a still lower .30 for TSS emissions, and, in terms of reliability those correlations did not reach statistical significance. Clearly, some mills with (relatively) less demanding permits (BC3, WA3) were among the best in actual environmental performance, while the opposite was true for GA3.

Second, the relative stringency of permit limits did not follow directly from which regulatory jurisdiction set them. For example, one Georgia mill had the fourth most stringent numerical permit for TSS, while another Georgia facility had the least stringent TSS permit. Nor did the relationship between permit limits and actual performance vary significantly across jurisdictions. Averaging the figures for BC mills, emissions were 29 percent as much as allowed by the regulatory permit; the parallel figures for Georgia and Washington mills were 29 percent and 36 percent respectively.

Regulatory Regime and Environmental Performance

We also sought to examine the relationship between *regulatory regimes*, viewed more holistically, and the environmental performance of pulp mills operating within those regimes. Underlying much popular and academic writing about regulation is a "deterrence model" of firm behavior, which holds that businesses abate environmental impacts only when compelled to

TABLE 4.2

Regulatory Jurisdiction, Permit Limits, and Mill-Level Emissions, 1998–99

(ordered by performance level)

BOD

Facility	Limit Rank	Limit (kg/d)	Performance (kg/d)	Performance Rank	Performance as % of Limit
WA4	1	4,023	1,271	3	32
GA3	2	5,455	4,663	8	85
BC4	3	6,080	1,000	2	16
WA1	4	6,964	3,848	7	55
GA1	5	7,045	2,367	6	34
BC3	6	7,592	993	1	13
BC2	7	9,060	2,302	5	25
WA2[a]	8	13,295	9,535	9	72
WA3	9	14,136	1,996	4	14

BOD = Biological Oxygen Demand. Correlation between limit and performance = 0.46.
[a]Using uncorrected WA2 figures, since limits take the production technology mix into account.

TSS

Facility	Limit Rank	Limit (kg/d)	Performance (kg/d)	Performance Rank	Performance as % of Limit
BC2	1	7,555	2,349	1	31
WA4	2	7,818	3,147	3	40
BC4	3	9,120	3,525	5	39
GA3	4	10,909	7,178	8	66
BC3	5	11,809	2,484	2	21
WA1	6	14,009	5,846	7	42
WA2[a]	7	21,477	12,173	9	57
WA3	8	24,909	3,487	4	14
GA1	9	26,364	3,637	6	14

TSS = Total Suspended Solids. Correlation between limit and performance = 0.30.
[a]Using uncorrected WA2 figures, since limits take the production technology mix into account.

do so by law and aggressive enforcement officials. In this model, firm-level variation in environmental performance depends on the interaction of (a) the stringency of official environmental regulations, (b) the likelihood that violations will be detected,[9] and (c) the consistency and severity of the penalties for detected noncompliance. From that standpoint, one would expect the best-performing pulp mills to be in the regulatory jurisdictions that have the most prescriptive and stringent legal rules, the most fearsome sanctions, and the strictest enforcement style. Other theories of regulation, however, argue that a legalistic style of regulation is likely to engender legalistic and political resistance, while a more cooperative, flexible style of regulatory enforcement will generate higher levels of compliance, at least if regulators have the credible capacity to invoke strong legal sanctions against firms that fail to cooperate (Bardach and Kagan 1982; Scholz 1984; Ayres and Braithwaite 1992). Whichever theory is correct, however, one would expect a significant correlation between governmental regulatory style and environmental performance of regulated firms.

Prior research indicates that the United States tends to employ a more legalistic, deterrence-oriented style of regulation than most other economically advanced democracies, whereas Canada, New Zealand, and Australia generally employ a more cooperative, negotiated mode of enforcement. American regulatory rules are far more detailed and are enforced more legalistically, resulting in more frequent and much larger regulatory sanctions. American rules generally require regulated enterprises to engage in more detailed record-keeping, reporting, and proof of compliance.[10] Comparing enforcement of environmental regulations for pulp and paper mills in the United States and Canada, Kathryn Harrison (1995) concluded that the American regulations were enforced more legalistically and more often resulted in penalties, and that compliance with BOD effluent standards was higher in the United States.[11] In the case of Australia, a series of ethnographic and archival studies suggest that regulators there traditionally rely heavily on cooperation and persuasion, with an almost complete absence of the kind of coercive enforcement that often occurs in the United States (Gunningham 1987; Grabosky and Braithwaite 1986). Moreover, compared to Canada, Australia, and New Zealand, pulp mills in the United States are much more vulnerable to privately initiated class-action lawsuits for discharges that cause harm to fish, natural resources, or human health—lawsuits that are expensive to defend and potentially punitive.

Although the level of regulatory prescriptiveness and legalism in U.S. regulatory enforcement varies a good deal,[12] corporate environmental affairs managers whom we interviewed at the end of the 1990s reaffirmed these conventional contrasts in national styles of regulation. For example, corporate officials at a corporation with mills in both Canada and the United States contrasted the "enforcement frenzy" in the United States with the partnering approach regulatory officials took in Canada, where, they said, "We can stay focused on the end result and the regulators work with us on a compliance schedule. Often the important thing is keeping an eye on the goal. In the U.S., they want the standard, and they want compliance today." Within the United States, some mill officials described the U.S. EPA as more legalistic than state environmental enforcement officials,[13] while some American states, such as Georgia (where three mills in our sample are located), have long had the reputation of adopting a less legalistic approach to enforcement than some other states, such as Washington (home to four sampled mills).

Yet these differences in regulatory style do not explain the differences in pulp mill environmental performance, at least when we use jurisdiction (admittedly a somewhat blunt indicator) as a proxy for regulatory style. The two graphs in Figure 4.1 show the average emissions of BOD, and AOX of pulp mills grouped by regulatory jurisdiction (1998–99). Nevertheless, our mill-level pollution data reveal no consistent difference among regulatory jurisdictions in the environmental performance of "their" pulp mills. No regulatory jurisdiction ends up with all "leaders" or all "laggards." Notwithstanding the presumably greater fearsomeness of U.S. regulatory enforcement, the sampled U.S. mills were as likely to be in the bottom half as in the top half of the environmental performance league in controlling emissions of BOD, TSS, and AOX. The mills in Washington, generally considered a "greener" state, did no better on average than those in Georgia. And variations among mills within each state were as large as differences across jurisdictions.

More formally, when we compare the average emissions of each type of emission in each jurisdiction, we find that there is no statistically significant difference among regulatory jurisdictions for BOD[14] or AOX,[15] although British Columbia and New Zealand differed significantly on TSS.[16] In British Columbia, regulations call for radical reductions in AOX by the end of 2002, and most of the mills there cluster closely in AOX emissions. But even so, two of the four BC pulp mills in our sample were slightly above the four-jurisdiction median on that pollutant. Similarly, we found there was no statistically significant relationship between regulatory jurisdiction and the extent to which pulp mills had invested in state-of-the-art pollution-control technology as of 1999.[17]

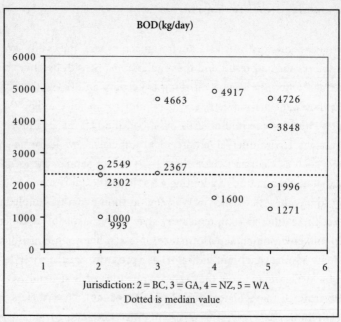

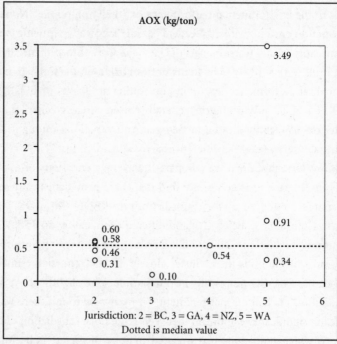

FIG. 4.1. Average Emissions of BOD and AOX Grouped by Jurisdiction

The weakness of the correlation between regulatory jurisdiction and firm-level environmental performance, we believe, reflects two important features of pulp and paper regulation and indeed of much contemporary environmental regulation. First, *within* all the jurisdictions in this study, there is considerable flexibility in regulatory requirements.[18] There is variation among mills within jurisdictions because regulators tailor facility-level permits and informal orders to individual mills' particular inputs, technologies, ecological environment, and investment cycles (e.g., delaying stricter permit requirements for old facilities until a scheduled upgrade of the mill's production processes). In no jurisdiction do regulations and regulators make all facilities march exactly together, as in close order drill; rather, like cowboys during a cattle drive, they prod a group of individuals in the same general direction.

Second, there are few striking differences in environmental performance *among* jurisdictions because all the "cattle drives" are moving in the same direction at about the same pace. By the mid 1990s, there was considerable convergence in the substantive pollution-control standards in all our jurisdictions.[19] New Zealand regulators noted that their rule-making process was expressly comparative and that regulators traveled to other jurisdictions to observe production practices and regulatory requirements.

Specific Regulatory Requirements and Environmental Performance

Notwithstanding the general convergence, all regulatory regimes are not identical. Some specific regulatory differences do help explain some of the firm-level differences in Table 4.1. For example, in the state of Washington, government regulations compelled pulp mills to install secondary wastewater treatment processes in the 1970s, while British Columbia did not require secondary treatment for mills discharging into coastal waters until the 1990s, when it also increased fines for violations of the Waste Management Act. One consequence was that in 1998–99, that is, at the time of the measures in Figure 4.1, Canadian coastal mills such as BC4, BC3, and BC1 had much newer, and hence closer to state-of-the-art, secondary treatment facilities than most U.S. mills, and hence lower BOD and TSS emissions on average. Similarly, in the early 1990s, British Columbia enacted a regulation that requires pulp mills to eliminate AOX emissions by the end of 2002

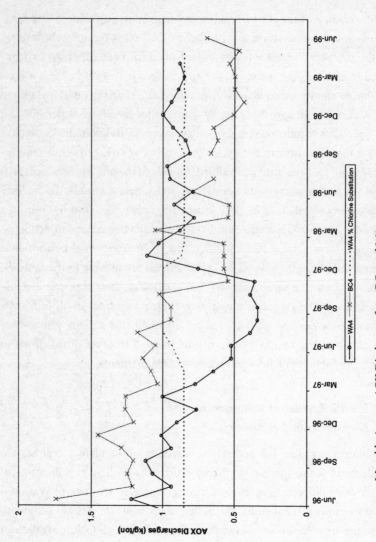

F I G . 4.2. Monthly Average AOX Discharges from BC4 and WA4, 1996–99

(Cashore and Vertinsky 2000)—a requirement that is more stringent and more imminent than the AOX limits set in the U.S. EPA's cluster rule. That surely helps explain the tighter clustering in AOX emissions among Canadian as compared to U.S. pulp mills, as shown in Figure 4.1.

Consider more specifically the AOX numbers for two facilities, WA4 and BC4. Both mills are run by relatively smaller companies. Both were experiencing difficulties in turning a profit in the latter half of 1990s. WA4 is in the state of Washington, BC4 in British Columbia.

Between June 1996 and April 1999, BC4 steadily improved its AOX discharges. When modifying its bleach plant in 1996, BC4 chose to add a peroxide tower rather than use a chlorinated bleach. The reason for choosing peroxide over chlorine dioxide (the standard approach to reducing use of elemental chlorine) was BC4's anticipation of a continuously and rapidly tightening regulatory license, particularly the British Columbia regulation requiring elimination of AOX discharge in mill effluent by December 31, 2002.[20] Thus BC4 reached 100 percent substitution by December 1997.

WA4, on the other hand, remained constant in its AOX discharges between June 1996 and April 1999, except for the summer of 1997, when the mill ran a trial at 100 percent chlorine substitution to determine what changes needed to be made to the facility to achieve that level continuously. But WA4 faced a longer "grace period" under the EPA's proposed regulation, the deadline for which was 2008, than BC4 did under British Columbia's 2002 regulatory deadline, and the latter standard was stricter. Hence WA4 felt able to delay ECF operations until it could make some additional capital investments in its chlorine dioxide system, eventually completed in June 1999. WA4 then began normal operations at 100 percent substitution, reducing AOX discharges to 0.3–0.5 kg/ton, a year and a half after BC4 achieved that level. Differences in current and near-future regulatory license requirements thus help explain the differences in AOX reduction by WA4 and BC4.

Yet as suggested by the significant variation in regulatory performance among mills in the same jurisdiction, regulatory license requirements only go so far in explaining variation in environmental performance. For example, BC4's permit limits in 1998–99 for BOD emissions were less strict than WA4's, yet BC4's actual emissions of BOD were slightly lower than WA4's and generally showed less variation from quarter to quarter. Moreover, in

June 1999, WA4 began operating at 100 percent ECF, *eight years* before the EPA's deadline. Thus while differences in the details of regulatory permits may help explain the remaining differences in environmental performance between those at the front and at the back of the herd of regulated mills, it seems that other factors, associated with the firms' economic and social licenses, are equally if not more important.

Economic Pressures and Differences in Environmental Performance

Logically, firms that are more profitable and have greater financial resources should be able to sustain better environmental records than firms in the same industry that are pinched for profits and financially strained. Research has confirmed this assumption: larger firms have often been found to be better environmental performers than smaller firms—partly because of their larger visibility and reputational concerns, but partly because they have more resources to spare for specialized environmental engineering and management (Haines 1997; Hillary 2000; Hobbs 2000). In terms of the "license" metaphor, one can think of larger, more profitable firms as having a less constraining economic license than smaller, less profitable firms.

For the most part, we were able to obtain financial data only for the large corporations that own the individual pulp mills in our study, not for each mill itself. Many of the parent corporations are vertically integrated, operating not only pulp mills (the subject of our research) but a variety of paper mills, and/or forestry divisions. We reasoned that although individual mills are expected to be financially independent to a considerable extent, they generally enjoy some degree of access to corporate financial resources for major capital investments. Moreover, since the mills' environmental failings might be attributed by the market or by regulators to the parent corporation, corporate-level resources can presumably be made available to deal with subpar environmental performance at particular pulp mills if corporate officials so desire or feel compelled to do so. We accordingly tested the proposition that mills owned by larger corporations and those with larger current profits and rising stock prices would have better environmental records than those owned by corporations with lower sales, smaller (or negative) earnings, and declining share prices.

TABLE 4.3

*Correlation Coefficients of Corporate Income and Income to
Sales Ratio with Mill-Level Environmental Performance,
Technology, and Management Style, 1998–99*

	BOD	TSS	AOX	Objective technology[a]	Subjective technology[b]	Managment Style
Corporate income–sales ratio, 1990–94	not significant	not significant	−0.96	0.84	0.63	−0.62[c]
Corporate income 1990–94	−0.61	−0.65	not significant	0.77	0.55[d]	not significant

NOTE: AOX = adsorbable organic halides; BOD = biological oxygen demand; TSS = total suspended solids.

[a]"Objective technology" refers to the number of more advanced technologies adopted by the facility.

[b]"Subjective technology" refers to managers' self-evaluation of their facility's technology compared to the state of the art.

[c]The sign is negative because True Believers were ranked 1 or 2 and Reluctant Compliers were ranked 7 (see Table 5.1 for more detail).

[d]Only statistically significant at a $p = 0.10$ level, all others statistically significant at a $p = 0.05$ level (2-tailed).

Our data provide some support for this proposition, provided that one assumes that it takes time for a corporation to translate economic good times into good environmental performance. First, we divided the mills in our sample into three categories—smaller, larger, and huge—based on the average annual sales of their corporate parents during the 1998–99 period. We found that average 1998–99 BOD, TSS, and AOX emissions did *not* differ significantly for each corporate size category. Similarly, we found no statistically significant correlation between either (a) corporate net income or (b) change in corporate stock price (up or down) and (c) environmental performance. Mills whose corporate parent was presumably experiencing milder economic constraints in 1998–99 did *not* have lower BOD, TSS, or AOX levels than mills whose corporate parents were doing less well in that period.[21] Nor did we find a significant correlation between 1998–99 corporate economic indicators and environmental control technology (using either "objective" or "subjective" technology measures).

On the other hand, as shown by Table 4.3, mills owned by corporations with larger profit margins (ratio of income to sales) and larger annual sales income in the early 1990s (1990–94) tended to have lower AOX emissions later in the decade (1998–99), and they also had better pollution-control technology. This may reflect the fact that it was in the early 1990s that pulp mills were making the investment decisions to comply with then-current political demands to reduce use of elemental chlorine and reduce contaminated effluent in general. More generally, it is plausible that due to the importance of costly technology investments for reducing emissions,[22] and the time lag for bringing new technology on line, corporate profitability at Time 1 (1990–94) has a stronger influence on environmental performance at Time 2 (1998–99).[23] Moreover, as shown in Table 4.3, corporate profitability in the first half of the 1990s was significantly correlated (−.62) with a more ambitious environmental management style in 1998–99.[24] And as we shall see in the next chapter, environmental management style appears to have an independent influence on environmental performance.

On some issues, particular firm-level economic differences help explain the relative environmental performance of certain mills. For example, due to variability in raw material and bleaching processes, some mills found oxygen delignification systems to be a profitable, win-win investment, while others did not.[25] Mills that installed oxygen delignification systems had significantly lower emissions of AOX in 1998–99 than mills that had not.[26]

As noted in Chapter 3, economic constraints also impose a ceiling on beyond-compliance environmental expenditures. And economic constraints do not fall evenly on all firms. GA3, operated by a relatively small corporation, was in the "second division" in control of BOD and TSS in 1998–99 and was a relative laggard in control of chemical spills. Yet its mill managers were extremely proactive in instilling a positive attitude toward environmental protection. At weekly production meetings, environmental performance (along with workplace safety) was at the top of the agenda. Signs noting the mill's environmental performance in the preceding period were posted throughout the plant. Yet economic license constraints kept GA3's environmental management from achieving higher levels of performance. With profits low, mill-level environmental managers had enjoyed little support from financial headquarters in obtaining funds for capital investment in new pollution-control equipment (they rated their current equipment as well behind the best available),[27] or even in new production equipment (which might also have improved their environmental performance). GA3 did a subpar job in control of particulate matter in its air emissions. With funding tight, even GA3's dedicated environmental management was not able to achieve a top record in spill prevention or water pollution control.

WA2 was even further from the leaders on virtually all the quantitative measures of environmental performance—BOD, TSS, AOX, number of spills, and both objective and subjective measures of environmental technology. Yet WA2's less than stellar performance cannot be attributed to tighter than usual economic license constraints. In the 1995–99 period, WA2's corporate parent was the second most profitable company in our sample, as measured by average income-to-sales ratio, and in 1998–99, it had the second highest average net earnings.[28] In this case, as in some others, neither regulatory nor economic license factors fully explain corporate environmental performance—which leads us to a discussion of the role of social license factors in that regard.

Social License Pressures and Differences in Environmental Performance

As discussed in Chapter 3, almost all the managers we interviewed referred to the influence of local environmental activists in the communities in which the mill was located. Some referred to instances in which they had been targeted by national or international environmental activist organizations. Unfortunately, we could neither find nor devise any systematic, objective measures of the *degree* of social pressure on each mill, that is, of the relative "stringency" of the terms of its social license. Local activists demanded different things from different mills. Moreover, different mills responded to (and reshaped) similar community demands in disparate ways, as discussed in the next chapter. We could not, therefore, compute a quantitative relationship between social license pressures and firm-level environmental performance.

A qualitative analysis, however, suggests that variations in social license pressures have significant effects on firms' relative environmental performance. Consider again the contrast between WA4 and WA2, as shown in Figure 3.1. WA4 is among the leaders in control of chemical spills, BOD, and TSS, and it does relatively well in controlling AOX. WA2 is one of the comparative laggards. Yet both mills are in the same U.S. jurisdiction and are subject to the same federal and state laws, administered by the same federal and state regulatory agencies, and hence, presumably, subject to similar regulatory license requirements. While we do not have financial data for WA4, which is part of a privately held corporation, it is a division of a smaller firm than WA2, with less financial depth. In the latter half of the 1990s, WA2 had a better profit margin than most of the corporations in our sample for which public data were available. Hence there are no indications that WA4's economic license is significantly "looser" than WA2's.[29]

The two mills do differ significantly, however, in the immediacy and intensity of the community pressures they experience concerning environmental performance. WA4 is located on the waterfront in a fairly large city, once heavily dependent on trade in forest products but now with a much more diversified economic base. WA4's blue-collar and largely industrial neighborhood has changed; the WA4 mill is very visible to the white-collar workforce in nearby downtown office buildings. The city is home to several environmental groups that pay close attention to the quality of WA4's receiving waters. WA4 purchased its mill in the early 1980s from a company notorious for its lack of concern for the local environment while "shipping the profits back East." The new owners found they faced an uphill battle in winning the trust of local activists and a local population who no longer needed or wanted a pulp mill on their doorstep. Thus the mill managers felt they needed to gain the community's trust. "I see most of the [environmental] groups two or three times a month," WA4's environmental manager told us. "Most important of all, what we say is what we do . . . I need their trust as much as they need ours. As soon as we violate it, all bets are off."

WA4's sensitivity to community pressure has at times prodded it to "beyond-compliance" measures. The company invited activists to all its permit negotiations with regulators, and it claims to have based its environmental priorities at least in part on those voiced by community activists. WA4's sense of vulnerability to community action is conveyed by this account by its environmental manager:

> We had a major spill when the effluent line to the bay ruptured. This was treated effluent, but it kept gushing, so we had to close the mill. There was lots of foam, and it was unsightly. Everyone was going to see this big, white foaming bubble floating in the bay, so we got a spill recovery company and put a boom around it. We sampled the water and phoned the regulators and the community. . . . When we have a violation, I call . . . the agency first, then the NGOs, [saying,] "This is what happened; this is the environmental damage."

WA2, in contrast, is the primary employer in a small company town, miles from the nearest large city. It experiences some local pressures—from owners of high-priced vacation homes, whose riverside view encompasses the plumes from WA2's pulp mill, and to some extent from the government. After a chlorine release from the facility required a partial evacuation of WA2's neighbors, the mill was obliged to install chlorine monitors both inside the mill and at the local fire department. Nevertheless, with its more isolated location, WA2 is not exposed to regular inquiries from local or regional environmental NGOs. WA2 managers do not voice the same sense of vulnerability to local pressures that WA4's managers do. They have not come close to establishing the same level of communication or dialogue with NGOs or regulatory officials that WA4's managers mention repeatedly. And unlike WA4, they do not refer to voluntary beyond-compliance measures they have taken to win the trust of NGOs and regulators. Thus WA2's less demanding "social license" appears to be a very important reason for the disparate environmental performance of the two mills.[30]

Table 4.1 omits effluent levels for AUS, a pulp mill located in Australia, because a significant proportion of its wastewater is piped to a public water treatment plant, and hence it is difficult to compare its BOD, TSS, and AOX to those of the other mills, whose effluent, after treatment, is discharged directly into receiving waters. Yet AUS's environmental performance in 1998–99 was excellent, and that too seems attributable in significant measure to social license pressures. For example, at the request of the local community, the mill had ensured that it did not increase its effluent volume when it expanded the facility's production capacity.[31]

Activism by environmental groups also clearly improved some firms' relative standing in terms of environmental performance. In Chapter 3, we described how demonstrations by Greenpeace, and the related adverse publicity, played a major role in inducing GA1 (in Georgia) and BC3 (in British Columbia) to sharply reduce pollutants in their pulp mill effluent.

Interaction of Social and Economic Licenses

In several cases, customers' demands wedded environmental concerns with economic pressure, helping to explain certain performance differentials among the pulp mills in our sample. For example, GA2 is the leader in our sample in eliminating AOX emissions, far exceeding the performance of the other U.S. mills—which are subject to the same general standard for AOX in the EPA "cluster rule." The company's decision to improve AOX performance was made in 1989 due to European customer concerns regarding dioxin in the diapers it produced. GA2 "[f]elt it's not good business to be in the middle of the [dioxin] controversy."

Similarly, as described earlier, consumer demand in Europe for chlorine-free paper played a significant role in inducing BC3 to make sharp reductions in its AOX emissions during the 1990s, achieving lower levels in 1998–99 than other mills in British Columbia (and indeed, lower than all mills in our sample save GA2). U.S. pulp mills, on the other hand, are generally not export-oriented and hence are more insulated from European demands for TCF and effluent-free paper (Norbert-Bohm and Rossi 1998, p. 230). With the exception of GA2, with its special customer concerns, the U.S. mills in our sample had below-average records in AOX reduction in 1998–99.[32]

Conclusion

Notwithstanding substantial convergence among the pulp mills we studied, significant mill-level differences in reduction of pollution persist. In this chapter, we have explored the extent to which variability in the circumstances in which the mills find themselves—that is, in the relative strictness of their regulatory, economic, and social licenses—accounts for those differences in environmental performance. No simple answer emerges, although it is clear that variation in license requirements goes a considerable way toward explaining some differences.

With respect to the *regulatory license*, for example, we found that British Columbia's lag behind the United States in requiring secondary wastewater treatment in mills at the edge of coastal waters helps explain the generally better BOD control by those BC mills in 1998–99, on average, because their treatment facilities were newer and closer to the "state of the art." Similarly, British Columbia's more imminent and more stringent regulatory deadline for elimination of AOX discharges helps explain why its mills, on average, had lower AOX emissions in 1998–99 than the U.S. mills in our sample.

Other interfirm differences in environmental performance could be attributed directly to the terms of their particular *economic license*. Mills whose products and customers were environmentally sensitive (such as GA2, selling paper diapers in western Europe) had particularly low AOX discharges. Some firms operating under serious economic license limits, such as those that were cash-strapped, told us this constrained their capacity to put in place appropriate environmental technology, and this was reflected in below-average environmental performance. Conversely, mills whose corporate parents had larger sales and higher profit margins in the first half of the 1990s, a period of intense social and regulatory pressures regarding chlorine, had better technologies and better environmental performance at the end of that decade.

Different *social license* demands often appeared to be particularly powerful in influencing differences in environmental outcomes. For example, the gap between the emissions of WA2 and WA4 described earlier was very much what one would have anticipated given WA2's remoter small-town location and WA4's location near the heart of a changing, more economically diversified city with lively environmental activists.[33] In a number of cases, our interview data suggested that a painful, well-publicized encounter with a major environmental group produced a sea change in the corporate approach to the environment.

On the other hand, these external license pressures clearly did not explain all the variation in mill-level performance. Substantial differences in environmental performance generally remained among mills in the same regulatory jurisdiction, often exceeding differences with mills in other jurisdictions. That is, differences in firm performance could not be explained by the "regulatory style" of any of the jurisdictions studied. No regulatory regime did uniformly better or worse than others in generating beyond-compliance corporate environmental performance. One reason, it appears, is that regulatory licenses were to some degree tailored to the technological and economic circumstances of particular mills, and we were not able to develop comparable indicators of the tightness of one mill's permit as compared to others.

Similarly, although the relative tightness of firms' economic licenses had some explanatory power, corporate economic resources, as measured by size and profitability, did not account for all the variance in mill-level environmental performance. Some smaller cash-strapped mills were outstanding environmental performers, and there was considerable variability among mills run by large corporations, as well as among smaller ones. While the remaining indeterminacy may reflect our inability to develop sufficiently precise and comparable measures of the relative "tightness" of each mill's economic license, our qualitative data as well as the analysis of management style in the next chapter, lead us to believe that economic variables, however well measured, are not likely to account for all intermill environmental differences.

With respect to firms' social licenses, too, we could not quantify the intensity of the social pressures each mill experienced. Hence we can provide only qualitative evidence concerning the relative importance of firms' social licenses in explaining their environmental performance. But here too it is very unlikely that differences in social pressures account for *all* the observed differences in how far firms move "beyond compliance" in environmental performance. Managers at different mills responded to similar social pressures in different ways. Social license pressures are not merely difficult to measure but inherently imprecise and malleable. That is, the intensity of social pressures depends on how they are interpreted and responded to and often reshaped by corporate managers.

The same indeterminacy and malleability (in varying degrees) affect the terms of firms' regulatory and economic licenses. Pulp mill managers, as we shall see in the next chapter, interpret their legal obligations in different ways, have different relations with regulators, and influence those regulators differently. Even the terms of the economic license are not entirely clear: what one firm may calculate to be a win-win beyond-compliance investment, another, with a different attitude toward environmental issues, may decide is too expensive.

In sum, it became apparent to us that the perceptions and attitudes of mill and corporate managements, and their interpretation of their license terms, acted as an important filter through which information about external licenses was sifted, guiding their responsiveness to conflicting external pressures. The next chapter accordingly explores the relationship between what we came to call "environmental management style" and differences in corporate environmental performance.

5

Environmental Management Style and Corporate Environmental Performance

Accounting to environmental managers at GA1, dramatic demonstrations against the firm by Greenpeace in the early 1990s were viewed as a "wake-up call" that changed their corporate managers' attitudes toward the company's environmental responsibilities, leading first to changes in corporate environmental management and compliance policies, then to improved environmental performance.[1] But mill NZ2, in New Zealand, responded to Greenpeace's campaign against it quite differently. The company sought court injunctions to restrain individual members of the environmental group. The company engaged in its own media campaign to counter Greenpeace's arguments. As NZ2's environmental manager described it: "We decided to take the battle to Greenpeace, and our PR guy enjoyed the scrap. We decided we can win this war. We can visit the schools before they do and build relationships with indigenous groups. It comes down to individuals and, over time, to trust." NZ2 does not acknowledge any change in its behavior to have resulted from the Greenpeace campaign, having preferred simply to "tough it out."[2]

The divergent responses of GA1 and NZ2 suggest that the influence of external pressures on environmental performance depends on an "intervening variable"—*managerial attitude,* or more broadly, what we call *environmental management style.* A firm's environmental management style affects the way it deals with the inevitable uncertainties of the terms of its licenses—how it learns about, interprets, and responds to diverse external pressures for environmental improvement, how it calculates the likely costs of resistance and the benefits of responding favorably, how it goes about communicating with critics and implementing environmental responses, how it perceives and responds to pressures from regulatory regimes and economic constraints—which like social license pressures always entail a significant measure of uncertainty. The logical inference is that firms subject to similar regulatory regimes, technological constraints, social environments, and economic pressures will vary in environmental performance. Some, as indicated by our data, go "beyond compliance" more consistently and further than others. To explain that variation, therefore, it seems sensible to examine, not only the terms of their licenses to operate, as we did in Chapter 4, but also the ways in which firms interpret, respond to, and seek to reshape those license constraints. That is the focus of this chapter.

Based on extensive interviews in 1998–99, we classified each mill's environmental management style on a scale of ideal types. We then correlated environmental management style with the quantitative measures of environmental performance discussed in previous chapters. The results are striking. Environmental management style was a more powerful predictor of mill-level environmental performance than was regulatory regime or corporate size and earnings. Before discussing those data, however, it is important to explain how we conceptualized and sought to measure corporate environmental management style, and then to illustrate the different ideal types.

In Search of Corporate Environmental Management Style

In discussions of emerging strategies of environmental regulation, considerable emphasis has been placed on corporate environmental management systems, conceived of as formalized procedures for making and implementing corporate environmental policies, auditing results, and responding to shortcomings. Yet it is not clear that adopting formalized management plans, which can be instituted for primarily symbolic reasons, actually produces improved environmental management, much less improved environmental performance (Nash 2001). Cary Coglianese (2001) has argued that managerial attitude—particularly what he labels "commitment"—is the key variable in shaping corporate environmental performance.

Similarly, in our field research, we sought to identify what we came to call "environmental management style" at each of the mills and corporations in our sample. By management style, we refer to a combination of managerial attitudes and actions that mark the intensity and character of each management's "commitment" to environmental compliance and improvement. We focus on both attitudes and implementing actions because we concluded that managerial attitudes toward environmental matters often could best be inferred from managers' accounts of the decisions and policies they had made, and actions taken, in response to particular regulatory, economic, and social challenges. We therefore based our assessment of each mill's "environmental management style" on (a) managers' "expressed attitudes" toward environmental problems; (b) managers' environmentally relevant actions and implementation efforts; and (c) their explanations for those actions.[3]

A business operation's environmental management style, we assume, is shaped by both external and intracorporate events—that is, by the demands and constraints that flow from its economic, regulatory, and social licenses over time and also by the attitudes of the leaders who shape the "environmental culture" of the enterprise. These are not mutually exclusive causal categories. Corporate officials' environmental attitudes typically evolve in response to external shocks and demands—although we assume those attitudes also can be influenced by the individual's education, hobbies, readings, families, and friends. Conversely, firm officials' environmental management styles, it became clear to us, influence the ways in which they perceive the demands of their externally generated license to operate and indeed can reshape those demands, at least in part. One implication of the complex genealogy of environmental management styles is that they are subject to change over time, sometimes quite abruptly in response to mergers or detected violations of their economic, regulatory, or social license. For the most part, however, our research method provides only a simple "snapshot" of each firm's environmental management style as we detected it in interviews in 1998–99.

To classify each firm's environmental management style, we relied on our interview data to score each firm on four related dimensions of commitment to environmental values: (1) firm managers' *environmental ethos*, including the extent to which they considered gains to their firm's environmental reputation to be economically desirable; (2) the intensity of managerial *scanning* for environmentally relevant information, including the search for win-

win expenditures identified as both environmentally good and economically desirable for the firm; (3) management's degree of *responsiveness* to environmentally relevant information, including demands from regulators, customers, neighbors, and environmental activists; and (4) the assiduousness with which the facility had institutionalized *implementing routines* to ensure high levels of environmental consciousness and control capacity (including activities such as self-auditing, employee training, and close integration of environmental and production-oriented training and decision-making).[4] We sought to increase the validity of our assessment of each firm on these dimensions by coding the qualitative data separately, so that all members of our research team agreed on the same characterization of the firm's environmental management style. Moreover, we took care to develop our measures of mill environmental management before we analyzed the objective pollution data for each mill, and indeed before we had even obtained the environmental performance data for some facilities. This separate assessment was designed to ensure that our knowledge of firm-level environmental performance did not influence our assessment of the firms' management style.[5]

We found it difficult, however, to agree on a single numerical score for each mill because of the large number of activities within each of the three categories and because we could not easily weight the categories in terms of importance. However, we found ourselves in substantial agreement when we grouped the companies more holistically in terms of ideal types,[6] while still drawing on the initially identified variables. Arrayed in terms of "shades of green," or level of commitment to aggressive environmental management, the typology consists of five ideal types—*Environmental Laggards, Reluctant Compliers, Committed Compliers, Environmental Strategists,* and *True Believers.* Each successive managerial "type" displays incrementally greater commitment to *compliance* (or "overcompliance") with regulatory requirements, *scanning* for environmental information and opportunities, *responsiveness* to regulators and environmental activists, and development of reliable *implementing routines* for their environmental policies.

In the following sections, we first briefly set out the five ideal types. We then illustrate the fit between the ideal types and our sample firms through a detailed examination of the characteristics of one firm in relation to each ideal type. Since the fit between reality and our ideal types was not complete, we take two further examples of firms "on the cusp" between two ideal types, to illustrate the problems in classifying a minority of firms in this way. We then locate the remainder of our sample firms within (or on the cusp of a combination of) ideal types, and describe briefly why each is categorized in a particular way. Finally, we examine the relationship between environmental management style and mill-level performance.

A Typology of Environmental Management Styles

In this typology, it is important to note, the ideal-types are not wholly distinct. Rather, the types are "nested," in the sense that each builds upon the type immediately preceding it, sharing some characteristics but also including additional features, which served to distinguish it from the preceding type. Although that ordering might seem to imply a developmental sequence from "less green" toward successively "greener' management styles, we do not mean to suggest that such a developmental trajectory (while it often does occur) is inevitable or even typical, or that firms might not, under some circumstances, move in the opposite direction.

1. *Environmental Laggards.* Management in these firms does not commit to consistent achievement of regulatory standards as an essential business goal or constraint. Managers have a negative attitude toward many regulatory requirements and comply only to avoid costly enforcement actions. They do not scan for opportunities for environmental innovation; moreover, they are slow to create specialized environmental management positions or procedures and, when they do so, those personnel and procedures are not closely integrated with production. Laggards do not seek to develop cooperative, open relationships with regulatory agencies or with local communities on environmental issues.

2. *Reluctant Compliers.* In contrast with laggards, reluctant compliers, as a matter of firm or facility policy, seek to meet the minimum standards prescribed by legislation and permits. They are more willing to establish environmental positions and procedures to keep up with regulatory requirements. However, they are not committed to invariant or "full" compliance; they are willing to countenance "shortcuts" or occasional permit exceedances, unless monitored closely and pushed hard by regulatory enforcement

officials, and they are inclined to interpret their permit obligations narrowly. They resemble laggards in feeling no moral imperative to comply and in their disinclination to scan broadly for win-win environmental investments, for they tend not to see economic or social benefits in compliance. They also resemble laggards in their disinclination to develop open and cooperative relationships with regulators or local community environmental activists.

3. *Committed Compliers* take their regulatory responsibilities seriously. They strive to maintain compliance even when there are opportunities for avoidance. They usually seek to build in a margin of safety, setting equipment and designing processes so that even an unanticipated emission does not put them in breach of their overall license requirements. They are more cooperative in dealing with regulators in the sense that they seek to demonstrate their reliability in complying with regulatory and permit requirements. Nevertheless, they are predominantly reactive in their dealing with environmental issues; their environmental agenda is set almost entirely by reference to current and imminent legal requirements. They do seek out "win-win" opportunities in a narrow and traditional accounting sense, but invest only in environmental measures that can be demonstrated ex ante to produce a profit in a reasonably short time. They may respond to pressures from local communities or other external stakeholders, such as customers, but they do so predominantly by reference to the terms of the legal license, believing compliance to be the fundamental indicator by which their environmental performance will be judged. Environmental spending is still regarded predominantly as a cost without compensating economic benefits, though its benefit to the environment is generally acknowledged.

4. *Environmental Strategists.* Compared to Committed Compliers, Environmental Strategists have a broader, more future-oriented conception of their environmental objectives, which they see as more closely linked to their business goals. As a matter of long-term business sense, they believe it is desirable to meet current and anticipated regulatory requirements fully, with a margin of safety. They often seek to overcomply with existing permit requirements in order to maintain a reputation as good environmental citizens with regulators, environmental activists, neighbors, customers, and financial markets. They also act strategically and proactively in their relationship with regulators, seeking to build a positive reputation for honesty and reliability

where they believe that will generate long-term economic benefits. However, they strive to reshape regulation (at its formulation stage) so as to minimize its economic impact upon them and provide them with greater flexibility.

Environmental strategists believe that in a range of circumstances, environmental improvements can lead to improved economic performance. Hence they establish highly professional environmental management departments that actively scan for and seek out win-win opportunities. They place emphasis on the integration of economic and environmental performance, establishing sophisticated internal control and auditing systems. They are willing to make substantial environmental investments that cannot be justified ex ante as directly profit-enhancing, but that can be viewed qualitatively as adding to the economic health of the corporation in the long term. For similar strategic reason, Environmental Strategists, as compared to the Committed Compliers, often accommodate to community demands, taking environmental measures that go well beyond legal compliance. However, Environmental Strategists also take initiatives designed to shape community attitudes, educating local interest groups and governmental officials about the firm's environmental policies and the constraints it faces. Information is also carefully managed, for fear that it might be misinterpreted, misunderstood and/or used against them by environmental groups or their competitors. For this reason, they have only very limited transparency, at least as compared to True Believers.

5. *True Believers*, like other firms, have to make decisions that ensure that they remain economically viable. Nevertheless, they approach those decisions with a distinctive attitude toward their environmental responsibilities, explaining their decisions on environmental issues not purely in pragmatic terms (the "business case") but also in terms of principle, as "the right thing to do." They see a reputation for environmental excellence as an important key to business success, as do many environmental strategists. They therefore adopt many of the same strategies as environmental strategists but make that goal more central to their corporate identity. They have an extremely broad perception of what constitute win-win opportunities. This makes them more inclined to define investment in beyond-compliance environmental measures as "good business decisions," even if the numerical payoff can't be calculated ex ante. True Believers constantly scan for such opportunities both

internally and externally and are prepared to invest in them both for the short and the long term. Because they believe that establishing trust with local communities is essential, they are more inclined than Environmental Strategists to accept the need to be fully transparent. Accordingly, they disclose whatever information the community requests about their environmental impacts, and they are even more inclined than Environmental Strategists to go beyond compliance in remedying environmental impacts that disturb their neighbors.

Applying the Typology

Real-world organizations, of course, are complex, multifaceted, changing entities, and few conform in all respects with any single ideal-typical set of managerial attitudes as outlined above. While some of the paper mills whose managers we interviewed seemed to fit comfortably within our ideal types, others were more difficult to classify, having most but not all the characteristics of a particular ideal-type, or sharing features of two or even three different types.[7] On the other hand, the very concept of an ideal type recognizes that entities in the real world will only approximate, rather than fully match, the ideal-type, so we remain confident about the usefulness of that approach and of our classifications of mills within it. In our accounts below, we shall show how companies within each ideal type perceived and handled issues relating to each of their licenses, dealt with uncertainty concerning license terms, and resolved conflicts between the terms of the different licenses.

Environmental Laggards

Based on our research in 1998–99, none of the facilities in our sample fitted the description of an Environmental Laggard. That is an important finding in itself. As discussed in earlier chapters, it suggests that by the end of the twentieth century in the United States, Canada, Australia, and New Zealand, the combination of economic, regulatory, and sociopolitical pressures had required all pulp mills, if they wished to stay in business, to make a commitment to capital-intensive technological modernization and adopt environmental control methods that bring them, at a minimum, into rough compliance with existing regulatory laws and requirements. Management attitudes and practices reflected that change. All had established environmental management programs of at least some level of sophistication. All seemed to fully accept the legitimacy of the regulatory regime for pulp mills' effluent and emissions.

Reluctant Compliers: WA2

We have already displayed some of WA2's pollution data,[8] observed that it experienced less intense social pressures than many other mills in our sample,[9] and noted that as of 1998–99, it was well below average for the pulp mills in our sample in terms of environmental performance. WA2 is part of one of the world's largest paper companies, with annual sales of over $6 billion. Nevertheless, the mill operates within a tight economic license. The corporation as a whole struggled with sharply fluctuating profits and losses in the 1990s and a substantial debt load, which it sought to address by rationalizing its manufacturing base, closing or selling a number of facilities. The combined pulp and paper mill at WA2 was a poor economic performer through much of the 1990s, suffering from weak pulp prices internationally. Nevertheless, it employs close to 1,500 people, is a major economic contributor to the local area, and is the largest taxpayer in its county. And in terms of environmental management style, it is the clearest example in our sample of a Reluctant Complier.

Our interviews with mill managers at WA2 made it clear that their approach to environmental decision-making was fundamentally reactive. Environmental considerations were viewed almost entirely as a cost lacking compensating economic benefits. According to the mill's environmental manager, "It's only once in twenty years [that] there's been a project that was [beneficial on both] economic and environmental [grounds]." This view was echoed by personnel at WA2's corporate head office, who reported that most environmental improvements involved a cost burden that was rarely compensated for by efficiencies in production or chemical usage. Back at the mill, WA2's environmental manager saw little virtue in investing in environmental technology for its own sake or because it might provide broader benefits, whether of an economic nature or in terms of satisfying stakeholders' demands. To her mind, environmental investments caused economic costs and cost-cutting production measures caused environmental costs: "Things that cut costs usually damage the environment. For example, an additive to the paper machine is cheaper, but it pours things [pollutants] off in the dryer because it's more caustic, and that leads to more releases and so to more costs."

Neither WA2 corporate officials nor the mill environmental manager mentioned any efforts to scan for innovations that might both save money and reduce environmental impact. The mill's environmental manager noted, however, that there was no lack of useful projects requiring attention: "We could do better on solid waste and on recycling. We could improve on current processes or on rehabilitating from the mistakes of the past and to modernize the process. [Money] could be used to clean up past issues such as PCBs still on site, asbestos, peeling lead paint. There are always things falling down that need demolishing." But she did not express any confidence in getting cooperation from mill or financial managers for environmental expenditures.

Against this backdrop, regulation was not just the principal but indeed the only driver of improved environmental performance at WA2. Consider the environmental manager's description of the decision-making process she would face were she to seek a capital expenditure for an environmental project:

> In terms of a business case, each individual part of the mill prepares capital budgets. That budget is submitted up the line. We seldom get even half of what we ask for given to us. . . . The most persuasive case is an order from the agency: Do this or we will shut the operation down. Below that, next in the hierarchy is where the agency has said this was required of you and you missed the deadline. Next down from that would be, this is required of you, but only in the future. Next down from that is "We'd like to do it but no one is beating us over the head to do it." But very seldom do you get money for this stuff.

Moreover, at WA2, the mere fact that a regulation had been enacted was not regarded as a sufficient driver of improved environmental performance unless that rule was also effectively enforced. As the environmental manager put it: "Resources flow to current needs. Inspections (in part) determine current needs. . . . We would be slackers without inspections. We'd be doing something else with our time and money. Without inspections in a particular area, we wouldn't pay attention to that area."

This managerial stance appears to have elicited a high level of monitoring and enforcement by WA2's regulators, redoubling the salience of regulatory enforcement in the minds of WA2 managers:

> We get something like eighteen to twenty-four inspections in a year. The majority are surprise inspections, when they just show up and say, "We want to look at X," and it's very effective. With a mill this size, it would take us weeks to disguise the problems, and so they pretty much catch you. . . . They come in with their guns loaded, and before they come in, they'd have been up to look at us from the hill and to look at the stacks, so when they come in, they know what they're looking at.[10]

Consistent with this attitude, WA2's environmental manager attributed almost every major environmental decision directly to regulation, although regulation itself was on occasion a surrogate for broader community pressure:

> Why were the steam strippers introduced? The answer is the state got lots of citizen complaints, and so their engineers say: "What are your capabilities at the mill?" So they got us on to a compliance schedule. They were also measuring the level of citizen complaints and asking: "Where [do] the TRSs [odor-causing chemicals] come from?" They developed a plan and executed it over several years.

The corporation did have a management system for tracking each mill's environmental performance, and each adverse incident was subject to an environmental investigation and to a root-cause analysis. However, the adoption of ISO-14000 had been contemplated but rejected, according to the mill environmental manager, because it "would be a big pain." And in many respects, WA2's environmental management system was narrowly focused. In contrast to the case with Environmental Strategists and True Believers, environmental training of employees was viewed at WA2, not as a practice having virtue in its own right (for example, in reducing spills and gaining tighter operational control), but rather as a necessary response to government regulation. Similarly, while corporate headquarters mandated periodic environmental self-audits, they were not used as a diagnostic tool for identifying failures and opportunities in environmental performance generally (as was the case with Environmental Strategists and True Believers). On the contrary, we were told, "It's the Legal Department who audit. They ask what are the rules, and it's focused on our legal compliance." And whereas Environmental

Strategists and True Believers invariably claimed that their internal standards were more demanding than government inspections, at WA2, government inspections set the corporate standard.[11]

In terms of social license, the environmental manager described a management that was reactive and only minimally responsive to other stakeholders. With its significant brand-name presence in consumer markets for some paper products, it might have been anticipated that the company would be sensitive to the potential impact of a poor environmental reputation on retailers buying its products[12]. Yet WA2 gave no indication of paying attention to potential consumer environmental concerns.

Historically, the mill had also been largely unresponsive to its local community. This had changed somewhat by the late 1990s, but largely as a response to regulatory pressure:

> The company used to own the town. In the 1960s, the company sold the town to the citizens, and there developed a drawbridge mentality. No one in the town knew what was happening in the mill or vice versa. In the last few years, we have tried to get in touch with the community. This started with SARA Title III [the community right-to-know law], and we began emphasizing it [communication] more as we headed towards our risk management plan and emergency response planning requirements [both required by regulation].

However, WA2's shift toward communication with the local community had not led to any substantial dialogue and only to modest attempts (e.g., through attempts to investigate odor complaints) to take seriously and accommodate to community concerns. As WA2's environmental manager put it: "[T]here are three to four town meetings in the last year. People ask questions. [What] it's done [is] to reduce citizen complaints, because they understand what we are doing. If we have a stone wall approach, they assume we are doing nothing. We have not always communicated very well."

In summary, WA2 is a Reluctant Complier, because as a matter of firm or facility policy, it does seek to meet the minimum standards prescribed by regulation. It has environmental positions and procedures to keep up with regulatory requirements. However, it is willing to countenance noncompliance where this would not be noticed by regulatory enforcement officials and if it thinks it can get away with it. It sees very little benefit to its economic license in environmental spending unless it is mandated by regulation and that regulation is enforced. It is disinclined to scan for win-win environmental investments and tends not to see economic or social benefits in compliance. It views its social license in narrow terms and is disinclined to develop open and cooperative relationships with regulators, the local community, or other environmental activists.

Committed Compliers: BC4

The pulp mill we designate BC4 is located in British Columbia. Part of a moderate-sized forest products corporation, BC4 is designed to produce approximately 700 tons of pulp per day and as of 1999 employed 330 people. Many of BC4's significant customers (some 30 percent of total pulp sales) are in western Europe, and in the 1990s, they generated some pressures on BC4 to reduce emissions of chlorine compounds (AOX). Customer concerns also contributed to BC4's decision to adopt an ISO-14000-certified environmental management system. On the other hand, in the latter part of the 1990s, the company was operating in the red and enjoyed little financial slack. Unlike most of the mills in our sample, it did not face a local community that pushed it hard for better environmental performance.[13] Yet BC4 took its regulatory license terms very seriously and tried very hard to comply with its legal obligations. BC4 is a good example of a Committed Complier.

For BC4 (as with a Reluctant Complier such as WA2), regulatory requirements—as opposed to a deeper commitment to environmental improvement as part of a business strategy—formed management's main environmental frame of reference. In 1998–99, BC4 mill managers described regulation as the "shrinking noose" that drove all major environmental expenditure. At corporate level, too, management reported that while some environmental projects might have some modest economic payback in the long term, "this payback does not drive the project, it's usually the need to stay in compliance with regulation."

However, unlike WA2, BC4 took its regulatory responsibilities very seriously. As the mill manager put it: "Regulation is the ultimate. You comply with the law. There is no way there is conflict with the law." BC4 thus routinely built a safety margin into its operating parameters so that even unanticipated excursions would be unlikely to result in a breach of its legal license.[14] Similarly, BC4 was willing to make substantial beyond-compliance investments in order to meet anticipated future regulatory requirements. For example, according to head office personnel, a decision to upgrade the bleach plant during the 1990s, while it did speed up production, was taken primarily "to get away from being on the edge of compliance."

In its relations with regulators, too, BC4 was far more cooperative than were Reluctant Compliers. As a British Columbia regulator put it, BC4's environmental manager "does what I ask. I don't have to justify myself six ways. They may not do it as quickly as I want, but it happens." Moreover, to BC4, the regulatory agency's capacity (or incapacity) to enforce those regulations and the risk of potential penalties were irrelevant. The BC4 environmental manager saw regulatory inspections themselves as superficial and unimportant in improving performance. Nevertheless, his view was that "[t]he regulations are out there and the implications of failing to meet them are too great from a public and market point of view. So we are more demanding of ourselves than the regulators are. . . . For us, our whole business is at stake." In his opinion, the periodic mill-specific reports published by BC regulators were "a pretty effective tool," because "[i]f you have recurring environmental problems, you come up on the list. It keeps you in compliance, because public pressure is more demanding than the regulatory agencies. . . . Agencies are more forgiving."

As these remarks suggest, BC4 managers felt the need to meet the demands of wider social stakeholder groups more keenly than Reluctant Compliers did. They had had sufficient encounters with environmental groups to be highly sensitive to the effects of adverse publicity on community relations and also on customer and consumer confidence in their products. Nevertheless, BC4 differed from Environmental Strategists and True Believers because even when responding to these broader social pressures, BC4's primary reference point was the regulatory license, which management viewed as the key external measure of acceptable environmental performance. The company feared that if it did not meet the legal standard, it might face informal sanctions imposed by the public, the media, and perhaps also by European markets. As the mill manager put it, "What drives [our environmental performance] is regulation."

Notwithstanding the company's concern to meet (or marginally exceed) regulatory requirements, BC4's approach to environmental issues was therefore more limited than that of Environmental Strategists and True Believers. BC4's environmental manager was well-integrated into the production process, attending daily and weekly production meetings, and was located in the same area as the production engineers. However, he was not involved in developing mill environmental or business policy, as environmental managers at Environmental Strategist firms typically were. Environmental management was seen as a lower-level technical position rather than a higher-level policy position. Equally telling was BC4's perception of the economic benefits of environmental investments. When describing the possible economic benefits of installing more modern, greener technology, BC4's general manager limited his list of benefits to largely tangible, quantifiable gains, such as speeding up or increasing production, decreasing labor costs, and decreasing materials costs. Absent from this accounting of what constituted a win-win investment were more qualitative benefits, such as improved reputation, winning greater regulatory flexibility, improving community relations, and enhancing the firm's public image—all factors typically mentioned by Environmental Strategists and True Believers. Similarly, compared to the Environmental Strategists in our sample, BC4's internal environmental audit program was relatively underdeveloped. It lacked any reciprocal audit arrangements with its sister mill, for example, whereas Environmental Strategists tended to use environmental specialists from other mills, who could look at their system with "new eyes" and provide new ideas. Even BC4's environmental training program for mill operators was substantially regulation-oriented.[15]

For BC4, the existing regulatory system was seemingly taken as a given. Company officials did not take exception to the current regulations or to the way they were enforced. And unlike Environmental Strategists, they appeared to have no strategy for negotiating with regulators over the terms of their license or for seeking regulatory flexibility.

BC4 resembled an Environmental Strategist in its responsiveness to customer concerns regarding environmental performance, even in ways that were not driven by its regulatory license. Because major European customers demanded elemental chlorine-free (ECF) pulp,[16] BC4, as noted in Chapter 4, had made the investment in becoming an ECF mill before being legally required to do so. In response to adverse publicity in Europe regarding BC4's parent corporation's forest practices, the parent company decided to implement a formal environmental management system (including at BC4) and obtain ISO-14000 certification. However, BC4's environmental manager viewed the company's ISO-14000 system in rather limited terms, as a valuable tool for helping to ensure that the mill remained in compliance with regulations and for responding to pressures from customers and regulators. In this regard, BC4 differed from Environmental Strategists, which spoke of ISO-14000's potential for facilitating continuous improvement, change in the corporate culture, and intensifying the search for win-win and beyond-compliance outcomes.

In summary, this Committed Complier took its regulatory responsibilities seriously and sought to maintain compliance even when there were opportunities for avoidance. It built in a margin of safety. However, management's environmental agenda was set almost entirely by reference to current and imminent legal requirements. It scanned for win-win opportunities in a narrow and traditional accounting sense. It was responsive to pressures from customers, neighbors, and regulators, but it responded predominantly by reference to the terms of the legal license, believing compliance to be the fundamental indicator by which its environmental performance would be judged. While generally acknowledging the environmental benefits that flowed from regulation, BC4 managers saw environmental spending predominantly as a cost, albeit with some compensating economic benefits.

Environmental Strategists: BC2

BC2's corporate parent (BC2corp) is a very large integrated forest products company. Its multinational operations include timberlands and wood products, pulp, paper, and packaging. The BC2 mill produces approximately 1,200 tons of market pulp each day, and another 1,200 tons per day of paper grade and specialty pulps. It is adjacent to a substantial township, which is no longer dependent upon the mill as a major source of employment.[17] Segments of the community are increasingly critical of the mill's presence and operations. BC2 is located on a river, which sustains a fishery, requiring good water quality.

During the 1990s, BC2corp felt that its reputation for ethical and environmentally responsible behavior was suffering as a result of rising negative perceptions of the forest and wood products industry. Since the company had a very substantial political profile in several countries, BC2corp management felt compelled to reassess its approach to environmental issues in order to recharge its reputation and to reach out to its stakeholders. At both the mill and the corporate level, BC2's environmental management style makes it a good example of an Environmental Strategist.

Like Committed Compliers, BC2 took very considerable steps to ensure that it was in compliance with all regulatory requirements, routinely building in a margin of safety. And like Committed Compliers, BC2 viewed its regulatory license not just as important in its own right but also as an index against which the company would be judged by social and political audiences. BC2 managers referred to the damage that adverse publicity related to noncompliance could do to the company's reputation and social license. However, BC2 differed from Committed Compliers in the extent to which it was willing to exceed present legal requirements. An independent industry observer gave us one example: "The government was trying to get rid of [a type of highly polluting burner used at pulp mills]. [BC2corp] said the government is right and decided to shut their own down. So they are trucking waste 200 miles at the cost of millions of dollars a year, while their competitors are still operating [the burners]."

Like other Environmental Strategists, BC2 also differs from Committed Compliers in the extent to which it strives to develop trusting and cooperative relationships with regulators. For example, both BC2 and British Columbia regulatory officials emphasized how the company had established a close (community activists suggested too close) working relationship with the regulator. As mill management told us:

> We disclose to local regulators even if we don't have to. We work closely with the regulators. They have a copy of our emergency response plan and so on. The culture of the company is "We care about the environment." . . . Positive relations with the regulators at all [BC2corp] mills is important, because our credibility is important, as is developing trust. And we are an important economic entity in the local area.

Developing a good relationship with regulators, it was assumed, increased the company's opportunity to influence the design of permits and new regulations. Corporate officials have been very active politically, commonly heading up industry association representations and seeking to modify or postpone proposed regulations that BC2corp did not regard as scientifically, environmentally, or economically justifiable.[18]

As indicated by the case of the burners mentioned above, BC2's environmental management style also differed from Committed Compliers in that it did not regard compliance with regulation (or regulation plus a margin) as the ultimate standard to which it aspired. Mill and corporate officials both asserted that there were often good strategic reasons for going substantially beyond regulation, particularly the need to protect the company's reputation and social license. One BC2 official told us: "Our behavior is predicated by the feelings of the local community. There is lots of activity associated with process management and driven by odor [which is not regulated with any specificity]. We had a local population of about 30,000, but it's now 80,000 and much more cosmopolitan. . . . We have spent $13 million at [the mill] on odor."

BC2corp officials also expressed a particular sensitivity to the possibility that adverse publicity on environmental issues might send negative signals to financial markets and threaten their relationships with customers in environmentally sensitive markets:

> Public opinion is huge. If the public is opposed to you, you risk shutdown. We became attuned to it twenty or thirty years ago with our forestry operations . . . now we do landscape forestry. It has a less visible impact and a better wildlife impact. Looking at it from a business standpoint, it's risk management. We became responsible environmental stewards because it's not in our financial interest to risk our operations being closed down.[19]

On the other hand, it was clearly not the case that BC2 spent money on the environment simply because it was "a good thing to do." Mill and corporate officials were adamant that money could only be invested in environmental issues when there was a demonstrable business case for doing so. As the mill manager stated: "We are in the business of making money. The shareholders look for a return. Why invest if no return? [. . .] Why invest in [our company] if treasury bonds would give you a better return?"

BC2corp environmental managers added: "What really drives us is the investment cycle. . . . making a technological choice to last thirty years against a backdrop of regulatory obligations, customer expectations, and political expectations. It is impossible to think of an economic enterprise going beyond compliance for the sake of it."

Thus like other Environmental Strategists, BC2 used a sophisticated calculus in determining its environmental strategy. The environment was essentially viewed as one issue among others that had to be managed efficiently and effectively for the long-term benefit of the company, and factored into overall corporate strategy:

> The fundamental thing . . . is blending a business strategy with an environmental strategy. We are a financial entity. We have fiduciary obligations to our shareholders. We need to make assets work financially. And we need a longer-term view because of the nature of the asset. . . . We start with a vision of the plant in three to five years—including an environmental and a community perspective. Then we do the business planning.

Decisions concerning environmental expenditures were determined according to similar criteria as other business decisions, that is, employing a systematic weighing of costs and benefits, prioritizing, calculating whether particular investments would be likely to achieve corporate financial targets, and making decisions based on the overall "business case." The "business case," however, included qualitative concerns such as enhancing corporate reputation, public relations, regulatory flexibility, and credibility with the community and regulators.

As an Environmental Strategist, BC2 was prepared to invest significant resources in searching for win-win solutions to environmental problems, for its officials believed that such solutions could often be found. For example, BC2corp had conducted an extensive review of its chemical purchasing procedures in the belief that it could reduce both waste generation (an environmental win) and waste disposal costs (an economic win). In fact, managers claimed, the review had a "dramatic impact on hazardous waste generation." In pursuit of win-win solutions, BC2corp also made considerable investments in technological R and D:

> We identified the path forward: how to eliminate dioxins and furans . . . and identified technologies to get there. . . . We did lots of experimental work and ended up with a phased program. . . . It was a 2.5-to-3-year process from thought

to feasibility, capital approval, design, and construction. It cost [approximately] $75 million. Is it delivering what we want? It took eighteen months to do that, because it was new technology for our employees.

Just how far Environmental Strategists like BC2 are willing to go beyond compliance is difficult to specify in the abstract. On the one hand, BC2 environmental managers acknowledge that even projects that could be demonstrated to provide win-win outcomes are not always implemented, because in each case environmental projects compete for capital with other projects, which may promise a higher return: "We want higher production rates, reduced chemical use, a better yield on wood, and we go for the project that promises most." On the other hand, BC2 was sometimes also willing to make substantial environmental investments that could not be justified ex ante as directly profit-enhancing. Some of these involved a political calculation about what was necessary to protect its social license (such as the decision to spend $13 million on odor), while others had an economic focus. BC2 managers found such decisions difficult to grapple with because of "the difficulty of having enough quantifiable data around the economic benefits." Yet in the extent to which it was prepared to do so, BC2 was noticeably different from Committed Compliers. As corporate management pointed out:

> Another company not wanting to spend as much capital as us may claim it's not prudent to do more than government requires—but they have missed a substantial part of the picture. We are saving via technology that saves on chemicals and is more efficient and results in a lesser wage bill and in less liability claims. It's a longer-term view, and we are getting better at justifying it to the markets.

BC2's commitment to integrating economic and environmental objectives led to a broader use of environmental management tools than Committed Compliers employed. BC2's audit process, for example, was not designed to achieve legal compliance alone: "The auditing function is to help understand deficiencies in our system. We track a number of major issues, and if we find we are not as good as best practice, then it becomes an opportunity."

Similarly, BC2's environmental management system was designed not only to ensure compliance and allay customer concerns but also to "control . . . costs better, . . . be more competitive, . . . [achieve a] lower incidents rate, [and] sustain . . . environmental performance."

Compared to Committed Compliers, BC2 was more proactive in its approach to community relations. In response to the local community's increased sensitivity to the mill's emissions, BC2 managers had arranged regular tours of the mill conducted by a staff member, who specialized in explaining the mill's production processes and environmental controls. Regular meetings, seminars, and forums were held with the community. The mill manager said that his "door was always open." There was also considerable evidence, such as the abovementioned $13 million investment in odor controls, that the mill had not only listened to community concerns but had also, in a major way, responded to some of them.

Yet there was also a sense in which the company was more concerned to *manage* community responses than to enter into a genuine dialogue.[20] Members of a local environmental group felt strongly that BC2 did not respond to their concerns, complaints, or requests for data. They cited a particular incident (of which they had video evidence) in which effluent from the mill had been discharged onto the river beach, where it was left for a number of months until the rains washed it away. Mill officials pointed out that the effluent had already been treated, and that while it might be unsightly, it was not a health hazard. Community group members disagreed, claiming that those who had walked near the effluent to take the video pictures developed sores on their legs.

BC2corp's careful management of external relations also extends to the management of information about discharges from its facilities. The company's annual environmental report aggregates all environmental discharge information, making it impossible for readers to obtain mill-specific information. The company prefers to respond only to specific requests for information about conditions at a specific location,[21] and, according to one corporate official, the company "consider[s] data that is not publicly available to be confidential." Even when the data requested are legally required to be made available, BC2corp has often required those seeking the information to obtain it from public sources rather than providing it directly. And notwithstanding BC2's claims that "our doors are always open," when it came to divulging information to local community groups, members of at least one of the latter felt that they often ran into a nontransparent brick wall.

BC2corp was proactive with respect to environmental issues that affected its relations with customers and ultimate consumers. The most salient example arose in the late 1980s, when the discovery of dioxins in pulp effluent and products became an important market issue among western European customers and consumers. That, according to BC2 officials, led to a number of beyond-compliance actions "to ensure dioxins do not exist in our effluent or our de-foamers." Nevertheless, BC2corp did not appear to be a True Believer, in the sense that its primary concern was always its economic stakeholders' specific opinion of its environmental performance, rather than a more generalized belief that good environmental performance eventually and inevitably brings economic reward. For example, in referring to the ISO-14000 environmental management system BC2 had adopted, a member of the management team told us: "14001 certification is market driven, especially from Europe and Japan. Our customers tell us they want fiber from sustainable forests. . . . It's about being able to access and retain a market, and if you have to take on a shade of green, so be it."

In this case, as in a number of other examples, BC2's environmental management style reflected the belief that in pursuing economic goals, the terms of the firm's social and regulatory licenses must not only be accommodated but exceeded. Yet as with other Environmental Strategists, BC2's efforts to accommodate those values are carefully calibrated, with the result that the firm's commitment to beyond-compliance environmental goals fall short of that of the mills we labeled True Believers.

The True Believers: WA4

The ideal-typical True Believer, as sketched earlier, may not be entirely achievable in the real world. Yet in terms of attitude and aspiration, some of the firms in our sample, while in some respects difficult to distinguish from Environmental Strategists, seemed to approach that mindset. WA4 was the one that most closely resembled the ideal-typical True Believer.

WA4 is owned by a privately held company, WA4corp. The WA4 mill produces pulp and paper with a total production capacity of approximately 1,200 tons per day. WA4 is located on the waterfront in a fairly large city and, as described earlier, has a demanding social license, the result of strong pressures from watchful local environmental activists and a concerned public.[22] Throughout most of the 1990s, when pulp prices were often low, WA4 also faced tough economic pressures, and it did not have the financial depth of companies like BC2 (or WA2, for that matter).

WA4 management's most distinctive characteristic was the extent to which they made the pursuit of environmental excellence and a commitment to the maximum feasible environmental protection a central component of their corporate identity, a rationale for their behavior, and a strategy for business success. This goal did not blind them to the need to succeed in economic terms, but it did fundamentally shape how they went about doing so. Their central assumption was the merger of business success and environmental performance. Of course, even True Believers do not make expensive changes in inputs, processes, or products when the costs of doing so appear to exceed their environmental benefits. However, compared to other firms, including Environmental Strategists, WA4 managers not only expressed more willingness to treat investment in environmental improvements as an important goal in itself but also seemed to perceive many more environmental expenditures as both "affordable" and "desirable."

In some respects, WA4's approach to regulation resembled that of the Environmental Strategists. WA4 established performance targets that were more demanding than the legally required limits in its regulatory permits, for example, and often introduced environmental improvements well in advance of anticipated regulation. Its officials also went to considerable lengths to establish relationships of trust with its regulators. They did so, first of all, to reduce uncertainty (so that in the event of ambiguity as to the terms of the license or whether it had been breached, the regulator would likely exercise its discretion in their favor) and, secondly, because a good relationship might help them negotiate more cost-effective outcomes. However, WA4 managers were distinctive in the extent to which they believed that conflicts between the demands of the firm's regulatory license and its economic license could be mitigated, and commonly overcome, by seeking out and implementing win-win solutions. This belief permeated their approach to compliance issues. For example, WA4 management commonly established tighter day-to-day pollution-control standards than those prescribed by its regulatory permit not only to build in a margin of error but also because they believed that this approach would bring its own economic rewards:

We track the environmental stuff that slows production ... we now have five or six key measurable factors to test our performance against. But compliance is not regarded as enough—the push is to an ever-higher level. By picking a target higher than regulation, you less frequently get upset conditions. You are not managing on the edge, so you get less downtime and use less chemicals, and need less maintenance. Keeping to the targets which are better than compliance also leads to reduced costs, and we use this information with the regulators and the community. This pays huge dividends.

Thus, to WA4 managers, there was a triple dividend involved in going beyond compliance: it would improve both their standing with regulators and the community *and* the firm's economic bottom line. Similarly, WA4 managers viewed the early implementation of technology to meet anticipated regulation as a way of gaining both an environmental and an economic advantage. For example, describing their decision to move to ECF pulp production, a WA4 official said: "We saw Europe react to bleaching. If it happens in Europe, it usually happens in the U.S.A. a bit later, so we adapted our plant. We spent millions more, and we did it far earlier and cheaper without having to retrofit."

WA4 also differed from the Environmental Strategists, albeit only in degree, in evaluating potential investments in environmental protection that do not have any demonstrated economic payback, or insufficient payback within a relatively short period. So broad was their belief that "what's good for the environment is good for the bottom line" that they perceived a great many environmental decisions, at least at operational level, as being sound economic investments.

At the same time, WA4's ambitions were much lower when it came to investments in very costly technology, which the company believed were beyond its grasp in the current economic environment; in this sense, it resembled an Environmental Strategist. For example, WA4 managers believed that the company's wastewater treatment system, installed in the 1970s, "is more or less [the] best available technology still ... Our treatment plant ... is very efficient in terms of comparing what comes into the plant with what goes to the discharge point." They added, however, that "new mills now tend to build bigger treatment systems with more retention and treatment time, and so get better results. ... Newer plants get better BOD per ton because they installed a larger treatment plant." WA4 managers were thus aware that enlarging their treatment plant would improve their BOD discharges, but had chosen not to do so. We are not suggesting that they should have done so, but would merely point out that even True Believers do not take every action they know will improve the environment.

Nevertheless, even in times of scarce capital funds, WA4 managers engaged in proactive and aggressive search for incremental win-win solutions and for continuous improvement in the implementation of the firm's environmental policies, for, as True Believers, they view that effort as an important element in improving profitability. The mill environmental manager noted:

> We feel if we are vigilant, push for continuous improvement, and try harder, we can stay competitive.... [In hard economic times], all capital expenditure becomes more modest and it becomes, "What can we do with existing processes? How can we reduce chemical usage, minimize energy use, and improve things like housekeeping efficiencies?" We keep experimenting and improving process control.

Similarly, WA4 managers, exemplifying the True Believers' characteristic melding of environmental and economic goals, emphasized that:

> In lean times ... there is more emphasis on tightening up and refining and tracking the process as a way to save money. When it runs smooth and avoids variability and upsets, you avoid a lot of environmental problems. So we are not asking for capital, but looking for win-wins to reduce cost and get the environmental benefits.

More fully than Environmental Strategists, WA4 placed a high priority on establishing and maintaining strong relationships with the local community. Managers were extremely proactive, energetic, and innovative in doing so, believing that a close and trusting relationship with the local community was essential to the mill's very existence. They made strenuous efforts to nurture and maintain such a relationship and emphasized the importance not just of communicating with local communities but of entering into a genuine dialogue with them. This implied considerable transparency on the company's part and a willingness not only to listen but also to respond to community concerns.

When WA4 first acquired the mill, local environmental activists were hostile and mistrustful. As one company official put it, "We were telling people we care, we'll invest, and that we have a stewardship commitment to the land, but the response was that 'talk is cheap.'" The company persisted in pursuing a policy of openness and community dialogue, however, as well as "walking the talk." A WA4 manager noted:

> We found we should not send our PR people out, it has to be staff: the environmental manager, the mill manager, who talk to local environmental groups. We gave up press releases and really started talking to people, and that started to make a difference. We were sharing financial information, our business plans, and our environmental plans. We allowed the community in to look at actual measurements of dioxin. Now it's a real dialogue. I see most of the groups two or three times a month. Most important of all, what we say is what we do. . . . I need their trust as much as they need ours. As soon as we violate it, all bets are off. I worked hard [for] ten years to build it, and [if] I screw up, it would erase ten years of good work.

Exceptionally, both workers and the community groups with which we spoke strongly supported WA4. As one of the latter told us: "It's a real honest dialogue with WA4. . . . They give you any information you ask for. When they include the community, they really listen and make changes to their programs. . . . They are honest about what they are willing and not willing to do."

An indication of WA4's responsiveness to community environmental concerns is provided by this story from one mill manager:

> When dioxin first showed up in 1991, when we renewed our wastewater permit, there were concerns from the community that a deal was done between the company and the government behind closed doors. We didn't like the permit limit, but we didn't want to appeal it, because that would send the wrong message to the community. We . . . asked, "What do *you* want in the permit?"—and so sent a message out and saved our reputation [with the community]. The public has the ability to appeal the permit. Nobody appealed, but it was very controversial. Every other pulp company in the state appealed their permit. . . . We dropped out of the industry association for similar reasons. The industry generally was in dinosaur mode and didn't want to disseminate information. We dropped out because they just beat on the desk and intimidated legislators.

Similarly, when WA4 experienced a serious chemical spill, managers not only took immediate and effective action to mitigate its impact, but also disclosed the problem to the local community at the very earliest opportunity. Contrast BC2's handling of an effluent spill (p. 115 above) with the account of WA4's environmental manager of a similar spill (p. 90 above). In WA4's case, the facility responded to a spill of treated effluent by containing and cleaning the spilled (and arguably harmless) material. In BC2's case, the same material was left on a beach after a spill until rains finally washed it away.

As a True Believer, and in striking contrast to BC2, WA4 was prepared to take whatever risks might flow from sharing information with regulators and environmental activists, beyond the disclosure required by law, in hopes of building a trustful and cooperative relationship. Rather than using dialogue to attempt to pacify or co-opt environmental activists, WA4 treated its interactions with the community as a process in which it would listen carefully and respond, perhaps reshaping corporate priorities.

To WA4, community relations served other purposes as well. The terms of the social license are inherently unclear, generating considerable uncertainty both as to what outsiders might consider a breach and what adverse consequences might stem from a perceived breach. For WA4, developing a strong and trusting relationship with local critics helped reduce that uncertainty—and hence increased the company's control over its destiny. While building social capital does not necessarily prevent conflict, WA4 managers felt it does diminish the chance that conflict would escalate into all-out warfare should adverse incidents such as "spills, tank failure, dioxin issues" occur in the future.

Similarly, establishing good community relations—even if it required disclosure of environmentally sensitive information—was seen as a means of minimizing the risk of costly lawsuits:

> Citizen suits are a big issue. But if you keep your information secret, groups go dig through the public records, unearth data, and initiate action. If we are more open with our stakeholders, they are not as likely to put forth those kinds of suits. So the environmental community provides a valuable service to industry by setting the standards and rewarding industry for getting up to the mark.

Furthermore, in the minds of WA4 managers, good community relations would facilitate governmental approval of potentially controversial decisions. A WA4 manager said that in talking to environmental activists, "We show them what the options are and the trade-offs. And if we can get assurances that the environmental groups will be happy, we are sure the government will buy in." Put differently, good community relations could sometimes be used to gain additional regulatory leverage. For example, WA4 managers believed that support from a prominent local activist had facilitated the state's relatively rapid approval of their innovative toxic waste cleanup plan.

Finally, in our interviews with pulp mill officials, only True Believers such as WA4 emphasized the importance *for environmental policy* of establishing a strong and cooperative relationship with their workforce, not only as a component of community relations but as an integral part of achieving operating excellence. This included a strong emphasis on extensive employee training in corporate environmental policies, including the importance of maintaining tight tolerances in effluent control and other potentially polluting processes. The integration of environmental excellence and overall quality control was repeatedly reflected in WA4 managers' observations:

> We have to be competitive. We set a standard of operating excellence—and pick a target. It permeates everything: maintenance, community activity, paper quality. If you put [a] standard out there, people will go for it. The workforce [is] your greatest asset. . . . There is huge value in a workforce that goes for excellence, that tackles the sense of environmental accomplishment and puts it right back into the business. You can't build it any other way. The key to making an environmental management program work is instilling it—getting everyone involved in the environmental management plan. The emphasis is on preventative maintenance—checklists and planned outages, rather than running it till it breaks. Keeping on top of tank integrity by testing . . . [for problems].

Thus the key feature of environmental management style for a True Believer such as WA4 is the conscious blending of the firm's social, regulatory, and economic license requirements, that is, seeing them as mutually supportive rather than as contending external pressures.

Two "Mixed" Types of Environmental Management

A few mills in our sample were difficult to categorize within the typology of environmental management styles discussed thus far. Some firms, for example, had many of the traits of True Believers yet displayed a somewhat lower level of commitment to environmental improvement or integration of economic and environmental goals than WA4, for example. Yet they more closely resembled WA4 than they did BC2 and other Environmental Strategists. We ended up classifying such firms as "less intense" True Believers. More difficult to classify were some firms that displayed the characteristics of two quite different types, as exemplified by the following two cases.

AUS: Part Reluctant Complier, Part True Believer. AUS's corporate parent (AUScorp) is one of the world's leading integrated packaging and paper companies, with over 150 plants around the world. During the period of our field research (1998–99), the company's economic situation was healthy.[23] The AUS pulp mill in our sample provides the raw material for a paper mill that has been built adjacent to it. No market pulp is sold. The pulp mill itself has a production capacity of approximately 1,200 tons per day. Together, the pulp and paper mills employ approximately 900 people, most of whom live locally. The mill is located on a relatively small river in a valley, which is quite heavily industrialized. In dry periods, its treated discharges amount to approximately 7 percent of river flow. While there is no local population situated in the immediate proximity of the mill, a significant community does exist some little distance away. Its principal environmental concerns have been odor and eutrophication of the river.[24]

In many respects, AUS environmental management exhibited the characteristics of a Reluctant Complier. As the mill environmental manager stated: "Compliance is the basic yardstick. The essential element of environmental responsibility is to be in compliance." The company conducted periodic risk assessments, which incorporated a concern for compliance, rating the mill according to a "compliance index"—a numerical assessment measuring actual compliance. In addition to regular compliance audits, environmental training also focused on compliance.

Yet AUS did not place a strong emphasis on maintaining any "margin of error." Managers acknowledged "clipping their limits" from time to time. At the corporate level, the AUScorp environmental manager defined regulatory compliance as achieving "material compliance" rather than absolute compliance in every aspect.[25] (This may be attributable to the local regulatory system, which emphasizes the ambient environment rather than discharge limits, although the pulp and paper industry is legally required to meet mill-specific discharge limits.) Whereas other companies told us that they would slow or close down production as they approached their discharge limit, AUS said it would continue operating and report any resultant noncompliance to the regulator after the event.

Moreover, AUS managers, at least at the corporate level, seemingly lacked any conviction that costly environmental innovations might also provide compensating economic benefits. They did not seek out win-win opportunities beyond those that were obvious in accounting terms. Both mill and corporate environmental managers complained that the company lacked any corporate environmental management plan, making it very difficult to do any long-term planning or build on previous work. As a result, "Everything has to be requested each time." The company had only moved a very limited distance toward integrating environmental and economic issues. Senior management viewed environmental concerns as an add-on rather than as a central business strategy issue. This was a matter of considerable frustration at the mill level. As the mill environmental manager suggested: "Continuous improvement *should* drive us . . . but we haven't got it happening yet. The logic and structure of the management system approach is not fully appreciated across the width of the corporation."

Mill-level officials also described their program of employee environmental training as weak, explaining that senior corporate-level decisionmakers had only limited awareness of environmental issues. From the perspective of mill managers, reactive due diligence concerns about personal liability were the essential drivers of environmental awareness and action at the senior corporate level. Nor did corporate officials seem sensitive to the possibilities of using its environmental credentials to protect existing markets or capture new ones. When we asked the corporate environmental manager where the company sold its paper products and who its customers were, his response was "God knows and who cares?"

The tensions between mill-level and corporate environmental concerns stood out most sharply in the sphere of community relations, where AUS's management style, dominated in this area by mill managers, resembled not that of a Reluctant Complier but that of a True Believer. AUS's mill entered into a genuine dialogue with the community and was extremely responsive and very transparent. That posture had evolved from painful past experience. As the mill environmental manager described it:

How did this community consultation arise? We got browbeaten into it. The [State Regulatory Agency (SRA)] took us to court on a major issue about odor. We had had various skirmishes with them. It was a confrontational period. But we took stock. We had a fairly good story, not perfect, but we were pushing the technology envelope. So there were two indignant sides, and the lawyers were enjoying it. Really, half the effort went on covering your backside, not really tackling the problem, just covering yourself legally. And the [SRA] was playing with community consultation, so we started to do it different.

Corporate management was not entirely happy with this evolution at the AUS mill. According to the mill environmental manager:

It was prickly for a while, awkward, and both sides knew it was not working. The directors have a due diligence responsibility. I had the job of talking to the community committee about what we were going to do to improve. But the [SRA] is sitting in and reserving the right to use anything you say against you. So the company lawyers said, "Admit nothing." It was a no-win situation by being cautious, so I went the whole hog—and the SRA held off. We told the community everything, all our dirty washing. Over the course of three or more years, the community became very supportive. I did get support from the general manager to go the whole hog, but Head Office had a distinct discomfort because of lack of familiarity with local concepts.

Having decided to embrace the ethos of community dialogue, AUS mill managers went to very considerable lengths both to ascertain and respond to community views and to make their decision-making more transparent:

In the old times, we scoped a project, put it together, got Board approval, then the project team did the costings, then it went back to the Board, and *then* we announced what we were going to do. Until then, maybe the regulators had an inkling, certainly the community didn't. Now, once we have done the preliminary scoping and got the preliminary OK, we brief the community committee, and ask their issues and concerns, then we take these on board. [For example], they wanted no more effluent, so the challenge was, can we do this and still build the new [equipment]? And because we knew this early, we could go to the designers and ask ways to achieve minimum water usage and how to offset this elsewhere in the plant. We achieved this, and got environmental approvals from the regulators and no objections from the community.[26]

In summary, like a Reluctant Complier, AUS sought to meet the minimum standards prescribed by legislation and permits, but without a strong commitment to "full" compliance. Its managers are disinclined to scan broadly for win-win environmental investments. However, in terms of shaping its social license, AUS was a True Believer at the mill level, obtaining corporate support for this management style on a project-by-project level, but struggling to achieve long-term corporate support for this attitude.

BC1: Part Environmental Strategist, Part Reluctant Complier. BC1 is a pulp mill owned by a diversified multinational corporation with interests in oil and gas, metal recycling, and shipping, as well as forest and building products and pulp and paper mills. Corporate sales in 1998–99 exceeded $3.5 billion, but this represented a substantial decline from the early 1990s, inasmuch as the corporation had sold off subsidiaries to pay down debt. The pulp mill BC1 produces approximately 1,100 tons per day and employs 900 people. It is located on an estuary adjacent to local fisheries. When the link between pulp-mill effluent and dioxins was first made in the late 1980s, low levels of dioxins were found in shellfish recovered near its operations. A local heron colony was also one of the first to be identified as under threat. At one stage in the early 1990s, environmental and fishermen's groups demanded the mill's closure. At the end of the decade, local environmental groups were still active in opposing the mill's activities and some were currently suing BC1 in court. BC1's environmental management style did not respond to these and other social, regulatory and economic pressures in consistent ways, however.

On one hand, BC1 had adopted an opportunistic approach to regulatory compliance. While generally in compliance with its environmental permits, indeed, by a considerable margin in some respects, BC1 managers evinced no moral imperative to comply. They took a narrow view of the mill's regulatory responsibilities, often seeking to avoid or minimize them, as far as this could be done without incurring penalties. According to the mill environmental manager: "Now we have got better legal people working for us. We know when we can push a point and when we can't. Our legal counsel was a leading prosecutor. He can put a spin effectively on what we do. He understands that what could be a black-and-white issue could be gray. He knows what's good enough [to avoid prosecution]."

In essence, rather than taking the view that 'If it's the law, we do it," the managerial attitude is: "That's the law. To what extent can we get around it?"

Similarly, BC1 was a Reluctant Complier in relations with both regulators and community environmental activists. It was disinclined to develop open, cooperative relationships with either. The mill's relationship with the community was particularly adversarial. While the mill management had belatedly taken small steps to reach out to its critics in the community, that approach was discouraged at corporate level and had been discontinued. At the time of our interviews in 1999, a representative of a local environmental/community group told us that "the estuary is knee-deep in dead material in which nothing will grow" but that no dialogue was possible because "community groups are not welcome at the mill." The mill environment manager concurred, saying, "This mill has done a horrible job of PR in the last decade. There is a huge trust chasm with the local community and animosity between the residents and the mill."

BC1's corporate management resisted many changes proposed or demanded by community groups, such as changes in BC1's plans for a solid waste disposal landfill in a difficult geological area, and had even refused to endorse some mill-level requests for modest environmental upgrades. The corporate resistance continued even though current plans and policies had provoked civil suits by community and environmental groups, and even though opposition to the planned landfill had compelled mill managers to consider the transportation of waste to another jurisdiction (at considerable expense).

Yet in other respects, BC1's environmental management style resembled that of Environmental Strategists. In many ways, BC1 worked hard to integrate environmental and business strategies in a carefully calculated way. As a BC1 manager put it, "Historically, it was very willy-nilly how we should spend money. Now we have lengthy documents and lay out priorities from an environmental perspective: what, when, and who will do it." BC1 had taken substantial steps to integrate environmental and production issues (including the adoption of ISO-14000), to develop a cost-benefit approach to environmental spending and some form of environmental accounting, and to establish what the mill environmental manager described as a "show me the numbers" attitude to environmental action.

BC1 also displayed an awareness of the desirability of unearthing win-win opportunities and scanned actively to find them. For example, discussing the firm's reasons for adopting an expensive oxygen delignification process, the mill manager noted: "Oxygen treatment reduces production costs, improves yield and is good for the environment." Far from BC1 standing still in environmental terms, a mill manager told us: "We are now getting into pollution prevention, spill containment, standard operating procedures to reduce fiber losses." And it was clear that mill management scanned widely to keep abreast of environmental risks and opportunities: "We look at trends, for example, in U.S. regulation, less so [in] Asia and Europe. So we anticipate: how will we get squeezed, and what should we take on to position ourselves?" Like other Environmental Strategists, management reported: "We do things when there is a business case to be made, when we can make money, plus if it's the law."

Yet BC1 was distinguishable from other environmental strategists in that it chose to adopt a very different strategy vis-à-vis compliance issues. It was not (as with the case of the Compliers) that BC1 managers failed to fully consider a broader range of options, or that their focus was narrow. Rather, they simply did not see their opportunistic approach to regulation, or their negative relations with the community, as likely to impinge substantially on their economic license. Hence, for them, minimizing compliance and responsiveness was a rational, strategic choice. BC1 also differed substantially from other Environmental Strategists in its narrow perception of the terms of its social license, which was underscored by its extreme disregard of community relations.

In sum, in applying this typology to our sample, we found that there were certain "break points" that distinguished the various management style categories. True Believers appeared to be morally driven and almost evangelical in their pursuit of environmental excellence. Environmental Strategists made strategic use of corporate environmental policy and most (but not all) of them believed that the current sociopolitical climate required them to be excellent environmental performers. Thus their commitment to excellent environmental performance appeared to be contingent on the sociopolitical climate, as opposed to the apparently noncontingent moral commitment of True Believers. Committed Compliers, while very similar to Environmental Strategists, tended to define all strategy and demands in reference to regu-

TABLE 5.1

Facility Environmental Management Style Rankings

TB = True Believer			ES = Environmental Strategist		
Facility	Rank	Style	Facility	Rank	Style
BC3	1	TB	GA1	3	ES
WA4	1	TB	BC2	3	ES
GA2	2	TB	WA3	3	ES
NZ1	2	TB	BC1	4	ES-RC

CC = Committed Complier			RC = Reluctant Complier		
Facility	Rank	Style	Facility	Rank	Style
WA1	5	CC	AUS	6	RC-TB
GA3	5	CC	WA2	7	RC
NZ2	5	CC			
BC4	5	CC			

latory requirements and to set goals wholly in terms of regulatory requirements, whereas Environmental Strategists' considerations were much
broader. All of these groups took compliance with the law for granted for
either moral or strategic reasons. Reluctant Compliers, however, tend to
comply because they do not want to get caught, and the consequences of bad
environmental performance, other than regulatory action and the adverse
publicity that might flow from it, were not generally taken into account.
Thus we found ourselves ranking facilities as shown in Table 5.1.

Environmental Management Style and Environmental Performance

Using the approach described above, we classified the environmental management style of each of the fourteen mills in our sample. We then calculated average environmental performance for each management style category. The results are striking. As shown in Table 5.2, BOD of the effluent was
substantially lower for True Believers than for Environmental Strategists,
whose scores were in turn substantially lower than the average for Committed Compliers, whose scores were substantially lower than the average for
Reluctant Compliers. The same relationship emerges, albeit somewhat less
dramatically, with respect to control of AOX and TSS (except that the Environmental Strategists did better than True Believers, on average, in controlling TSS). The correlation between environmental management style and

TABLE 5.2

Management Style and Environmental Performance

(average discharge, 1998–99)

Environmental	True Believer		Environmental Strategist		Committed Complier		Reluctant Complier	
Performance	Value	n	Value	n	Value	n	Value	n
BOD (kg/day)	1,288	3	2,304	4	3,607	4	4,726	1
TSS (kg/day)	4,510	3	3,439	4	6,155	4	7,212	1
AOX (kg/ton)	.44	3	.46	3	.57	2		0

NOTE: BOD = biological oxygen demand; TSS = total suspended solids; AOX = adsorbable organic halides.

environmental performance was .76 for BOD, .66 for TSS, and .57 for AOX. And a separate analysis reveals that True Believers and Environmental Strategists bettered their permit limits for BOD and TSS by a significantly larger percentage, on average, than did Committed and Reluctant Compliers.[27] Thus in a cross-sectional analysis in 1998–99, environmental management style was a much more powerful predictor of mill-level environmental performance than regulatory regime or corporate size and earnings.

One reason environmental management style is associated with better environmental performance is that True Believers and Environmental Strategists tend to invest in better pollution-control technology. The correlation between management style and the "subjective technology" measure (based on managers' self-evaluation) is .67; with the "objective technology" measure, it is .53. Higher-ranked "subjective technology" is in turn correlated with control of BOD (.68), TSS (.69), and AOX (.8).[28]

But better technology is far from the only reason for better environmental performance by Environmental Strategists and True Believers. Much of their edge, our interviews suggest, stems from a dedicated approach to day-to-day environmental management (what we have called "implementation") and more active scanning for win-win measures that both improve environmental performance and cut costs. Both WA4 and WA2, for example, achieved large, sharp reductions in BOD and TSS in their effluent in the 1970s after installing the secondary treatment facilities required by their regulatory licenses. In subsequent years, neither mill's regulatory permit limits for those pollutants were tightened significantly. But over those years, WA4, a True Believer in terms of environmental management style, achieved steady, gradual declines in BOD,[29] whereas WA2, a Reluctant Complier, did not. A recurrent theme in our interviews with managers at WA4 was that such environmental achievements had only been possible through a commitment to effective employee training, preventive maintenance, systematic environmental management, and "operating excellence."

For six facilities—three who were True Believers or Environmental Strategists, and three who were Committed or Reluctant Compliers—we were able to trace average and maximum monthly figures for BOD and TSS over the 1990–99 period. All the facilities in the former group improved their environmental performance over the decade, while the improvement for the latter group was either nonexistent or negligible. This too indicates the importance of management style in producing step-by-step incremental improvements.

One important indicator of effective environmental management is the incidence of inadvertent spills of pulping or bleaching chemicals.[30] Such spills often stem from inadequate maintenance, subpar training (as reflected in failure to follow precautionary procedures or inadequate response to emergencies), or poor planning. Table 5.3 shows the relationship between mill environmental management style and the incidence of chemical spills in 1998 through 1999. Two measures of spills are used: the first row shows the annual average number of all chemical spills per facility reported to regulatory officials, the second the annual average of all "big spills."[31] Strikingly, the True Believers had perfect records, exceeding those of Environmental Strategists (who bested Committee Compliers on the first measure, but not the second).

In addition, Environmental Strategists and especially True Believers also do a better job of building "reputational capital" with regulators and with environmental activists (in local communities and nationally), which appears to pay off in attaining more flexibility in regulatory permits. Again, the contrast between WA4 and WA2 is instructive. To control dioxin emissions, both WA2 and WA4 were required by state regulators to develop a control program. But while the permit given WA4 (a "True Believer" with good relations with the regulatory agency) required it simply to submit a detailed engineering report within eighteen months, WA2 (an obvious "Reluctant Complier") was required by the same agency to (a) submit a preliminary re-

TABLE 5.3
Management Style and Average Number of Chemical Spills
per Year, 1998–99

	True Believer	Environmental Strategist	Committed Complier	Reluctant Complier
All spills	0	1.5	3.5	3
Big spills	0	0.5	0.5	0

NOTE: Data only available for the seven U.S. facilities.

port within six months, (b) submit a final scope of work document within eight months for agency review and approval, and (c) submit an engineering report for review and approval within ten months. In terms of transaction costs, this means that less of WA4 environmental managers' time is spent writing reports and more on supervision, problem-solving, and production.

The True Believers' cooperative relationship with environmental activists also can lead to quicker, less costly environmental problem-solving. A WA4 manager told us, for example, about his mill's dispute with regulatory officials concerning a Superfund (hazardous waste) site on property the firm had acquired. The government was reluctant to sign off on anything, he said, while the company wanted to proceed with a cleanup plan. "But the environmental groups mobilized behind us and that got EPA and [the state regulator] in the room and to achieve the first settlement of [a] Superfund site in the country without litigation. . . . It saved us millions of dollars." Similarly, according to a GA2 manager, when the mill was facing a potential community-based challenge to the permit change it was negotiating with regulators, "We asked the community, 'What do *you* want in the permit?'— and we found we could accommodate this and actually probably saved $1 million on legal fees in avoiding potential community litigation. We saved a ton on money and our reputation."

Conclusion

Inevitably, regulated enterprises experience some of the terms of their regulatory, economic, and social licenses to operate as ambiguous or potentially malleable. Just as inevitably, therefore, the impact of those external drivers on corporate environmental performance is mediated by the attitudes and environmental management styles of individual companies and facilities. In this chapter we have thus noted considerable variation in the perceptions of management at different mills and found that this in turn had significant implications for corporate environmental behavior. While management at some mills made very considerable efforts to stay well ahead of regulatory requirements and to maintain good relations with regulators, others did not. Some took the view that economic benefits would flow from certain environmental improvements, and therefore pursued win-win outcomes, while others were skeptical about the existence of such opportunities or viewed them in very narrow terms. Equally large differences were found in how different firms interpreted the terms of their social license and the extent to which they took community concerns seriously.

We sought to encapsulate these differences in environmental management style in a typology—ranging from Laggards, to Reluctant Compliers, Committed Compliers, Environmental Strategists, and True Believers. After categorizing each pulp mill in our sample on that scale, we found that there was a very significant correlation between corporate environmental management style and mill-level environmental performance. Management matters, and it matters a good deal.

Yet environmental management style operates within important economic constraints. It is far from omnipotent in shaping environmental performance. The correlation between environmental management style and environmental performance, while quite significant, is not overwhelmingly powerful. As noted in Chapter 3, no mill in our sample, including the True Believers, had adopted environmental improvements that were vastly better than those employed by the Reluctant Compliers. As of 1998–99, none ran a commercially viable totally chlorine-free (TCF) operation or a totally "closed-loop" mill, with no discharges to the environment. None had developed a consumer market for unbleached paper products.

Nor is it easy to disentangle environmental management style from the external pressures that a firm faces, for the latter clearly plays a role—one that we found difficult to define systematically—in shaping the former. Consider, for example, the relationship between environmental management style and the firm's economic situation. Two mills in our sample that were struggling economically through the 1990s were nevertheless True Believers in terms of environmental management style and had good or excellent environmental performance scores. Nevertheless, for the sample as a whole, we found that corporations that had larger sales and profit margins in the first half the 1990s were more likely to be Environmental Strategists when we conducted our fieldwork in 1998–99, while firms that were less profitable in that period were more likely to be Committed Compliers. The quality of pollution-control technology, too, is strongly correlated with economic performance, and as noted earlier, it was the mills whose corporate parents did well financially in the 1990–94 period that had the better environmental performance, on average, in 1998–99. Finally, it is important to remember that regulatory action and social pressures were the principal triggers for those expensive investments in pollution-control technology, as visible ecological impacts and the environmental activism generated by the dioxin scare in the late 1980s and early 1990s led to more stringent regulatory standards for AOX (and in Canada for BOD and TSS).

We are left, therefore, with a complex, multivariate explanation for interfirm differences in environmental performance.[32] We explore the implications of these findings in the following chapter.

6

Conclusion

Over the past decade, a considerable literature has developed on the "greening of industry." At the heart of the field lies the question, "What are the determinants of greening?" For without an empirically grounded understanding of when and why profit-oriented businesses are willing to go beyond compliance with environmental law, or how far they are willing to do so and with what limits, it is impossible to disentangle wishful thinking and ideological exhortation from the kind of realistic expectations on which governmental and social policy can sensibly be based. Notwithstanding some valuable case studies (generally confined to environmental leaders) and some less illuminating survey evidence, adequate empirical answers have not been forthcoming.[1] As we demonstrated in Chapter 2, we still know little about why individual corporations behave the way they do in the environmental context, about why some companies, but not others, choose to move beyond compliance, or what motivates them to do so, about what the most important influences on environmental outcomes are, or what social policy tools are likely to prove most effective in achieving improved corporate environmental performance.

In this book, we have sought to advance the empirical understanding of these questions by studying fourteen pulp and paper manufacturing mills in British Columbia, Australia, New Zealand, and the states of Washington and Georgia in the United States. We have used a combination of qualitative and quantitative data gathered in 1998–99 to examine a number of alternative explanations for variation in "environmental performance" over time and across business corporations. We have particularly focused on the role of regulatory regimes, economic variables (such as firm-level economic incentives and resources), political and social pressures, and corporate environmental management and attitudes.

Our data and analyses have shown that the relationships between these variables and environmental outcomes are complex. This very complexity makes it desirable to both summarize and integrate our main findings, which we do in the first part of this chapter. In the second part, we explore their broader implications and lessons for social policy and regulatory design.

Understanding Corporate Environmental Performance

To explain corporate environmental performance, we have argued, it is useful for analysts (and corporate managers themselves) to view business enterprises as simultaneously motivated and constrained by a multifaceted "license to operate." We found that corporate managers, at least in closely watched industries like pulp and paper manufacturing, viewed each facility's license to operate as including not only its regulatory permits and legal obligations but also an often-demanding "social license" and a constraining "economic license." The regulatory, economic, and social licenses are monitored and enforced by a variety of stakeholders, who commonly seek leverage by exploiting a variety of license terms. Environmental groups not only enforce the terms of the social license directly (e.g., through shaming and adverse publicity) but also seek to influence the terms of the economic license (e.g., generating consumer boycotts of environmentally damaging products) and of the regulatory license (e.g., through citizen suits or political pressure for regulatory initiatives). Thus the *interaction* of the different types of license often exceeds the effect of each acting alone. The terms of some legal license provisions extend the reach and impact of the social license by directly empowering social activists or by giving them access to information that they can use to pressure target enterprises. Conversely, a company that fails to respond appropriately to social license obligations risks a tightening of its regulatory license when frustrated community activists turn for help to politicians and regulators.

The terms of each strand of the "license to operate," however, often are far from clear. Moreover, proactive corporate officials sometimes can reshape some license terms—by providing information to and negotiating with regulators or environmental activists, by engaging in community outreach and education, and by scanning for technologies and procedures that simultaneously cut costs and improve the firm's environmental performance. Yet this very complexity, interactive nature, and malleability of the various license terms frustrate efforts to find objective measures of the relative stringency of one facility's license to operate as compared with another's.

Nevertheless, we attempted to examine the direct relationship between each strand of the license to operate and mill-level environmental performance. Of necessity, we could employ only rough proxies for the inherently complicated regulatory, economic, and social licenses. And we measured facilities' environmental performance—also a variegated phenomenon, consisting of action against many kinds of environmental risks—primarily by using quantitative data concerning serious kinds of water pollution and spills, which was available for most mills only for the latter part of the 1990s. This analysis, while necessarily simplistic, did produce some interesting insights into why some mills went further beyond compliance than others.

Understanding Convergence

Evaluations by government bodies and industry associations, along with our own measures, have all confirmed the same general conclusion: over the past thirty years, there has been a dramatic reduction in the polluting emissions of pulp mills in all the jurisdictions studied—on the order of 80 or 90 percent for several leading measures of water pollution in wastewater.[2] Moreover, there has also been a considerable narrowing of differences between environmental "leaders and laggards" in levels of pollution control. All of the mills in our sample were generally in compliance with their regulatory permits; this too confirms the findings of other recent studies of the pulp and paper industry. None of the mills we studied were regulatory laggards in the sense of being ignorant of or systematic evaders of their regulatory licenses. All of the mills for which we could obtain quantifiable regulatory permit limits had gone beyond compliance, reducing the discharge of key water pollutants to levels well below those specified by their permits.[3]

Changes in all strands of the pulp industry's license to operate, at least in economically advanced democracies, help explain both the overall decline in pollution and the general convergence of environmental performance across individual mills. Most striking, perhaps, was the convergence across the countries and the firms we studied in the *terms* of each of the individual types of license. When interviewed in 1998–99, firms with operations in more than one jurisdiction did not regard their regulatory license as being materially different in different jurisdictions. They referred to differences of enforcement style and philosophy in the different regulatory regimes, but they also observed that when the regulatory license was ratcheted more tightly in one jurisdiction, other jurisdictions commonly followed that lead.[4] Similarly, while many mills reported that they had experienced far less social pressure in an earlier era, all now experienced some such pressure. Communities and environmental advocacy groups tended to act as de facto regulators, thereby further diluting the importance of different enforcement styles. As one mill manager put it, "the implications of failing to meet the regulations are too great from a public or market point of view, so we are more demanding on ourselves than the regulators are." Finally, the advent of globalization, and an extremely competitive world pulp market has diminished variability in the economic licenses of pulp mills. Institutional investors and financial analysts today are likely to judge all firms by common criteria.

Just as important, there has been a convergence *among* the different types of license. Just as the regulatory and social licenses have demanded tighter controls on emissions, the economic license in an increasingly competitive world market has become more demanding, pushing all the firms studied to concentrate on cutting costs and improving profits. The tougher regulatory and social licenses have substantially improved the environmental performance and attitudes of all the firms; in our sample, we did not find a single true laggard, and we found only one true Reluctant Complier.

But the economic license has simultaneously constrained how far firms can go in a "green" direction. Due to economic constraints—especially overcapacity in the world market for pulp and the weakness of customer demand for unbleached paper or totally chlorine-free paper—none of the mills in our sample had leapt far ahead of the others by abandoning pulp bleaching or running a totally chlorine-free (TCF) operation; one mill (BC3) that had tried TCF had lost too much money in doing so and retreated. Economic license constraints helped explain why none of the firms in our sample had done the innovative engineering or made the very costly investments that would be necessary to operate a completely "closed-loop" mill, with no discharges to surrounding waterways, and why none had abandoned bleaching of paper at all as a way of reducing use of potentially polluting bleaching chemicals.[5]

At the same time, financial markets today are more likely to react adversely to firms that get adverse publicity for regulatory noncompliance or avoiding environmental liabilities. Because both regulators and financial analysts take heed of demonstrations and protests against pulp mills, firms can justify paying heed to the social license in terms of economic risk management. The net result of accommodating to the demands of the three different types of license is that a firm can afford neither to drop too low nor aim too high: hence the considerable convergence in performance revealed by the statistics.

That convergence, however, has drifted more or less steadily toward better control of effluent in the pulp industry. The primary engine of that movement, we believe, has been periodic "tightenings" of governmental regulatory licenses. The law on the books (and in each mill's permit) is a benchmark for enforcers of both the social and economic license. Exposure of substantial legal noncompliance is taken by both community activists and professional investors as a justification for skepticism about the environmental good faith or the competence of mill managers. And that, of course, strengthens the capacity of regulatory license requirements to overcome economic license restraints.

The largest reductions in pulp mill discharge to water of harmful pollutants have stemmed from investments in expensive technologies, particularly secondary wastewater treatment facilities, oxygen delignification systems, and the substitution of chlorine dioxide for elemental chlorine as a bleaching agent (which often required construction of a chlorine dioxide plant). Economic license constraints often affected the timing of those installations, as firms often successfully argued that they should coincide with periodic rebuilding or updating of primary production equipment. But sooner or later, the regulatory license has trumped economic demands, partially through the implicit promise that all competitors would be obliged to make the same investment. And indeed, one of the most striking findings in our research has been the extent to which major investments in prevention and control technology have been made in response to pending or anticipated regulatory rules.[6]

Understanding Variation

Convergence in environmental performance in the pulp and paper industry, while impressive, has not been complete. At the end of the twentieth century, we found significant differences among the mills we studied. The difference between best and worst performers was substantial: on some measures, such as BOD, TSS, and AOX, laggards emitted between three and four times more pollution than leaders. While some pulp mills in our sample were emitting less than 20 percent of the BOD and TSS allowed by their regulatory permits specified, others were in the 60–85 percent range. Thus we were left with an important puzzle. Why have some pulp mills done a better job in reducing pollution than others?

No simple answer emerges from our data, which point toward a complex, multivariate explanation. Corporate environmental behavior and motivation are extremely complex. They involve the interaction of numerous variables, each difficult to measure, and more resistant still to quantification, modeling, and regression analysis. Nevertheless, our interview and statistical data do generate a considerable number of insights for theories of regulation and corporate environmental behavior—relevant not just to the particular industry sector we studied but also to other highly regulated, heavily scrutinized, and mature industry sectors, and perhaps to others as well.

Variation in Firms' Licenses to Operate. Notwithstanding substantial convergence in the terms of the various license requirements, significant variation between the licenses of different mills helped explain some of the differences in their environmental performance. With respect to the *regulatory license*, for example, we found that British Columbia's lag behind the United States in requiring secondary wastewater treatment in mills at the edge of coastal waters resulted in better BOD control by those BC mills in 1998–99, on average, because their treatment facilities were newer and closer to the "state of the art." Similarly, British Columbia's more imminent and more stringent regulatory deadline for elimination of AOX discharges helps explain why BC mills, on average, had lower AOX emissions in 1998–99 than the U.S. mills in our sample.[7] Other interfirm differences in environmental performance could be attributed at least in part to the terms of mills' particular *economic license*. For example, a mill whose products and customers were environmentally sensitive (GA2, selling paper diapers in western Europe) had low AOX discharges. Some firms operating under serious economic license limits, such as those who were cash-strapped, told us this constrained their capacity to put in place appropriate environmental technology. Conversely, mills whose corporate parents had larger sales and higher profit margins in the first half of the 1990s, a period of intense social and regulatory pressures regarding chlorine, had better technologies and better environmental performance at the end of that decade.

Different *social license* demands often appeared to be particularly powerful in influencing differences in environmental outcomes. For example, the gap between the emissions of WA2 and WA4, described earlier, was very much what one would have anticipated, given WA2's more remote, small-town location and WA4's location near the heart of a changing, more economically diversified city with lively environmental activists. In a number of cases, our interview data suggested that a painful, well-publicized encounter with a major environmental group produced a sea change in the corporate approach to the environment. More diffuse community pressure also prodded some firms to beyond-compliance measures, such as substantial expenditures on odor reduction measures. In several cases, customers' concerns, in the wake of Greenpeace's campaign in western Europe complaining about dioxin in pulp-mill effluent wedded environmental concerns with economic pressure—helping to explain lower AOX emissions on the part of some of the mills in our sample.[8]

On the other hand, more global measures of the relationship between the different strands of the mills' license to operate did not correlate closely with contemporary variation in mill-level environmental performance. With respect to the regulatory license, for example, pulp mills' environmental performance did not consistently reflect the regulatory jurisdiction in which they operated or the type of regulatory regime they faced. On none of our measures did facilities cluster tightly by regulatory jurisdiction. Even the mills in British Columbia, where regulations called for radical reductions in

AOX by the end of 2002, were not uniformly below the sample average. Notwithstanding more fearsome legal sanctions in the United States and the allegedly more legalistic U.S. approach to regulation, U.S. mills were as likely in 1998–99 to be below as above average. Similarly, we failed to detect any significant statistical relationship between regulatory jurisdiction and the extent to which pulp mills had invested in state-of-the-art pollution control or pollution-reduction technology. One reason, we conclude, is that convergence in regulatory licenses has by and large come to outweigh regulatory divergence. Just as significant, there is considerable flexibility in regulatory requirements *within* all the jurisdictions in this study, for regulators have tailored facility-level permits and informal orders to individual mills' inputs, technologies, surrounding environmental exigencies, and investment cycles.

With respect to economic variables, too, the relationships between corporate economic license and mill-level environmental performance, while suggestive in some cases, as noted above, were often inconclusive. One mill that sold pulp to be made into food containers, which one might expect to trigger especially strong market-related concerns about reducing use of elemental chlorine as a bleaching agent, operated at only 60 percent substitution, below average, and had not installed an oxygen delignification system, a leading-edge technology in reducing chlorinated organics. We discovered no significant statistical relationship, for example, between general economic conditions in the pulp industry, as measured by highs and lows in pulp prices, and various mill-level measures of pollution reduction and control of chemical spills. Similarly, we found *no* statistically significant correlation between average 1998–99 emissions and corporate economic resources, as measured by total sales or profit margin of the mill's corporate parent in 1998–99. Although mills owned by corporations with larger profit margins (ratio of income to sales) and larger annual sales income in the early 1990s generally had lower BOD, TSS, and AOX emissions late in the decade, and also had better pollution-control technology, some of those correlations did not reach the level of statistical significance.[9] Corporate profitability in the first half of the 1990s was correlated $(-.62)$[10] with more ambitious environmental management style in 1998–99, but that association did not persist when we used 1995–99 measures of profitability. Some of the best-performing mills in terms of the environment were "true believers" in terms of environmental management style, despite struggling financially throughout much of the 1990s.

Finally, although a demanding social license was said by many managers to have been a trigger for certain beyond-compliance environmental measures, it is important to note that managers at different mills responded to social pressures in different ways. Some reacted to community or NGO demands with resistance rather than responsiveness. And this suggests that environmental management style—the attitudes and modes of thought that guided corporate and mill-level policy, not social pressure alone, is a key variable in determining the capacity of social pressures to shape corporate environmental performance.

Variations in Firms' Environmental Management Style. The different responses of firms to apparently similar social and regulatory pressures, plus our findings about the effects of corporate economic resources, suggest that the influence of the regulatory, economic, and social licenses on environmental performance depends on an "intervening variable"—managerial attitudes, or the combination of attitudes and executive action we call "environmental management style." When we classified each mill's environmental management style on a scale extending from Environmental Laggard through Reluctant Complier, Committed Complier, and Environmental Strategist to True Believer, and then correlated environmental management style with environmental performance, the results were striking.[11] Average emissions for True Believers were substantially lower than those for Environmental Strategists, whose scores were substantially lower than the average for Committed Compliers, whose scores were substantially lower than the average for Reluctant Compliers.[12]

True Believers and Environmental Strategists, we found, also tend to invest in better pollution-control technology. They also achieve larger incremental gains in environmental performance by virtue of a more dedicated approach to day-to-day environmental management (what we have called "implementation"). True Believers, we found, thus have fewer costly and environmentally harmful accidental spills of pulping chemicals. Moreover, they appear to scan more actively for win-win measures (which both improve environmental performance and cut costs). Environmental Strategists and especially True Believers also do a better job of building reputational capital with regulators and environmental activists (in local communities and nationally), which appears to pay off in attaining more flexibility in regulatory permits. In addition, True Believers and Environmental Strategists show a pattern of continued improvement in environmental performance over time, whereas Committed Compliers and Reluctant Compliers do not.

Yet firms are still constrained by the terms of their licenses. Thus environmental management style is far from omnipotent in shaping environmental performance, and it may well be shaped in part by the firm's economic situation. A firm that pushes the boundaries of its licenses too far will be punished: by regulators (if there is serious breach of the terms of a permit), by markets (if behavior goes beyond what is perceived by investors and analysts as economically rational), and by communities or NGOs (if behavior goes far beyond what is perceived as socially acceptable). As noted earlier, no mill in our sample, including True Believers, could ignore the capital constraints imposed by its economic license. And where the economic license was tight, even True Believers were not very far ahead of the Committed Compliers, for example, in adopting costly new environmental protection measures. Our data suggested that the attitudes of True Believers and Environmental Strategists resulted in incremental gains in the reliability and imaginativeness of day-to-day implementation of relatively standard corporate environmental policies, as well as a broader definition of what constituted economic gain from the installation of environmental equipment.

Moreover, although we are convinced by both our statistical and fieldwork data that "management matters," our methodology did not enable us to explain precisely why firms approximated one ideal type or another. As a working model, we assume that this is the outcome of interaction between external factors (e.g., license requirements) and internal factors (e.g., corporate culture). There was much to suggest that firms with different cultures behaved very differently. We were struck for example, by the behavior of a "corporate raider" that operated two mills in our sample. In each case, its attitude to the local community was confrontational in circumstances in which many other mills had gone to very substantial lengths to appease and establish trust with community groups. But to more fully tease out why different environmental management cultures arise would take a far more detailed and intensive study of a number of firms, including not just leaders (as a few studies have done)[13] but also laggards (which are apt to refuse access to social scientists).

Understanding Corporate Greening

Our findings shed some empirical light on the literature on regulation and compliance and on the greening of industry, both of which we surveyed in Chapter 2. For example, a number of environmentalists and legal scholars presume that variation in environmental performance can be substantially explained by differences in regulatory regimes, particularly the stringency of their environmental rules and facility-level permits and the aggressiveness with which they are enforced. Yet we found that no regulatory jurisdiction is doing noticeably better or worse than the others in improving environmental performance among the pulp mills it seeks to control.[14]

Most strikingly, the purported greater prescriptiveness and deterrence orientation of U.S. environmental regulation did not produce better environmental outcomes on the part of U.S. mills.[15] At least in this closely watched industry, debates about coercion versus persuasive, compliance-oriented enforcement strategies are not of the essence, for once the terms of the regulatory license are established, firms have a variety of reasons to comply, over and beyond the efforts of enforcement agencies. Community and NGO vigilance in particular often has been the key to the salience and the threat, in managers' eyes, to their regulatory license, regardless of regime regulatory style.

In this industry, too, we find little empirical support for the more romantic versions of the "greengold thesis," which asserts that there is a happy coincidence between what is good for the environment and what is good for business. On the contrary, particularly with respect to investments in costly new pollution-control or pollution-reduction technologies, win-win solutions do not abound. The best example we encountered was the introduction of oxygen delignification, adopted by some mills partly because it promised operating cost reductions as well as pollution reduction. But many other mills calculated that oxygen delignification in their operations would not pay off on either dimension. Most major environmental improvements in the past few decades, such as those resulting from the installation of secondary treatment systems for wastewater and 100 percent substitution of chlorine dioxide for elemental chlorine in pulp bleaching, were driven by regulation (or anticipated regulation),[16] since they entailed large capital investments and increases, not decreases, in operating costs, and did not result in a clear competitive advantage on the sales front. Most other new environmental technologies are extremely expensive, with no short-term payoff or demonstrable strategic advantage.[17] Significantly, none of the companies in our sample had moved "outside the box" in terms of new bleach technologies or closed-loop production and none saw any natural market advantage in doing so.

Thus to the extent that substantial improvements of the environmental performance of the sector depend on the introduction of costly new technologies, they are not likely to be generated by economic pressure that elicits corporate scanning for win-win opportunities. That appears rather to be the comparative advantage of government regulation, which can (as it has in the pulp and paper industry) serve as a coordinating mechanism, encouraging investment in new environmental technologies by implicitly promising firms most willing to go along that that their competitors will be required to make similar investments.

On the other hand, our research indicated that firms in the pulp and paper industry enjoyed much greater opportunities to achieve win-win outcomes in terms of process and operational changes, such as diligent supervision and training that resulted in better maintenance and tighter process controls—which in turn reduced chemical spills, thereby minimizing downtime, waste, and trouble with regulators and the community. Put another way, the "greengold" thesis had greater resonance when it came to the benefits of good housekeeping and a systematic approach to environmental management. But even in this realm, we found that *perception* was all-important. Some firms adopted vigorous environmental management and training systems and did a great deal more than was required by law, in the belief that it made good economic sense to do so, and/or because they believed it would protect the other terms of their license to operate. But other mills seemed singularly unimpressed with the idea of win-win outcomes and remained reactively driven by regulation and other social forces. It appears that management matters far more than the rhetoric of win-win.

Our research does not provide support for the various stage models of corporate greening that assert or assume that firms will go through a progression (in the view of some, a natural evolution) from laggard to compliance, to compliance plus, to environmental excellence.[18] On the contrary, the constraints of the economic license (not least, the pressures to cut costs, the judgments of financial markets, and the unwillingness of consumers to pay a price premium for environmental excellence) are likely to keep them far short of the last of these stages. As we have seen, any company that strays too far from the terms of the economic license is likely to be brought back into line. For example, since consumers have thus far been unwilling to pay a price premium for totally chlorine-free paper, even companies that have the technology to go down this path do not use it because it is uneconomic to do so. Neither is it the case that firms will all, sooner or later, progress to at least a higher (albeit not the highest) stage of environmental performance.[19] For notwithstanding increasing convergence in environmental performance, our study has also demonstrated substantial continuing variation and no evidence of any natural trend to higher stages of corporate greening.

On the other hand, our findings resonate with the various theories that emphasize the importance of a firm's social standing and in particular its economic stake in maintaining its reputation for environmental good citizenship. Firms in our sample, particularly larger firms with a high public profile, or even smaller ones highly dependent on the goodwill of the local community, tended to be highly sensitive to negative publicity and vulnerable to informal sanctions and shaming. And their behavior was shaped by a far broader range of stakeholders within the "organizational field" than regulators alone. Local community concern and pressure were particularly important in this respect.

Finally, our findings also lend considerable support to those who attribute importance to managerial attitude. However, whether a "greener" environmental management style derives from the sources mentioned in the literature—such as "charismatic green leadership," internal corporate culture, the nature of the firm's market niche, or other variables—was not apparent from our research, which would have had to have taken a very different form if we had sought to address such issues.

To what extent can our specific findings in this study be generalized to firms in other industries? No definitive answer can be ventured, of course. Much depends on the extent to which the other industries resemble the pulp and paper industry on at least some important dimensions.

The pulp and paper industry, for example, is subject to close environmental scrutiny, by communities as well as by regulators—especially because one component in its effluent, dioxin, has been the subject of great publicity and is particularly frightening to much of the public. It is capital-intensive and characterized by high asset specificity (that is, mills can't easily switch to other products, and companies cannot lightly abandon their huge sunk costs in current technologies). At the same time, it is intensely competitive. Firms in the Northern Hemisphere are threatened by lower-cost producers in Southeast Asia, and investors do not see the industry as a particularly attractive one; thus environmental managers have to fight especially hard for funds for beyond-compliance measures. Moreover, potential win-win innovations by one facility can be copied by others relatively easily, so that the gains from innovation may be short-lived. It is difficult for firms to capture additional market share by creating distinctive, "greener" products.

These characteristics are not unique to pulp manufacturers. To at least some extent, they are mirrored by other mature heavy industries, such as metals, chemicals, and other commodities. But it is also important to underscore the complexity of the analytical scheme we have developed to explain firm-level environmental performance. The relative tightness of the terms of a firm's regulatory, social, and economic licenses, the interaction among those license terms, and the firm's reaction to them, inevitably varies from firm to firm, as well as across industries. Thus we do not advance a crisp, highly determinative formula for predicting or explaining firms' environmental performance. Rather, our claim is that the analytic framework that arose from and pervades this study is theoretically applicable to virtually every industry, and thus can aid in comparing and understanding other regulatory contexts and firms too.

Policy Implications

Our findings have a number of implications for regulatory design and social policy and suggest a number of instruments and strategies by which governments and others can most effectively change corporate environmental behavior. In analyzing the type of intervention that might be necessary, it is useful to begin by asking, "To what extent are firms likely to undertake environmental improvements voluntarily?"

Although there were a range of situations in which most of the firms we studied were willing go beyond compliance, they did so for the most part because of their perceptions of their license conditions and as a matter of risk management. Their beyond-compliance investments were mostly of the kind that we have termed "margin of safety" and "anticipatory compliance" measures, although some (in response to intense social license pressures) fell into the "good citizenship" category. It was government regulation, social pressures, and occasionally consumer action that drove environmental behavior, coupled with management's varying perceptions of the scope for win-win outcomes.

For these reasons, it would be unwise to assume that a purely voluntary approach will achieve further improvements, particularly in the case of Reluctant Compliers and Committed Compliers, which make up almost half our sample of firms. Even in the case of environmental strategists or true believers, their more ambitious good citizenship and win-win investments did not emerge across the board and were relatively limited. The evidence suggests that absent some substantial tightening of their license terms or some external shock precipitating a shift in management style, or both, many mills may simply remain at the stage of environmental progress that they have currently achieved.

In terms of regulatory design, the separate regulatory, economic, and social strands of the business enterprises' license provide a useful analytical framework for identifying the points of greatest leverage over corporate environmental performance.

Using the Regulatory License. It is important to reemphasize our finding that the largest improvements in corporate environmental controls of water discharges were associated with tightening regulatory requirements and intensifying political pressures. The big jumps in wastewater environmental performance in pulp manufacturing were the products of *regulation-driven technological change.* That is, technology changes occurred in order to meet more stringent performance standards.[20]

As noted earlier in this chapter, further technological change is also likely to be driven by regulation.[21] Yet governments are understandably reluctant to base performance standards on new technology that is unproven, for should the unproven technology fail, other jurisdictions will not adopt the requirement, and local industry may be put at a competitive disadvantage. More fundamentally, determining the appropriate technology on which to base a regulation is a costly and risky process for a government agency. The problems are exacerbated by information asymmetry: it is in the industry's interests to exaggerate the costs and impracticality of technological change, yet government is highly dependent on information supplied by the industry in making a determination on these matters. Thus governments are understandably reluctant to mandate substantial leaps forward in technology-based environmental performance in the absence of either major public pressure (as occurred with respect to dioxins) or the demonstrated economic viability of new technology.[22]

Nevertheless, even without specifying more stringent performance standards, regulatory agencies are able to influence the development of new technologies by specifying their long-term goals and engaging industry officials in a dialogue about pathways and timetables for achieving them. For example, the U.S. EPA notes in the preamble to its cluster rule that it "believes that the mill of the future will approach closed-loop operations"[23] and suggests an avenue by which this objective might be achieved.

The implied government capacity to make such technologies, once developed by leaders, mandatory for all firms provides some incentive for leaders to experiment and innovate, thereby obtaining first-mover advantages.[24] It also provides some incentive for laggards not to fall too far behind current industry practice, so as to avoid costly retrofits if new technology becomes required. That is, regulation can stimulate greener technological innovation and adoption of innovative technology by creating a dynamic, increasingly stringent regulatory environment and decreasing uncertainty. While large shifts in the political climate toward more lenient regulation could derail the process,[25] in recent decades, regulation in general, rather than any particular regulation, has been able to herd industry toward excellence by imposing a regulatory trajectory that forces facilities to anticipate a future of more stringent demands, in which new environmental and health impacts will have to be addressed.[26] This effect is intensified because regulations, health and environmental concerns, and technological innovations in any jurisdiction commonly ripple through to other jurisdictions by virtue of the process of "regulatory modeling."[27]

The "herding process" can be facilitated by the provision of good information about the relative environmental performance of regulatory leaders and laggards. For the most part, regulatory systems' performance in this regard has been disappointing. In conducting this research, for example, we faced tremendous difficulties in obtaining accurate and accessible data that could usefully be compared over time and between facilities.[28] Good evaluations of government or corporate policy require accurate, *comparable* outcome data. Monitoring requirements can provide such data if they take into account more than the compliance of a particular facility at a particular point in time. Monitoring requirements could allow for evaluative research and policy analysis if care is taken to ensure that the data collection they require allows for comparison over time and between facilities, and if the manner in which the data are reported assures data quality and facilitates accessibility.

More broadly, some regulatory agencies have sought to nurture innovative, cost-effective solutions and to build in continuous improvement by developing a "performance track": an alternative to traditional regulation that is offered to environmental leaders who agree to implement an environmental management system, to consult with and provide information to local communities, and to achieve beyond-compliance environmental outcomes negotiated with the regulator.[29] Underlying such approaches is the belief that such flexibility will "harness the power of competition to stimulate profitable clean technology and other environmentally beneficial innovations."[30] For example, mill GA2 signed an agreement with the U.S. EPA under which it committed itself to maintain superior environmental performance and to serve as a benchmark for the EPA in setting effluent guidelines under the cluster rules. In return, it was given significant regulatory flexibility, as well as operational and capital cost savings, including flexible control of hazardous air pollutants, flexible air permitting for trials of new products, and fewer reporting, monitoring, and recordkeeping requirements. It was also offered greater predictability of regulatory requirements over a fifteen year period.

On the other hand, negotiating flexible permits is costly and risky for both agencies and regulated firms.[31] Thus far, at least in the United States, they have proved feasible only in the limited number of cases where environmental and economic paybacks are sufficient to overcome their considerable cost to develop, administer, monitor, and assess, and where both agencies and facilities have sufficient reputation capital to overcome social actor opposition.[32] WA4, for example, was able to obtain a "bubble permit"[33] for its operations because of its heavy investments in its reputation with both regulators and social actors, while RF, already a superior environmental performer, was eager to obtain the much broader benefits described above.

Leveraging the Social License. Another central finding of our study was that business firms' social licenses provide a particularly powerful point of leverage. Community and environmental advocacy groups in particular tend to act as effective watchdogs and de facto regulators, shaming and otherwise pressuring companies into beyond-compliance environmental performance. While they can sometimes play this role in the absence of any form of state intervention, their effectiveness is enhanced by various forms of facilitative government regulation. In particular, rules that require facilities to inform the public of environmentally significant actions, and to disclose the results of monitoring, redress some of the inherent information asymmetries that occur between regulators, regulatees, and the public and allow social actors to most appropriately target their actions.[34]

For example, in Indonesia, under the PROPER PROKASIH program, regulators rank the performance of individual facilities using surveys, a pollution database of team reports, and independent audits. An enterprise's pollution ranking is readily understandable by the public, being based on color coding (gold and green for the best performers, black, blue, and red for those not in compliance). The program has reportedly been very successful in improving the environmental performance of participating firms.[35] In our study, we found that in British Columbia, mills were particularly mindful of avoiding breaches that might result in poor standing in a periodic government-published report that functioned much as a mill-by-mill environmental scorecard. In the United States, the Toxic Release Inventory, which simply obligates firms to publish their total estimated emissions of potentially hazardous chemicals, has created strong incentives to reduce the use of such chemicals.[36]

Moreover, our research indicates that government actions that *procedurally* empower local communities can have significant effects. In New Zealand, mills reported having become much more responsive to community environmental concerns after communities were given the legal right to challenge the terms of each facility's "consent" (permit), and thereby gained the power to delay the introduction of new processes or technology. In an Australian jurisdiction, similar effects flowed from a new law that obligated firms to prepare and comply with an environmental improvement plan, including a commitment to consultation with local communities.[37] In Canada and the United States, the permitting process has long been open to the public and allowed for public comment on permitting decisions. Such public access has been extended in the United States through programs such as Project XL and the Environmental Leadership Program, which make it a condition for providing greater regulatory flexibility that participating companies provide information to, and consult with, local communities.

The Economic License and Environmental Performance. Turning to the economic license, we described earlier how its terms operate as a constraint on environmental leadership. Our interviews with financial institutions, industry analysts, corporate lawyers, and company officials in the pulp and paper industry suggested that the unwillingness of investment analysts and the financial community to take account of environmental issues is changing only very slowly. However, not all aspects of the economic license militate against improved environmental performance. Scholars and environmental activists have suggested that governments and NGOs can act to mitigate some of the harsher impacts of the economic license by facilitating provision of information to the market, enabling it to make more accurate evaluations as to the environmental credentials and liabilities of different firms. There is some evidence that markets do punish environmentally "bad" firms and reward "good" ones in terms of their stock price,[38] perhaps because good environmental management may be regarded as a useful indicator of good management generally. However, other studies find no such effect.[39] We found little evidence of this effect in our study, discovering instead that several doses of adverse publicity about one firm's environmental record had no significant effect on its stock price.[40]

Nevertheless, governments may be able to add greater legitimacy and potency to the dissemination of relevant information to the market. For example, the U.S. Securities and Exchange Commission requires all publicly traded companies to report their environmental liabilities for both hazardous waste cleanup and environmental legal actions. However, there has been an extremely low disclosure rate.[41] Information standards can obviously only be effective to the extent that the information they require is in fact provided.

Similarly, the launching of private efforts to improve the provision of data to the market may also have a positive impact on corporate environmental performance. For example, lists of certified "green" firms, such as the Dow Jones Sustainability Group Index (DJSI) may, over the long term, encourage small companies to strive to be listed on the index. In addition, if investing based on the DJSI provides a reasonable return on investment (as seems to be the case),[42] such indices might lead to a less reactive approach on the part of financial analysts and provide incentives for corporate environmental leadership.

The economic license can also be influenced by consumer preferences. Were consumers to cease demanding bright white paper, pulp mills would abandon environmentally damaging bleaching technologies.[43] In theory, that process could be accelerated through independent certification and labeling schemes that call consumers' attention to products made in environmentally preferable ways, such as unbleached paper. Realistically, however, while such labeling schemes may have value in some areas, such as the sale of up-market wines, they face a much harder task in the realm of basic commodities such as pulp or copy paper. A more promising first step, therefore, would be for governments, as major purchasers of paper products, to lead the market toward dramatic reductions in the use of bleaching chemicals by insisting on buying only (or mostly) bleach-free paper products. Similarly, in circumstances where unbleached paper is unsuitable, government could provide leadership by purchasing pulp with high recycled-paper content. However, the fickleness of government in obeying its own rules may make companies reluctant to invest heavily in such initiatives, while others (and the industry association itself) have often been involved in systematic attempts to derail such government initiatives. Despite an executive order in 1993 for the U.S. federal government to purchase recycled paper, actual purchasing behavior did not change until 1998, after a second executive order, and only after tremendous pressure to do so was applied by various environmental groups.[44]

Policy can most directly influence the economic constraints faced by industry (and activists) by making it cheaper for industry to comply or go beyond environmental compliance (and cheaper for activists to participate in the regulatory process and obtain information). This could be done through direct subsidies, grants, tax incentives, and other transfers of money to both industry and community and environmental organizations. For example, governments can fund research consortia to find new and innovative technologies. They can also provide tax incentives for companies that install more environmentally friendly technology. And they can provide grants to activist organizations that allow them to pay staff to develop expertise or attend public hearings.

The points of leverage provided by the different strands of firms' license to operate are not, of course, mutually exclusive. Since the causes of inadequate environmental performance are complex, multifaceted, and contingent upon a range of external factors, they are unlikely to be amenable to a simple or single policy fix. Policy-makers need to employ a substantial toolkit and to leverage change at a number of different pressure points. Combinations of instruments, harnessing a broader range of social actors, are likely to provide the most promising approach. What combinations are likely to work best in what circumstances is itself a complex issue, which one of us has explored at length elsewhere.[45]

One of our strongest findings is that management style matters. By corporate environmental management style, we should reiterate, we mean something more than the adoption of formal environmental management systems, such as ISO–14000. Environmental management style includes a set of managerial attitudes toward environmental issues and actions that go beyond the formulation and systematic implementation and evaluation of environmental policies. It includes such variables as how open and responsive managers are in dealing with regulators and environmental groups, how imaginatively and energetically they scan for win-win opportunities, and what kind of calculus they employ in evaluating the business benefits of investments in environmental improvements. What distinguished high-performing True Believers and Environmental Strategists from, say, Committed Compliers was not whether or how often they conducted systematic self-audits, or how they developed environmental management systems, but how they conceived the purpose and function of such audits or systems.

If management style is important in explaining environmental outcomes, an important policy question is whether management style is amenable to influence by the levers of public policy, and if so how? Unfortunately, government intervention on this front is risky without knowing a great deal more about *why* management attitudes in different firms approximate different ideal types. And in this regard, our research, limited to cross-sectional comparisons at one point in time, as opposed to detailed firm-by-firm histories, produced no definitive knowledge. The managers we interviewed identified a number of influences on their behavior, largely in terms of the various license conditions described earlier. But why they reacted so differently to these different pressures, we cannot say. How government policy-makers might be able to change corporate environmental management style remains an elusive, but undoubtedly important, empirical and policy issue.

Finally, our research suggests that environmental management style alone cannot guarantee superior environmental performance. Indeed the data suggest that external license factors—regulatory and social pressures, and economic constraints and resources—that both interact with (and often shape) management attitudes are crucial in determining environmental performance. If those license conditions are not congenial, measures focused on management style alone are unlikely to make a large difference. To paraphrase Marx, companies make their own history but not in circumstances of their own choosing.

REFERENCE MATTER

Notes

1. Point-source pollution occurs at a particular place, such as a discharge pipe from an industrial facility, as contrasted with nonpoint-source pollution from diffuse sources, such as storm water runoff from roads, parking lots, or agricultural fields.

2. In its 1992 Water Quality Report to Congress, the EPA stated: "Often we associate water pollution with images of oil spills or raw sewage and toxic chemicals spewing from pipes at industrial facilities and sewage treatment plants. Although point-source discharges still produce some pollution, most are controlled with specific permit conditions that they usually meet. Currently, less visible nonpoint sources of pollution are more widespread and introduce vast quantities of pollutants into our surface and ground waters. Nonpoint sources deliver pollutants to waterbodies in a dispersed manner rather than from a discrete pipe or other conveyance. Nonpoint sources include atmospheric deposition, contaminated sediments, and many land activities that generate polluted runoff, such as agriculture, logging, and onsite sewage disposal" (U.S. EPA 1992).

3. See, e.g., Chertow and Esty 1997; Gunningham and Sinclair 2002.

4. As to the variability of corporate responses to similar external pressures, see, e.g., Arthur D. Little, Inc. 1995 and Nash 2000, and for a broader analysis in the comparable area of occupational health and safety, see Haines 1997.

5. Most studies of regulation focus on the behavior of regulatory agencies, or on aggregate results for larger populations of firms. See, e.g., Kagan 1993, Verweij 2000, Scruggs 1999. Studies of individual corporations, too, rarely include outcome data.

6. Vogel 1986; Kagan and Axelrad 2000.

7. We chose our subnational jurisdictions in the United States and Canada for two reasons: (a) they had significant pulp and paper sectors, and (b) at least one mill in the jurisdiction had a reputation among our initial informants for environmental excellence. In the United States, we concentrated on Washington and Georgia in part because they are generally regarded as having different regulatory cultures and

because by focusing on just two states, we could sample several mills within each, thus holding the regulatory jurisdiction constant while searching for facility-level explanations of differences in environmental performance. In Canada, we focused on mills in British Columbia.

8. See, e.g., Baylis, Connell, and Flynn 1998 (postal questionnaire to 420 manufacturing and processing companies).

9. See, e.g., Hoffman 1997 and Prakash 2000. See also Ghobadian, Viney, Lui, and James 1988 (survey and analysis of four firms). A more sophisticated methodological approach is taken in Florida et al. 1999, which involved a much larger number of firms and comparison of "matched" enterprises. This study, however, has a different focus from our own, being concerned with internal organizational factors.

10. See, e.g., Greening and Gray 1994 (postal questionnaire to 451 companies), with 27 percent response rate.

11. While all the facilities we studied used the same primary production technology, many facilities also had secondary production technologies on site. For example, some facilities manufactured only wood pulp, whereas others manufactured both pulp and paper, and still others had lines that manufactured recycled paper.

12. On AOX, see p. 10.

13. Thus, of the fourteen facilities in our sample, three were chosen based on their reputation for excellence (thus determining the choice of subnational jurisdiction), eight were chosen on the basis of their jurisdiction alone, two on the basis of their reputation for being average or below average, and one because it was owned by the same company as two other mills in the study. The sample includes both smaller independent operations and mills owned by large transnational corporations.

14. Out of fourteen facilities, we interviewed HQ people at eleven, regulators at ten, and activists at six. In some cases, we have conducted follow-up telephone interviews with mill personnel and relevant regulatory officials.

15. The mill-level data on BOD, TSS, and AOX are not easily available to the public in accessible form, amenable to cross-mill comparison. Thus we were able to obtain some data for all fourteen mills, but not the same set of data for all mills. Time periods over which the reported emissions data were averaged (daily, monthly, or annual) often varied from jurisdiction to jurisdiction. And the time period for which various kinds of data were available for different mills varied (e.g., thirty years, ten years, two years, one year).

16. For an overview see U.S. EPA 1995. This report was completed under the Office of Compliance Sector Notebook project as one of eighteen sectors subject to detailed analysis covering a range of issues including: "general industry information (economic and geographic); a description of industrial processes; pollution outputs; pollution prevention opportunities; Federal statutory and regulatory framework;

compliance history; and a description of partnerships that have been formed between regulatory agencies, the regulated community and the public." See also Thompson and Graham 1997.

17. Bleaching is used not only to increase the whiteness or brightness of the pulp but also to provide greater color stability, improve its cleanliness, and alter the physical properties of the pulp to suit particular end uses. Bleaching normally entails exposing the pulp to between three and five progressive cycles of bleaching and water washing, each of which generates both chemical and organic wastes.

18. Pearson 1972, p. 470.

19. U.S. National Research Council 1996, p. 78.

20. Seegert et al. 1997.

21. Collins 1994.

22. The American Forest and Paper Association (AF&PA) notes in its December 2000 Progress Report: "In 1999, AF&PA member companies discharged less than 0.4 kilograms of AOX per metric ton of chemically bleached pulp. This represents a 90 percent reduction since 1974" (American Forest and Paper Association 2000, p. 5).

23. "[I]n 1994, conflicting comparisons of the impacts of TCF and ECF effluents were reported, but there was general agreement that any differences were relatively minor. . . . Although the world's leading producer of TCF pulp, the Swedish firm Sondra Cell, insists that TCF is environmentally preferred to ECF, even they acknowledge that the differences are 'small' and 'difficult to see'" (Harrison 2002, p. 77).

24. Industry researchers believe that ECF is also compatible with closed-loop systems (Harrison 2002).

25. See generally Maureen Smith 1997.

26. Seegert et al. 1997; Sibley 2001.

27. Chen et al 2001; Dube and MacLatchy 2000; Karels et al. 1999; Karels and Oikari 2000; Karels et al. 2001; Munkittrick et al. 1998; Parrott 2000.

28. Munkittrick et al. 1998.

29. Larsson and Forlin 2002; Munkittrick et al. 1998.

30. Kovacs et al. 2002; Sibley et al. 2001.

31. Some U.S. water pollution laws preceded this but did not have a major impact on the industry. Nor, in the early days, did the Clean Air Act.

32. See Doering et al. 1992.

33. Gifford and McFarlane 1990.

34. However, the result specified in regulation is almost always achieved by implementing the model technology.

35. In Canada, both federal and provincial governments have the power to regulate pollution by virtue of the British North America Act of 1867 and the Constitution Act of 1982.

36. Primary water treatment plants often resulted in pollution transfer from one medium to another, as when the removed suspended solids became a solid waste sludge deposited in landfill sites.

37. British Columbia 1994. See also Stanbury 1993.

38. Some Australian states where unemployment is high and that are more dependent upon large resource-based projects have tended to have weaker regulatory standards. Moreover, in some circumstances, substantial exemptions from such regulatory requirements have been granted to major pulp mills, arguably as a result of political pressure. For example, one mill was able to announce with pride that "we have initiated our own programs to control water contamination and were able to relinquish ministerial exemptions covering our operations in 1990" (implying that, until 1990, they had needed exemptions from the legal minimum standard).

39. Thus Doering et al. characterized the Canadian approach as involving "intermittent enforcement leading primarily to a process of negotiations with all the confusion and inconsistency that that entails" (Doering et al. 1992, p. 3). Harrison, in a study of enforcement of pulp mill regulations in Canada, has similarly documented how, "when mills failed to abide by their negotiated compliance schedules, federal and provincial officials time and again negotiated deadlines for compliance rather than going to court" (Harrison 1995), p. 227. The relative laxity of Australasian environmental enforcement agencies has also been documented (Gunningham 1987). This is in stark contrast with the enforcement approach at the federal level in the United States, where "the EPA sets standards for which compliance is feasible and then enforces these standards relatively vigorously" (Magat and Viscusi 1990).

40. In addition, Canada mandated Environmental Monitoring Studies of the receiving water environment, and prohibited the release of effluent that was acutely lethal to fish. See the Pulp and Paper Mill Chlorinated Dioxins and Furans Regulations of 1992, promulgated under the Canadian Environment Protection Act. For a summary see Stanbury 1993. British Columbia took a more drastic approach, announcing that it would require zero emissions of AOX in 2002.

41. See Sonnenfeld 1996.

42. Australia's federal guidelines for the first time established air and water emissions limits, solid waste disposal standards, and site suitability criteria for new mills, which were also required to monitor the level of dioxins in the water where they released effluent. In 1995, the guidelines were reviewed and the requirements lowered. See further Allison and Sakai 1992.

43. The RMA specified minimum national standards for water and discharge permits, so that New Zealand industries wishing to utilize a given water resource must meet the national standards as well as those appropriate for the water's purpose as determined by regional authorities. The act does not set out national effluent standards

nor receiving water quality criteria specifically for pulp and paper operations. But under the Organochlorines Programme established in 1995, the NZ Ministry for the Environment proposed National Environmental Standards for dioxins, planned for introduction in 2002/3. See generally Allison and Sakai 1992, and New Zealand 2000.

44. Tier 1 requires a level of environmental performance more stringent than basic BAT standards. Tier 2 requires the adoption of elemental chlorine-free pulp processes, and Tier 3 requires the adoption of totally chlorine-free (TCF) or "closed-
loop" pulp processes. Those who are willing to escalate to the higher tiers are given
more time to come into compliance and to amortize their costs.

45. It should be noted, however, that some environmental activists regard current
national standards as too weak to protect or improve receiving water quality and
point to successful industry association lobbying to prevent the adoption of more
stringent cluster rule standards originally proposed by the EPA. Consequently, they
argue that facility permit limits may in some cases be grossly inadequate.

46. Coglianese 1999; Nash and Ehrenfeld 1999.

47. Hoberg 1999 in particular has documented the very substantial extent to
which Canadian regulatory policy has been influenced by the United States: "The
most frequent pattern is emulation, where value convergence combined with US
leadership leads to Canadian borrowing of US policy innovations" (p. 107).

CHAPTER 2

1. See, e.g., Becker 1968; Stigler 1970; Miller and Anderson 1986. There is empirical
as well as theoretical support for this deterrence-based theory of compliance. According to Regens et al. 1997, "We also find that pollution control investment is
positively related to the EPA enforcement budget, suggesting at the very least the industries believe that the EPA will increase its investigatory efforts as their budget increases" (p. 695).

2. Kagan and Scholz 1984. In terms of the management literature, the rational
actor model is closely associated with the strategic planning school approach. The
latter, too, assumes that managers act according to a fairly narrow economic calculus, that they are able to obtain near perfect information both about their own organization and about the wider economic and business environment, and that they
have very considerable discretion in how they implement their preferred strategy
within the organization. Whittington 1993.

3. Certainly there have been arguments that firms should behave ethically and in
a socially responsible manner, but it was assumed that there would generally be no
financial advantage in doing so, albeit that their reputation might be enhanced.

4. Nehrt 1998.

5. See Scruggs 1999; Verweij 2000; Aoki and Cioffi 2000; Aoki, Kagan, and Axelrad 2000.

6. On the payoff for regulatory flexibility, see Bardach and Kagan 1982; Ayres and Braithwaite 1992; Gunningham and Grabosky 1998; Edward Weber 1998.

7. See Gunningham and Grabosky 1998 for a description of the Responsible Care initiative by the chemical industry; Rhone 1996 on forestry stewardship plan; Aoki, Kagan, and Axelrad 2000 for description of voluntary plan in water pollution by Japanese electronics manufacturers.

8. For a general review, see OECD 2000.

9. See, e.g., Fisse and Braithwaite 1983; Braithwaite 1989.

10. Morag-Levine 1994; Sabatier and Mazmanian 1983. Almost half the American manufacturing firms surveyed in Florida and Davison 2001 had undertaken programs to reduce local environmental impacts such as odor and dust, which generally are not closely regulated by federal or state regulatory laws.

11. Fowler 1995.

12. Emergency Planning and Community Right-to-Know Act, 42 U.S.C. 11001 et seq. (1986).

13. Braithwaite and Makkai 1991.

14. Suchman and Edelman 1997, p. 71. As further summarized by Hoffman 1997, in a work applying it to corporate environmental practice, institutional theory suggests that the corporation is a "socially based organization, seeking the subjective goals of survival and legitimacy rather than the supposedly objective goals of efficiency and profit maximization [and that] it is dynamic and complex and subject to social influences" (p. 13). On this view, decisions are mediated through the firm's institutional environment, with the result that they are influenced by the relevant "organizational field" (e.g., regulators, interest groups, capital markets and relevant financial institutions, local communities, the media, etc.) which to varying degrees will not only shape the firm's choices directly but will "also make institutional demands on the firm through the establishment of rules, norms, and common conceptions of behavior" (p. 29).

15. See, e.g., Smart 1992; Schmidheiny 1992.

16. Porter 1991, p. 8.

17. See generally Bhat 1996; Gunningham 1994.

18. For a summary, see Gouldson and Murphy 1998, pp. 2–3, and references therein.

19. See, e.g., Hajar 1995; Mol 1995.

20. See Porter 1998; Baylis, Cornell, and Flynn 1998. However, both Porter and the ecological modernization theorists acknowledge that there may be more scope for win-win outcomes in some sectors and circumstances than in others.

21. A survey of production managers in German business corporations concerning the effects of environmental protection measures indicated that "in 65 percent of all production divisions [that responded to the questionnaire], cost reductions have been achieved through modifications to manufacturing processes, production cost reductions in 49 percent, and energy and material cost reductions in about one third of companies" (Steger 1993, p. 162).

22. For example, many studies in this area are largely descriptive and exploratory and focus on leaders rather than the variation between leaders and laggards. See, e.g., Shrivastava and Scott 1992, pp. 9–21. Others confine themselves to survey evidence or are very preliminary in nature. See, e.g., Tsai and Child 1997, pp. 17–18. For a broader analysis of the limitations of existing research see Fuchs and Mazmanian 1998.

23. Based on a survey, Richard Florida and Derek Davison (2001) estimate that 24 percent of American manufacturing plants with more than fifty employees have adopted environmental management plans and 28 percent have a formal pollution prevention plan.

24. Mehta and Hawkins 1998, p. 65. See also Prakash 2000, pp. 9–10: "[F]or most [multinational enterprises] operating in industrialized countries, compliance with domestic environmental regulations is often a nonissue though previously many have resisted complying with laws."

25. See Walley and Whitehead 1994.

26. See ibid.

27. The most recent, detailed, and arguably most balanced analysis suggests a more complex picture in which, in some contexts, business commitment to improving environmental performance beyond compliance enhances profitability, and in others in which it does not. See Reinhardt 2000.

28. For example, in a McKinsey survey, 92 percent of CEOs and board members stated that the environment should be one of their top three management priorities, and 85 percent claimed that one of their major goals should be to integrate environmental considerations into business strategy (Walley and Whitehead 1994, p. 49). See more generally the initiatives and publications of the Global Environment Management Initiative (GEMI) at www.gemi.org.

29. Nash and Ehrenfeld in Coglianese and Nash 2001c, p. 79.

30. Newman 1993; Winsemius and Guntram 1992; Roome 1992; Greeno 1991; Hunt and Auster 1990.

31. Newman 1993.

32. More than forty such models have been identified. See Mauser 1996.

33. Roome 1992.

34. See, e.g., Hass 1996. Hoffman 1997 draws on the "new institutionalism" literature in organizational behavior to argue that corporations tend to emulate the

organizational structures and practices of the most economically and politically successful entities in their "organizational field," finding that petroleum and chemical companies have followed a similar evolution of environmental practices in the past three decades.

35. Ghobadian et al. 1998.

36. Schaefer and Harvey 1988.

37. Ghobadian et al. 1998, p. 15.

38. Prakash 2000, pp. 138–39. The 33/50 program is an EPA initiative calling for voluntary reductions in releases of seventeen high-priority toxic chemicals. EPA's goal was to reduce releases into the environment by 33 percent by the end of 1992 and by 50 percent by the end of 1995, measured against a 1988 baseline. The program achieved its goal in 1994.

39. See, e.g., Baylis, Connell, and Flynn 1998, pp. 150–61, noting, at p. 153, the "widespread generalization that industry is homogeneous in its response to [external] demands."

40. This in turn connects directly to the broader literature concerned with the management of corporate change. See, e.g., Peters and Austin 1985; Schein 1995.

41. R. Gray et al. 1995.

42. See, e.g., Florida et al. 1999.

43. Nash 2000.

44. Opportunity: Porter and van der Linde 1995a and Estrada et al. 1997. Threat: Walley and Whitehead 1994.

45. Some managers clearly share this point of view. In a recently completed comparative study, officials in two Japan-based multinational manufacturing companies asserted the view that worldwide environmental standards probably will become steadily more stringent over time: their firm, therefore, sought to gain a competitive advantage by becoming a leader in developing technologies and management systems for reducing pollution. Aoki and Cioffi 2000; Aoki, Kagan, and Axelrad 2000. See generally Porter 1991; Porter and van der Linde 1995a, 1995b. See also Sanchez 1997 for a brief review of the literature.

46. See Sanchez 1997 for a brief review of the literature.

47. Gladwin 1993, pp. 52–54. See also Ghobadian et al. 1988, p. 17.

48. For example, Yosie and Herbst's study on how corporations are integrating business methods with environmental management lists as the main motivators of excellence: economic benefits; corporate commitment and values; reputation enhancement; regulatory requirements; customer and stakeholder expectations; the contribution of EHS issues toward strategic differentiation of the company; and improved employee relations. Of these, only corporate commitment and values can be classified as an internal rather than an external driver.

49. Thus in a survey of seventy-eight of the largest companies in the United Kingdom, Ghobadian et al. (1998) were told that specific requirements set by customers
regularly were granted precedence if they conflicted with the company's environmental policy. In our study, too, pulp and paper mills generally have been unwilling
to cut use of bleaching chemicals when customers insist on bright white paper.

50. See Bowen 2000.

51. Reinhardt 2000.

52. Suchman and Edelman 1997.

53. Ibid., p. 919.

54. The industry association position can be maintained either by direct economic pressure (companies that sell their pulp to other industry members can be
threatened with a boycott) or by moral pressure ("if we let them pit us against each
other on environmental issues, where will it all end?").

55. See, e.g., Harrison 1999b.

56. Florida et al. 1999.

57. Ghobadian et al. 1998, pp. 16–17.

58. The potency of the social license can be increased, we observed, when the legal
regime grants rights of standing to sue either a company or a regulatory agency, requires broader public access to facility-level permits and emissions reports, requires
companies to consult with local communities, and allows activists to participate in
the decision-making process for permits. In addition to criminal sanctions and administrative notices (and civil penalties in the United States) companies that breach
their legal obligations are also vulnerable to either individual or class actions from
citizens injured as a result of the facility's illegal activities. In the case of local residents, they can oppose any expansion of the facility by both legal and political
means, thereby slowing or halting its economic growth.

59. "[L]ocal communities have the ability through the political process to create
the regulations that allow you to do business," one senior corporate official pointed
out. "[W]e operate under a license from the public in every place we do business, so
we have to be sensitive to public concerns."

60. Gladwin 1993, p. 39.

CHAPTER 3

1. Armstrong et al. 1998, p. 123. As indicated in nn. 2 and 3 below, these figures
are broadly consistent with subsequent and arguably more independent sources. In
the United States, the American Forest and Paper Association (AF&PA) adds that
new bleaching processes have achieved a 90 percent reduction in chlorinated organics since 1975 (AF&PA 2000, p. 5). The volume of water consumed per unit of pulp

production fell by 70 percent over the past 40 years (Armstrong et al. 1998), p. 123. Total energy consumed per ton of pulp fell 30 percent between 1972 and 1999 (AF&PA 2000, p. 12) and sulfur dioxide emissions per ton of pulp produced fell 65 percent between 1980 and 1989 (ibid., p. 6).

2. BC regulators also reported that in the 1990s, the survival rate of fish exposed to pulp mill effluent improved from 50 percent in 70 percent effluent to 99 percent in 100 percent effluent.

3. Note that this improvement in environmental performance cannot be attributed to changes in production, as can be seen in Figure 3.1: the greatest improvements in environmental performance occurred while production levels were basically stable.

4. The EPA's "Sector Facility Indexing Project," comparing "significant noncompliance" as detected by inspections and industry reports, found that in 1998 and 1999, American pulp mills (N = 244) had lower levels of significant noncompliance—4.3 percent for clean water regulations, 0 percent for RCRA (solid waste), and 21 percent for clean air requirements—than most other "dirty" industrial sectors (petroleum and metals manufacturing and smelting) (Stanley 1999). An EPA study of pulp mills in southeastern states in 1982–84 found 6 percent in "significant noncompliance" with permit levels, and that four of the fifty-six mills in the study created most of the instances of significant noncompliance (Magat and Viscusi 1990, p. 343).

5. McClelland and Horowitz 1999 also found that in the pulp and paper industry "there is widespread and substantial overcompliance with the relevant regulations" and "that plants incurred substantial costs to overcomply." On the other hand, many environmentalists regard the permit limits themselves as too permissive, so that even when overcomplying, facilities can still be discharging pollutants at levels that cause (sometimes severe) environmental harm.

6. At their worst, pulp mills in the 1960s killed all fish in the immediate vicinity of their discharges, and all other oxygen-breathing species. These severe effects on dissolved oxygen concentrations were the first environmental issues to be addressed by new or revivified regulatory regimes in the 1970s. By the 1980s, all oxygen-breathing life was no longer under threat downstream of pulp mill discharges. At one pulp mill in North Carolina, dissolved oxygen concentrations in the mill effluent improved 91 percent between 1987 and 1995, resulting in an 81 percent improvement in species richness (Seegert et al. 1997). But while modern production processes and secondary treatment of pulp mill effluent prevent acute toxicity in fish and invertebrates, fish in laboratory settings still show adverse effects due to exposure to pulp mill wastes. These include problems with enzymes involved in normal growth and development, including changes in blood levels of reproductive hormones (Munkittrick et al. 1998)

and changes in population structure (Larsson and Forlin 2002; Munkittrick et al. 1998).

7. These findings might not be true for some facilities in other jurisdictions, such as Sweden, where much of the technical research regarding promising new technologies is being conducted.

8. Regulatory regimes do not evolve in isolation. On the contrary, jurisdictions commonly model their legislation on that of other jurisdictions. Indeed, a study of global business regulation, found that "in all the countries . . . visited for this research, substantial parts of national environment protection laws were modeled from other nations' laws" (Braithwaite and Drahos 2000, p. 291). And Kathryn Harrison (2002), in a comparison of environmental standards setting in the United States, Canada, and Sweden notes that "There has been considerable convergence in both regulatory standards and industry performance." Of course, there is often a time lag between when one jurisdiction adopts a particular regulatory solution and it is taken up elsewhere, but in a industry like pulp and paper—with a high environmental profile, plus relatively standard processes of production and environmental technologies—it is hardly surprising that substantial intergovernmental modeling took place.

9. Henriques and Sadorsky 1995; Rappaport and Flaherty 1991; KPMG 1996.

10. Norberg-Bohm and Rossi 1998 attribute the sharp reductions in use of elemental chlorine (a source of dioxin emissions) in American pulp and paper mills in part to EPA regulations based on the U.S. Clean Water Act. Ashford et al. 1983 concludes that regulatory stringency is the single most important factor in eliciting investment in innovative environmental protection technological changes. Thornton 2001 found that large reductions in pulp mill BOD discharges were due to changes in technology induced by regulatory requirements.

11. Kagan 2000.

12. The EPA sent out a letter to state water regulatory agencies saying that it intended to regulate dioxin and organochlorines in pulp mill wastes. In Washington, this letter was sent on to each pulp mill. States were also instructed to start addressing the issue.

13. Some environmentalists argue that over the past few years, the regulatory process has ossified, and that further tightening of the regulatory license is unlikely. On the other hand, most (but not all) managers in our sample envisage periodic further tightening of their regulatory license in the future.

14. Thornton 2001.

15. Although the partial adoption of elemental chlorine-free (ECF) technology in the United States preceded rigorous federal regulation, pulp manufacturers anticipated that ECF technology, or more, would be required of them. They were right: in

1993, EPA proposed regulations with possible model technologies based on ECF (and other more rigorous) technology. Moreover, as early as December 1990, British Columbia had adopted a very stringent AOX regulation, which suggested that U.S. regulators might follow suit. By the time the EPA's final rule was promulgated in April 1998, the EPA noted, "Since the proposal, some facilities have modified their processes. There has been a substantial move toward ["best practicable technologies" mentioned in the 1993 proposed rule] elemental chlorine-free bleaching . . . oxygen delignification and extended cooking"(63 FR 18517).

16. B.C. Reg. 470/90.

17. See, e.g., Kubasek 1996.

18. Under some statutes, not only can citizen suits be brought for current or ongoing violations of regulation, but citizens can also sue a corporation for failing to comply with emergency reporting requirements (see, e.g., Coyle 2000).

19. Bubble licenses allow for single aggregate permit limits for an entire facility rather than separate limits for each piece of equipment at the facility. A bubble permit allows managers the flexibility to run one piece of equipment at high pollution levels if they can compensate for this excess by running other pieces of equipment at low pollution levels.

20. This example is described in somewhat more detail on p. 120.

21. Joyce and Thomson 1999, p. 441.

22. In addition, mill officials were exploring the possibility of treating the waste to make it a reusable commodity. "There might be opportunities," the firm's environmental manager said. Thus social license pressures can sometimes instigate a search for "win-win" alternatives.

23. For the United States, 43 FR 7572, Feb. 23. 1978, as amended at 43 FR 34785, Aug. 7, 1978, established emissions limits for total reduced sulfur (TRS) from pulp mills. The EPA's Cluster Rule characterizes TRS as having health-related as opposed to merely esthetic impacts.

24. While water color is not currently regulated, it is not necessarily only an aesthetic issue. Some of the sublethal effects found in fish are believed to result from the plant chemicals released during the pulp processing, and color may be a good indicator of the load of plant chemicals in effluents.

25. European demand for TCF paper, at least in the late 1990s, was not so strong as to enable producers to charge a premium for TCF pulp. Hence even mills like BC3, with the ability to operate TCF, felt economic pressures to back off from eliminating all chlorine as long as regulations allowed them to do so.

26. Norberg-Bohm and Rossi cite Young 1993. See also Knickerbocker 1994.

27. While the reason for the sale is unknown, and perhaps should not be entirely attributed to the switch to TCF pulp, the sale of the Samoa mill does indicate that it

was not seen as a valuable part of Louisiana-Pacific's future, and the failure of other facilities to adopt TCF technology indicates that it was not seen as an important technology by the industry. Even in Sweden where a number of mills produce TCF pulp, TCF capacity has stagnated while ECF capacity has continued to expand.

28. Milton Friedman cited in Murphy and Thomas 1999, p. 5.

29. Schmidtheiny and Zorraquín 1996.

30. Gentry and Fernandez n.d., p. i.

31. A number of pulp and paper companies have been subject over the years to shareholder resolutions about their continuing use of chlorine, and while it is difficult to establish conclusively whether such resolutions have changed industry practices, some informed observers assert that this is the case.

32. See Epstein, Palepup, and Krishna 1999.

33. For example, a 1994 survey of London financial analysts found that most doubted the significance of environmental factors in arriving at their financial assessments and took the view that such factors were essentially ethical or moral considerations lacking relevance to their evaluations ("City Analysts and the Environment: A Survey of Environmental Attitudes in the City of London," *Business in the Environment and Extel Financial Ltd.*, Nov. 1994, quoted in Gentry and Fernandez n.d.). A 1997 American survey was only a little more positive about the perceived connection between environmental and economic performance (Gentry and Fernandez n.d., p. 13).

34. See Lanoie, Laplante, and Roy 1997.

35. For example, a review of Goldman Sachs's *Paper and Forest Products Monthly*, an investment research bulletin, for 1999 revealed extremely few references to environmental performance as a significant criterion in evaluating a firm's economic performance within the sector.

36. For a more positive analysis of the *future* role of financial markets, see Schmidtheiny and Zorraquín 1996.

37. According to a World Resources Institute study, at least half of thirteen U.S. paper and pulp mills studied faced potential environmental liabilities that could cost shareholders as much as 10 percent of their equity. See "Pulp Fiction? Firms Hide Liabilities, Group Assets," *Investment News* 4, 3 (Dec. 18, 2000).

38. Similarly, one analyst pointed out that while he and his peers took very little interest in a company's environmental record generally, they did take serious notice of how much it was likely to cost a company to come into compliance with new regulations. In the case of the U.S. EPA's Cluster Rule, for example, a great deal of interest was expressed in how much capital expenditure might be incurred, and in speculating on which mills might be forced to close rather than invest the money necessary to ensure compliance. According to one senior corporate official of a very

large and sophisticated corporation: "At the time we were spending to anticipate the cluster rule, it was about 15–20 percent of our total capital expenditure, and the market sat up and took notice, and we had to explain it. But today it's much lower than that, and so spending $10 million here or there is not going to be noticed by the market."

39. Gentry and Fernandez n.d., p. 9. Consistent with that analysis, a 1997 analysis of the relationship between proactive environmental action (as measured by Toxic Release Inventory data) and industry analysts' 1–5 years earnings-per-share performance forecasts documents a significant negative relationship. While this does not necessarily indicate that environmentally proactive firms lose money over the longer term, it does suggest that, at the present time, analysts appear to systematically anticipate that green firms will have lower earnings-per-share over the *short term* (one to five years) (Cordiero and Sarkis 1997).

40. Eamer 1998.

41. In 1989–95, the annualized income to shareholders of the twenty-six largest publicly traded companies in North America looked like this: five companies had negative returns; five companies made 0–5 percent; ten companies earned 6–10 percent; and six companies returned 11–15 percent. Eamer 1998.

42. N. Craig Smith 1990, pp. 175–76.

43. See Ballian 2000.

44. See Lanoie, Laplante, and Roy 1997 and studies cited therein. Cf. Harrison 1999a.

45. For discussions of various aspects of consumer boycotts, see N. Craig Smith 1990; Friedman 1991; Fahey 1992; Joyner 1984; Harper 1984. See also generally Gunningham and Grabosky 1998.

46. See Meidinger 2001.

47. See, e.g., Greenpeace 1992.

48. For suppliers of electronic components, for example, see Aoki, Kagan, and Axelrad 2000.

49. To obtain ISO–14000 certification, a company must demonstrate that it has established and employs a formal environmental management system, which must include provision for clear lines of corporate responsibility for environmental issues plus the institutionalization of regular self-analysis of the firm's environmental impacts, articulation of environmental policies, employee training, auditing, and response, organized to achieve continuous improvement in environmental performance.

50. See Chapter 4.

51. See, e.g., Schmidtheiny and Zorraquín 1996.

52. Other mills, particularly those that used different types of wood or had different customer demands, had declined in the 1990s to install oxygen delignification, which their analyses indicated would not be cost-effective for them.

53. It should be noted that when environmentalists say "chlorine-free," they generally mean totally chlorine-free (TCF), that is, no bleach product containing any chlorine is used—no elemental chlorine, no chlorine dioxide. When industry says chlorine-free, it means elemental chlorine-free (ECF), using chlorine dioxide as a substitute. Most industry environmental managers and regulators contend that the environmental benefits of moving to TCF operations would be minimal.

54. The correlation between corporate profitability in 1990–94 and AOX was −0.96.

55. For an analysis of the relationship between profits and environment in a European context, which also suggests that the relationship is a complex one, see http://www.environmental-performance.org/analysis/index.php.

56. Market pulp prices fluctuated over the 1981–99 period, averaging $700 per ton, but there were several extended periods, including in the 1990s, in which they languished between $500 and $650 a ton.

57. One mill (WA3) was an exception, in that its emissions of BOD and TSS were better in times of above-average pulp prices than in times of lower pulp prices, and the same was true for another mill (WA1) with respect to TSS.

58. The chemical spill analysis was based on quarterly data for seven U.S. facilities from 1982 to 1999. Four facilities had a higher proportion of spills during "good times" (e.g., when pulp prices were higher than $700 per ton) than during bad times. The opposite was true, however, for three mills. Aggregating the data for all facilities, we found more spills per quarter in good times (5.04) than in bad times (3.18). The same overall pattern is found if we look only at 1989–99 data.

59. There are other, noneconomic reasons, too, for mills to eschew the pursuit of TCF operations. Canadian regulators argued early, and eventually convincingly, that the environmental performance of ECF mills is as good as that of TCF mills in the sense that the effluent from TCF mills also has adverse effects on fish and other life in receiving waters (Harrison 2002). The speculation is that the changes in fish are due not to the organo-chlorine or other bleach-chemical residues from ECF plants but to residues of chemicals extracted from the wood itself during the pulping process. Thus from the standpoint of most mills, "going all the way" to TCF operations is not necessarily being a better environmental performer.

60. British Columbia, as noted earlier, promulgated a regulation requiring zero AOX emissions from pulp mills by the end of 2002. Many BC pulp mill officials questioned the rationale for that requirement (see the preceding note), and also

questioned both the technical and economic feasibility of achieving zero discharge levels. They therefore also questioned whether the regulation would remain politically viable.

61. See OECD 1999; Thornton 2001.

CHAPTER 4

1. Averages were of all available data for the 1998–99 period. Averages for different facilities therefore do not cover exactly the same time period.

2. Unlike AOX, BOD, and TSS are measured in kg/day, not in kg/ton of production. The AOX measure thus "controls for" different levels of production; it is a measure of the relative thoroughness or pollution-reduction-efficiency of the mill. The BOD and TSS figures focus on the mill's actual impact on receiving waters, regardless of level of production. All environmental performance figures are not available for all mills. For example, no *comparable* figures were available for AUS. This mill discharges the majority portion of its effluent to a public treatment facility, rather than (as other mills do) directly into surface water near the plant, after treatment in the facility-owned treatment works. No BOD or TSS figures in kg/d were available for GA2, and we were unable to obtain AOX figures for WA1, NZ1, GA1, or GA3.

3. WA2, more or less a "laggard" on Table 4.1, does have one production line that employs a technology that is "dirtier" than that used by the other mills. However, as noted in the preceding note, we have attempted to correct WA2's figures to account for this difference.

4. Sublethal effects on fish, for example, include gross deformities and reproductive effects (Harrison 2002).

5. Our economic data were not as detailed as we would have liked, in that they related to corporate, not mill-level, finances. Moreover, as we shall emphasize again later, our statistical tests are limited by the small number of firms in our sample, so that one or two aberrant cases undermine the search for statistically significant relationships.

6. Reviewing the files for one mill in the British Columbia environmental agency, we noted that the mills reported much more information on emissions, and more often, than was specified by the regulatory permit, for regulatory officials supplemented the permit with informal requests.

7. For example, in British Columbia, limits are given in mg/L. Changing these limits to kg/day figures requires assuming a constant volumetric flow rate.

8. At the suggestion of a number of regulatory scholars, we also tried to use data from the U.S. Toxic Release Inventory to measure environmental performance

among U.S. pulp mills in our sample, but we found it difficult to interpret the data with any degree of confidence. Facilities are allowed to provide their own estimates of their releases, but such methods are not standardized, and facilities may vary in the number of processes and outputs covered. No two facilities reported on exactly the same set of chemicals. In addition, the definitions of chemicals themselves have also changed over time. The further back in time, the more such definitional inconsistencies can be found, making it difficult to discern improvement in releases from the early 1990s to the late 1990s. Moreover, if one limits data comparisons to improvement over later periods with more consistent data reporting, such as the period 1994–99, companies that were early adopters (before 1994) of good environmental practices would compare badly to those that adopted such practices between 1994 and 1999. Finally, enormous variations in releases are reported without any obvious explanation. We had no means to determine whether such large discrepancies were real or an artifact of data entry or the estimation procedure used by the facility. We therefore decided not to use the TRI data as a comparative environmental performance measure.

9. "We also find that pollution control investment is positively related to the EPA enforcement budget, suggesting at the very least the industries believe that the EPA will increase its investigatory efforts as their budget increases" (Regens et al. 1997, p. 695).

10. The contrast between U.S. and other nations' regulatory styles emerges from detailed case studies of a variety of regimes of social regulation, from coal mine safety (Braithwaite 1985), workplace safety (Kelman 1981; Wilson 1985; Wokutch 1992), and nursing home quality of care (Braithwaite 1993) to various kinds of environmental regulation (Vogel 1986; Aoki and Cioffi 2000; Aoki, Kagan, and Axelrad 2000; Dwyer, Brooks, and Marco 2000; Axelrad 2000; Verweij 2000).

11. Harrison drew on studies in the United States by Magat and Viscusi (1990) and in Canada by Thompson (1980), Victor and Burrell (1981), and Environment Canada (1975, 1977, 1980, 1982, 1984). Her finding resonates with other comparisons of environmental enforcement in the United States and Canada (Hoberg 1999).

12. The permits for pulp mills in the State of Washington that we obtained reflect a great deal of tailoring to particular firms' technical and economic situations. On the other hand, in the 1990s, Environment Canada prodded provincial governments to step up the intensity of implementation of standards for pulp mills (Harrison 1996). And British Columbia's regulations calling for total elimination of AOX from pulp mill effluent by 2002 are *more stringent* than AOX regulations in the United States.

13. One company official in the State of Washington told us: "There is a contrast between the state and federal agencies. Suppose, for example, we release chlorine every Tuesday. The state would see it and ask, 'What's going on?' By the third time

we did it, they would write us an order and say we won't go away until you solve the problem. That is, they would insist we reduce the pollution and limit the risk. In contrast, the federal EPA would allow the excursion to continue until it was so serious [that] it enabled them to impose a large penalty. They would then come in and want a million-dollar fine."

14. Single factor ANOVA, $F = 0.913$, $p = 0.476$.

15. Single factor ANOVA, $F = 0.338$, $p = 0.843$.

16. A single factor ANOVA found that not all jurisdiction averages were the same ($F = 4.199$, $p = 0.046$), and a multiple comparisons test (Tukey) found only British Columbia and New Zealand were significantly different ($q = -4.971$; q crit at 0.05 is 4.529).

17. As noted earlier, we ranked facilities in terms of a 1–5 scale on a variety of control technologies (e.g., use of oxygen delignification, percentage of reduction of use of environmental chlorine for bleaching, type of secondary treatment plant for effluent). In addition to this "objective" technology measure, we asked environmental managers to rank their own facilities' control technologies compared with the best available. On both measures, there was generally more difference within jurisdictions than across jurisdictions in the technology rankings of mills. For example, although BC and NZ mills are above average on both measures, each jurisdiction has both higher-ranked and lower-ranked facilities.

18. For example, in Washington, the lowest limits among our sample facilities were 29 percent of the highest limits for BOD and 33 percent for TSS (see Table 4.2).

19. Harrison 2002.

20. Another possible reason is that BC4 sells "market pulp" (whereas WA4 sells its pulp to paper mills owned by the same corporate parent), and many of BC4's customers were in western Europe, where environmental activists made some headway in the 1990s in generating consumer demands for "chlorine-free" paper. In this respect, the interaction of BC4's social and economic license, as much as the regulatory license, may have explained why it sought higher levels of chlorine substitution than WA4 did in the latter half of the 1990s.

21. The correlation between corporate size (as measured by annual sales 1998–99) and mill-level emissions was −0.10 for BOD, 0.24 (TSS) and 0.03 (AOX). The correlations between corporate net income (1998–99) and mill-level emissions were 0.21 for BOD, −0.05 (TSS), and 0.46 (AOX), none of which were statistically significant.

22. One of the strongest correlations in our data is between mill-level "subjective technology" scores and environmental performance—.68 for BOD, .69 for TSS, and .80 for AOX (all statistically significant). Some might wonder whether it could be that firms that are more profitable are so because they have not invested much in environmental controls. For example, WA2 was the second most profitable firm and

NOTES TO CHAPTER 4

among the worst in terms of environmental performance. We believe that in aggregate, the data do not support this hypothesis. Facilities WA3, BC2, and GA2 were among the best environmental performers in our sample, and their parent company the most profitable in the 1995–99 period. On average, more profitable mills had better environmental performance than less profitable mills.

23. It is likely that we found no statistically significant correlation between corporate profitability in the early 1990s and BOD and TSS emissions in the late 1990s because by the early 1990s, most mills, particularly in the United States, had already made the major capital investments that brought those figures down. See Figure 4.1.

24. It should also be emphasized that economic success was not the only source of stronger environmental management. Some "True Believers" were struggling financially through much of the 1990s. The correlation between 1998–99 environmental performance and corporate profitability (income sales) in 1995–99 was much lower (.16) than the correlation between 1990–94 profitability and performance (.62), and the 1995–99 correlation was not statistically significant.

25. Oxygen delignification is an extension of the pulping process that reduces the use of bleaching chemicals (Norberg-Bohm and Rossi 1998, p. 233). Some analyses have suggested that oxygen delignification is cost-effective for mills that use softwood pulp but not for users of hardwood (ibid., p. 236).

26. Mean AOX emissions for mills with and without oxygen delignification were 0.386 kg/ton and 0.755 kg/ton respectively. These averages are significantly different (t-value = 2.46, p = 0.02).

27. In our "objective measure" of technology, too, GA3 rated last in our sample of firms.

28. In the early 1990s, however, WA2 had one of the lowest income-to-sales ratios in our sample. WA2's lack of profitability in that period, when many other mills were investing in costly new pollution-control and AOX-reducing technologies, may help explain why it lagged in technology and environmental performance later in the decade, even as its earnings picture improved dramatically.

29. Moreover, both WA2 and WA4 are also paper product manufacturers, and hence their economic license is similar in that they are not primarily sellers of market pulp.

30. Mills BC4 and GA3 present a similar story. Both faced strong economic pressures to improve profits and cash reserves, but managers at BC4 were conscious of their mill's visibility to middle-class motorists on a nearby highway and recalled dramatic demonstrations at their mill and at their parent corporation by environmental activists. GA3, not located near a major population center, had not experienced such social license pressures. BC4 had decidedly better environmental performance than GA3 according to all our measures.

31. See p. 125 for more detailed description of AUS's efforts.

32. At the same time, it is also clear, as noted earlier, that European demand for TCF paper, at least in the late 1990s, was not so strong as to enable producers to charge a premium for TCF paper. Hence even mills like BC3, with the ability to operate TCF, felt economic pressures to back off from eliminating all chlorine-based products, as long as regulators still allowed their use.

33. Almost all our respondents acknowledged that a "mill in the boondocks" with an economically dependent local community could be anticipated to have a very relaxed social license compared to one located near (or visible to) an environmentally conscious middle-class community that no longer depended upon it for its economic well-being.

CHAPTER 5

1. See Chapter 3.

2. In 1998–99, NZ2 had the weakest record in our sample for control of BOD and TSS emissions, although it was in the middle of the pack with respect to reduction of AOX emissions.

3. By "actions," we mean managerial actions such as how often facilities trained employees, how readily they shared information with community groups, etc.

4. Our identification of these variables, and of the construct "environmental management style" is consistent with the method of theory construction articulated in Glaser and Strauss 1967.

5. There are, of course, risks that our classification of firms may fall short of reliability. First, where we attempt to measure attitudes, we might have confused rhetoric with reality (companies may only purport to have a particular attitude). However, that danger was substantially countered, we believe, by combining the attitude and action measures. Thus where we examined attitudes directly, we were able to see if the attitude was congruent with corporate actions (for example, if a firm claimed to be committed to compliance, did it have adequate compliance monitoring strategies in place). A second risk is that where we treat actions as a surrogate for environmental attitudes, these actions might be explained by factors unrelated to attitude. For example, aware of our interest in environmental performance, an interviewee might have explained action X (for example, installing an oxygen delignification system) on grounds that it would significantly reduce use of bleach chemicals used and hence chlorinated organics in wastewater, whereas the dominant reason may have been that the reduction in bleach chemicals simply saved money. To address this concern, we looked for consistency throughout the interview in terms of the explanatory stories that we were told regarding each environmental action de-

scribed and in comparing all the actions described throughout the interview. We also pledged that individual respondents and facilities would not be identified in our research, which reduced incentives for interviewees to try to "spin" the answers to our questions.

6. See generally Max Weber 1968 [1922].

7. Sometimes, there was a substantial disparity between the attitude of mill and corporate management, which was the most common explanation where firms fell between two ideal types. The environmental attitudes of several mills, as we shall see, changed over time, often due to particular external shocks—sudden "contractions" of their regulatory, economic, or social licenses.

8. See pp. 42, 43, 76.

9. See pp. 89–90.

10. Similarly, corporate officials at WA2's corporate headquarters attributed the level of environmental action at WA2 as being due substantially to the diligence of regulatory officials in this particular jurisdiction. One official indicated that the company had "far worse" mills in jurisdictions where regulatory enforcement was lax.

11. The WA2 environmental manager explained: "We take the results of the [government] inspections as the equivalent of an audit. So we take inspections as an audit tool and the corporate level department has an audit to compare our performance to other mills' performance in the company. We track our environmental incidents, violations, spills, and these are reported to the top of the corporation. Some get to be reported within twenty-four hours."

12. To ensure that the supply chain is "green," environmental activists have in recent years often targeted retailers, rather than producers. For example, "Protesters unfurl a banner from a crane near the Home Depot headquarters in Cobb County today," the *Atlanta Journal and Constitution* reported on Oct. 28, 1998 (p. 01a). "Five activists from the Rainforest Action Network scaled the construction crane as part of a campaign urging Home Depot to stop selling products made from old-growth wood." Subsequently, Home Depot "led industry as the first retailer to join the Certified Forest Products Council demonstrating our commitment to third-party independently certified products" (www.homedepot.com, environmental milestones, 1999).

13. BC4 was unusual in that the nearest significant community was far enough away not to be able to smell the mill, and in any event, was characterized as "a forest town," where the main sources of employment were the sawmill, logging, and related activities, and, as a result, the community was "historically more forgiving." There have been two sources of social pressures on the mill in recent years. Environmental activist actions, taken against the parent company's forestry operations, rather than

the mill, were the first. According to the environmental manager, the firm's response included the decision to adopt ISO–14000 as a means of gaining some environmental credibility. The second source of social pressure was from the urban public, who, although they did not come close enough to the mill to smell it, had a clear view of the mill from a highway that led past BC4 to a resort. Diminishing the mill's visual impact was first on the wish list of both the environmental and general managers. However, little action had actually been taken in this regard.

14. As mill management pointed out: "You set your boundaries stricter than the regulations just to be sure to be in compliance . . . you set margins tighter than the regulations just to get your margin of error."

15. Describing BC4's training program, its environmental manager said. "Every employee gets environmental awareness training . . . and every three to four years, we do a blitz. . . . If there have been new regulations, it's an opportunity to get it out to people."

16. ECF pulp production reduces the amount of dioxins and other chlorinated organics in mill effluents.

17. The original decision to situate the mill in this area was driven substantially by political considerations, with the government of the day wanting to provide employment and using its control over forest resources as leverage to persuade the company to locate there.

18. According to mill officials: "[Governmental] regulation does not inhibit us from doing anything. It sets a minimum level. Our concern is it's very prescriptive—we are concerned is there a scientific justification for the environmental benefit that goes along with it? Is there an economic justification for the benefit derived from certain things?"

19. "We are operating on public land with our timberlands and the government wants to know for sure that you are managing government resources appropriately and therefore we certify [to ISO–14000] all timberlands in [this jurisdiction] and will certify all our mills as well," a BC2corp official noted.

20. One BC2corp manager thought that the reason BC2 installed odor controls was the desire "to pacify the community. . . . Location and geography has a lot to do with it. We have another mill, a small one in the boondocks with only a tiny community, and there is no pressure there for change." It might be noted that most technical people in the pulp industry view odor as a nuisance issue alone, arguing that the unpleasant-smelling emissions do not damage human health or harm ecosystems. Thus it could be argued that if there is not much complaining about the smell, it is not necessary to spend substantial sums on reducing it. However, see Morag-Levine 1994 for an argument about the inadequacy of nuisance-based systems for dealing with odorous industrial fumes.

21. In justification of this policy, a BC2corp manager told us, "Every location has its areas of sensitivity. . . . We have a problem with how the data might be used, contextualized."

22. As noted in Chapter 4, WA4 purchased the mill in the early 1980s. Its predecessor had developed a reputation for indifference to environmental concerns, and WA4 faced what appeared to be an uphill battle in winning the trust of local activists and a local population who no longer wanted or needed a pulp mill on their doorstep.

23. In 1998–99, AUScorp's share price increased 15 percent (compared to an overall market average increase of 10 percent for the same period). Its after tax profit also rose 15 percent to nearly U.S.$200 million on sales of a little over U.S.$4,000 million. While some of the company's products, such as corrugated packaging, do not require brand identification, others clearly do.

24. Eutrophication results from the discharge of nutrients (nitrogen and phosphorus) into a river system. The nutrients promote algal growth, which in turn results in the depletion of dissolved oxygen in the water.

25. The AUScorp environmental manager told us: "I don't think compliance means 100 percent of requirements 100 percent of the time. That would be highly desirable, but in reality we are dealing with an imperfect system. . . . So you can expect times when you are not able to control your process. It's a false expectation to think that one side/aspect of your business is going to perform differently from other aspects. You are always going to have flaws. You can't expect perfect environmental performance but still make imperfect paper from time to time. As in our private lives, we make mistakes, it's wrong to expect perfection. *It doesn't mean you don't strive to reach perfection*" (emphasis added). He noted also: "The . . . valley itself meets the [relevant ambient air quality requirement for the airshed], so to put it in perspective, [we are less concerned about] . . . numerical noncompliance which has no measurable impact on the receiving environment. And that should be the driver."

26. The environmental manager at the mill also noted: "Having worked with the community, once you've shown your operations have a very low impact, they're mainly interested in ensuring that things don't get worse. They want a program to ensure you're moving in the right direction. . . . So if we are doing something to demonstrate incremental, slow change, it would go a long way. The *predictability* is the issue. Corporate [management] has to put its hand in its pocket. Here's a million here, millions there . . . But we can't answer: 'What are you going to do about thus and such next year?' There is a community expectation that water quality will improve . . . asking for more to go to the river would unleash a holocaust against us."

27. We grouped the mills into two categories, True Believers together with Environmental Strategists, and Committed Compliers together with Reluctant Compli-

ers, and for each mill we compared (a) average BOD and TSS emissions, 1998–99, with (b) the mill's regulatory permit limits for those effluents, and computed how far below (b) the figure (a) was for each, in percentage terms. See Table 3.1. The TB + ES group's emissions averaged 24 percent of permit limits for BOD, compared to 57 percent for the CC + BC1 group. The correlation between management style and percentage below limit was 0.67 for BOD and 0.63 for TSS, both of which are significant.

28. The "objective technology" correlations within environmental performance are somewhat lower (.6 for AOX), probably because those measures are based on a narrower range of technologies than the "subjective technology" measures and are focused on particular emissions.

29. The downward trend at WA4 was sufficient to result in a 50 percent improvement in environmental performance in a fifteen-year period (Thornton 2001).

30. Chemical spills (such as of pulping liquors) that reach a pulp mill's wastewater treatment system can kill the bacteria that are relied on to destroy organic matter in the effluent, or overwhelm the bacteria's ability to degrade the organic matter in those spills. The result would be an increase in BOD discharged into receiving waters.

31. Big spills are those measuring more than 100 units, regardless of the unit of measure, because more hazardous materials tend to be measured in smaller units.

32. Our sample is too small, unfortunately, to enable us to perform a multivariate regression analysis. And our qualitative interviews, which revealed the complex interaction of often company-specific factors that shaped both environmental management style and environmental performance, leave us with little confidence that a small sample quantitative analysis would result in definitive or striking findings, particularly based on the difficult-to-assemble and inevitably rough quantitative indicators we were able to construct.

CHAPTER 6

1. On the empirical limitations of the existing literature, see Fuchs and Mazmanian 1998.

2. See Chapter 3, pp. 41–42.

3. See Chapter 3. Also the OECD states: "It appears that many mills are well ahead of the permit or regulatory limits that are set. This inference is drawn from information on the range of discharges of the principal pollutants from the process, per ton of production.... Many mills have discharges that are low compared to the levels that are set in regulations or targets. However, information on permit limits was only supplied for a few mills in each country. Nevertheless, few mills are expected to have low permit discharge limits. This suggests that other factors than permit limits are driving the pollution control programs at mills" (OECD 1999, p. 16).

4. Regulatory regimes do not evolve in isolation. On the contrary, jurisdictions commonly model their legislation on that of other jurisdictions. Certainly there is often a time lag between when one jurisdiction adopts a particular regulatory solution and it is taken up elsewhere, but in an industry with as high an environmental profile as pulp and paper, in which the processes of production are relatively standard, as is the range of technologies for addressing them, it is hardly surprising that substantial modeling took place.

5. We do not mean to imply that economic license constraints absolutely preclude further environmental innovation: had we looked at other jurisdictions, such as Sweden, we might have found more innovation despite economic constraints, or lower economic constraints due to government subsidization of research efforts. On occasion, the economic license can even push in a green direction when customers or suppliers demand better performance due to health or environmental concerns.

6. Not only did regulation account for significant technological change, but it was regarded as an inevitably "tightening noose." A number of managers viewed regulation as paramount in bringing about long-term environmental improvements. Some cited the personal responsibilities of senior officers or managers, who in most jurisdictions are also liable to penalties as individuals. Others were influenced by their vulnerability to either individual or class actions from citizens injured as a result of the mill's activities. Many were concerned with the informal punishments that might accompany breach of regulations, not least, negative publicity and shaming. And of course some were influenced by all of these factors.

7. The differences between British Columbia and the United States in discharges, it should be noted, did not pass a test of statistical significance, reflecting the relatively small number of mills in the calculation and the intrajurisdictional variability in discharges.

8. Pulp producers "around the world have spent billions of dollars adopting new technologies, modifying old ones, and developing local innovations to meet growing environmental demands, expectations and regulations" (Sonnenfeld 2002, p. 1).

9. See Table 4.3 and related text.

10. The correlation between environmental management style and environmental performance was .76 for BOD, .66 for TSS, and .57 for AOX.

11. See Table 5.1.

12. Prakash 2000; Hoffman 1997.

13. The same result was found by OECD 1999, a ten-country study of the pulp and paper industry.

14. Indeed (eliminating GA2, whose low AOX score reflected special market incentives), the U.S. mills' average AOX emissions were slightly worse than the average.

15. An Organization for Economic Co-Operation and Development study of the

pulp and paper industry in 1999 reported: "With respect to bleaching, pollution prevention measures have been taken to reduce the quantities of chlorine gas used. In
some cases it has been totally replaced by chlorine dioxide. In other cases, even chlorine dioxide has been eliminated, and no chlorine compounds are involved in the
production of pulp. In this area, mills have gone far beyond the AOX levels set in
their permits. *These developments appear to be more market driven than environmental
permit/regulation induced*" (OECD 1999, p. 17, emphasis added). We note that it is
difficult to distinguish between anticipated regulation and responses to market or
social pressures, which at very least affect estimates of the nature and likelihood of
regulation. However, at least in the United States, the *total* substitution of chlorine
dioxide for elemental chlorine has probably been induced by anticipated regulation.
Mills in the United States have long argued that lower levels of substitution are adequate to protect health and the environment, and it is unlikely that they would entirely eliminate elemental chlorine if not required to do so.

16. See Norberg-Bohm and Rossi 1998. This is not to deny that pulp mills will invest in major technologies that also have environmental benefits, such as oxygen delignification in some circumstances, but the general picture is one of incremental
change with incentives too limited for firms to take risks to adopt major technological change.

17. See Chapter 2.

18. This finding is consistent with Ghobadian et al. 1998.

19. The academic literature on regulation draws a distinction between regulations
that specify "performance standards" (e.g., maximum emissions for particular sub-
stances) and regulations that mandate the use of specific control technologies
("technology standards"). Michael Porter and Claus van der Linde have argued that
performance standards can foster innovation because they free up an enterprise to
respond to a regulator's requirement in the way it best thinks fit. In evidence they
cite the relative success of the Scandinavian and U.S. governments in achieving
emissions reductions in the pulp and paper industry. The Scandinavian companies,
under a performance-based regime, "developed innovative pulping and bleaching
technologies that not only met emission requirements but also lowered operating
costs." U.S. companies, in contrast, did not respond to regulation by innovating because U.S. specifications or technology-based regulations did not permit companies
to "discover how to solve their own problems" (Porter and van der Linde 1995, p.
129). However, in the State of Washington permits we reviewed, we found that mills
were not generally required to install particular technologies, but that they were required to meet performance standards, although these in turn were based on certain
model control technologies. This most often led to the installation of the model
technology. In addition, where permits did require the installation of a specific tech-

nology, this requirement had usually been arrived at after negotiations between the regulator and regulatee, or only applied if certain conditions were met. Similarly in all the jurisdictions in our study, pulp mills' environmental developments generally were driven by *performance* standards rather than by governmental mandates to use specific technologies. These findings are in keeping with a ten-country OECD study of the pulp and paper industry, which states: "The permitting processes followed impose release conditions, including limits. These are developed on the basis of existing technology capable of meeting the limits. Mills are permitted to choose what equipment to install to meet the limits. Flexibility is granted in enabling them to do this in the most cost effective manner. Specific technologies are not mandated. In some cases, permit conditions include the installation of specified equipment. It is noted that this is attained through prior discussions between the permitter and permittee. The specification therefore reflects an agreement between the parties, and not the mandating of equipment" (OECD 1999, p. 15).

20. For a discussion of the relationship of regulation and technology in a somewhat similar context see Ashford and Heaton 1983.

21. Ashford 2002 notes that stringent and focused regulation has stimulated fundamental changes in product and process technologies in the chemical producing and using industries (p. 1422).

22. 63 *Federal Register* 18535.

23. Note Porter and van der Linde's characterization of U.S. pulp and paper regulations in the 1970s, which they argue, prevented U.S. companies from realizing first mover advantages because it "ignored a critical principle of good environmental regulation: Create maximum opportunity for innovation by letting industries discover how to solve their own problems" (Porter and van der Linde 1995, p. 129).

24. Some environmentalists argue that in the past few years, the regulatory process has ossified, and that further tightening of the regulatory license is unlikely. On the other hand, most (but not all) managers in our sample envisaged periodic further tightening of their regulatory license in the future.

25. Finnish pulp mills have found that this "dynamic incentive [to reduce averages below limits in order to avoid accidental short-term exceedences] has, however, been reduced by the fear expressed by many interviewees that discharges far below the permit limits are likely to result in tighter permit" (Mickwitz and Hildén 2001, p. 13).

26. In an industry with as high an environmental profile as the pulp and paper industry, in which the processes of production are relatively standardized, substantial modeling apparently takes place. For example, a number of our respondents pointed to the close relationship between United States and Canadian environmental regulations particularly, but similar technology-related regulatory solutions could also be

found in New Zealand and Australia. On the process of regulatory modeling generally, and its importance, see further Braithwaite and Drahos 2000, ch. 25.

27. For example, some facilities would report pollutant discharges in efficiency units (pounds per unit of production), others in concentration units (pounds of pollutant per liter of water), and others in impact units (pounds per day). However, the data required to make the conversions (production per day, discharge volume per day) between these units were often not provided. Even when production figures were given, frequent changes were made as to how production levels were reported, so that consistency over time and between facilities was difficult to maintain. Sometimes, although the same parameter was being monitored, the laboratory analytic techniques differed. Or different parameters were used to try to measure a similar environmental problem (chlorine discharges v. adsorbable organic halides v. dioxin).

28. While most jurisdictions required that data be collected relatively frequently, there was no consistency as to how often data were reported. Facilities were sometimes required to take daily measurements but only report annual averages. Data were also difficult to obtain, sometimes requiring a visit to the local regulatory agency and copying down the numbers on the company's report. Electronic data were available in some jurisdictions, but the data quality was not always as good as one would wish. For example, the U.S. EPA's Permit Compliance System contains discharge monitoring report data for all permitted facilities in the United States. However, a value of 4.3 1,000lbs/day is often entered into the database as 4.3 lbs/day instead of 4,300 lbs/day. Automated data quality routines ought to be able to identify such problems.

29. Examples of this approach include various Clinton-Gore Reinventing Environmental Regulation initiatives, most notably Project XL and the Environmental Leadership Program, the Wisconsin Green Tier Proposal (Wisconsin Department of Natural Resources 2000) and the EPA's Performance Track (U.S. EPA 2000).

30. Maureen Smith 1997, p. 9.

31. Because companies clearly have more information about their facilities' environmental performance problems and potentials than do regulators and social actors, unique, flexible permits require a high degree of expertise on the part of regulators and social actors who wish to assess (a) the appropriateness of permit conditions, and (b) the *comparative* performance of facilities with different permit requirements. Moreover, obtaining such permits requires more thought and work (and hence expense) *for facilities*, and they are therefore only worth their while if they result in substantial savings on compliance.

32. Such regulatory flexibility systems are common in some jurisdictions, such as Sweden and New Zealand (OECD 2000, pp. 36–37), small jurisdictions that do not need to regulate thousands of facilities. In addition, these jurisdictions still have na-

tional technology-based guidelines or regulations on which specific permits were based. In the United States, regulatory flexibility programs have met with only very limited success. Overly high transaction costs, a failure to overcome mutual mistrust, the lack of a statutory base, and a vague definition of "better" results have been identified as particular weaknesses. See, e.g., Edward Weber 1998, Steinzor 1996 and 1998, and Susskind and Seconda 1998. For a broader critique of environmental flexibility initiatives, see Davies and Mazurek 1996.

33. Bubble permits are of particular use in air pollution, because while wastewater is relatively easy to collect into a common stream for treatment (or a separate stream for recirculation back into the process), air emissions are difficult and expensive to collect and transport without leaks; thus each piece of equipment is often treated as a separate source.

34. See, e.g., National Academy of Public Administration 2000, which calls for an information-rich, flexible, and performance-driven strategy. See also Clarke 2001.

35. A recent study that examines the program over time suggests that community pressure, negative media attention, and increased likelihood of obtaining ISO–14000 certification are the major stimuli for improved environmental performance. However, the provision of increased environmental information to plant managers is also a significant factor, and the authors cite factory managers learning more about their own plants' pollution emissions and abatement opportunities as a key impetus for abatement (Afsah et al. 1997).

36. See further Gunningham and Sinclair 2002, ch. 8.

37. Kleindorfer and Orts 1996; Afsah et al. 1997; Hamilton 1993.

38. Day et al. 1997 found no significant abnormal returns for the forest products industry in the stock market for two events of environmental importance that they studied (the 1993 executive order stipulating that paper purchased by the government meet minimum stands of recycled content, and the 1987 announcement that pulp mills were a major source of dioxin in waterways and that trace amounts of dioxin could be found in most paper products).

39. The sign of the correlation is negative because the least ambitious management style was scored 7, while the most ambitious style was scored 1.

40. See analysis of GA1 in Chapter 3, p. 69.

41. "A 1992 survey of SEC registrants with the SEC found that 62 percent of respondents had not accrued known environment-related exposures on their financial statements. A 1996 study of environmental disclosure by companies involved in initial public offerings who were known CERCLA potentially responsible parties [i.e., might be responsible for hazardous waste cleanup] at one or more sites found a non-reporting rate of 54 percent, as compared to a non-reporting rate of 61 percent for currently registered companies. Additionally, a 1998 study conducted by the Office of

Enforcement and Compliance Assurance (OECA) on the disclosure of environmental legal proceedings, . . . for the years 1996 and 1997, found a non-reporting rate of 74 percent" (memorandum from Mary Kay Lunch, director of the Office of Planning and Policy Analysis, EPA, Jan. 19, 2001 [http://es.epa/gov/oeca/oppa/secguide.html]).

42. See Cerin and Dobers 2001.

43. For a brief period at the turn of the 1990s, companies exporting to environmentally sensitive European markets did pay considerable attention to these sensitivities, but as the premium price for TCF pulp dissipated, so too did the incentive for those companies to change their own technologies.

44. Greenwire [an environmental newswire], Oct. 18, 1996, ENVIROS, COUNTIES URGE FEDS TO BUY GREEN. It was not until February 1998 that the GSA announced that it would only sell recycled paper (Greenwire, Feb. 27, 1998, RECYCLING: FED AGENCY WILL PROVIDE RECYCLED PAPER ONLY). The Government Purchasing Project (GPP) notes on its website that "Executive Order 13101 was signed by Clinton in 1998 as a follow-up to Executive Order 12873 to strengthen 'buy-recycled' initiatives in the federal government. The new order eliminated the loopholes for availability and price, requiring copy and writing paper purchased to contain 30 percent post-consumer content when available, and mandating at least 20 percent post-consumer content in all purchases. . . . Compliance in federal agencies with buy-recycled laws has greatly improved over the years. For recycled copy paper, for example, compliance is up from a mere 12 percent in 1994 to 98 percent in 2000" (http://www.gpp.org/eo_13101.html; Sept. 12, 2002).

45. Gunningham and Grabosky 1998.

References

Afsah, S., A. Blackman, and D. Ratunanda. N.d. "How Do Public Disclosure Pollution Control Programs Work? Evidence from Indonesia." Resources for the Future: http://rff.org/CFDOCS/disc_papers/pdf_files/0044.pdf.

Afsah, S., B. Lapante, and D. Wheeler. 1997. "Regulation in the Information Age." NIPR working papers. World Bank.

Aldrich, Howard E. 1979. *Organizations and Environments*. Englewood Cliffs, N.J.: Prentice-Hall.

Allison, Robert W., and K. Sakai. 1992. "Australasian Mills Face Environmental Pressure to Cut Chlorinated Organics." *Pulp and Paper*, Nov. 1992. Ministry for the Environment, New Zealand: http://www.mfe.govt.nz/issues/waste/orgamo.htm at 23.07.01.

American Forest and Paper Association [AF&PA]. 2000. *Environmental, Health and Safety Principles Verification Program, Progress Report*.

Aoki, Kazumasu, and John Cioffi. 2000. "Poles Apart: Industrial Waste Management Regulation and Enforcement in the United States and Japan." In *Regulatory Encounters: Multinational Corporations and American Adversarial Legalism*, ed. Robert A. Kagan and Lee Axelrad. Berkeley: University of California Press.

Aoki, Kazumasu, Robert A. Kagan, and Lee Axelrad. 2000. "Industrial Effluent Control in the United States and Japan." In *Regulatory Encounters: Multinational Corporations and American Adversarial Legalism*, ed. Robert A. Kagan and Lee Axelrad. Berkeley: University of California Press.

Armstrong, Douglas A., Keith M. Bentley, Sergio F. Galeano, Robert J. Olszewski, Gail A. Smith, and Jonathon R. Smith Jr. 1998. "The Pulp and Paper Industry." In *The Ecology of Industry: Sectors and Linkages*, edited by Deanna J. Richards and Greg Pearson. Washington, D.C.: National Academy Press.

Arthur D. Little, Inc. 1995. "Hitting the Green Wall." Editorial by Rob Sheldon and Jonathon Shapley in *Perspectives*.

Ashford, Nicholas A. 2002. "Government and Environmental Innovation in Europe and North America." *American Behavioral Scientist* 45, 9: 1417–34.

Ashford, N., and G. Heaton. 1983. "Regulation and Technological Innovation in the Chemical Industry." *Law and Contemporary Problems* 46, 3 (Summer): 157.

Ayres, Ian, and John Braithwaite. 1992. *Responsive Regulation. Transcending the Deregulation Debate.* New York: Oxford University Press.

Ballian, J. 2000. "The Environmental Push Me-Pull-Me." *Safety Health Practitioner* 18, 3 (Mar.): 46–48.

Bardach, Eugene, and Robert A. Kagan. 1982. *Going by the Book: The Problem of Regulatory Unreasonableness.* A Twentieth Century Fund Study. Philadelphia: Temple University Press.

Baylis, Robert, Lianne Connell, and Andrew Flynn. 1998. "Sector Variation and Ecological Modernization: Towards An Analysis at the Level of the Firm." *Business Strategy and the Environment* 7: 150–61.

Becker, Gary. 1968. "Crime and Punishment: An Economic Approach." *Journal of Political Economy* 76, 2: 169–217.

Bernstein, Marver. 1955. *Regulating Business by Independent Commission.* Princeton, N.J.: Princeton University Press.

Berube, M., J. Nash, J. Maxwell, and J. Ehrenfeld. 1992. "From Pollution Control to Zero Discharge: How the Robbins Company Overcame the Obstacles." *Pollution Prevention Review,* Spring 1992: 189–207.

Bhat, Vasanthakuram. 1996. *The Green Corporation: The Next Competitive Advantage.* Westport, Conn.: Quorum Books.

Bowen, F. 2000. "Environmental Visibility: A Trigger of Green Organizational Response." *Business Strategy and Environment* 9: 92–107.

Box, George, E. P. Jenkins, M. Gwilym, and G. C. Reinsel. 1994. *Time Series Analysis: Forecasting and Control.* 3d ed. Englewood Cliffs, N.J.: Prentice-Hall.

Braithwaite, John. 1985. *To Punish or Persuade: Enforcement of Coal Mine Safety.* Albany: State University of New York Press.

———. 1989. *Crime, Shame, and Reintegration.* Cambridge: Cambridge University Press.

———. 1993. "The Nursing Home Industry." In *Beyond the Law: Crime in Complex Organizations,* ed. Michael Tonry and Albert J. Reiss, Jr. Chicago: University of Chicago Press.

Braithwaite, John, and Peter Drahos. 2000. *Global Business Regulation.* Cambridge: Cambridge University Press.

Braithwaite, John, and Toni Makkai. 1991. "Testing an Expected Utility Model of Corporate Deterrence." *Law and Society Review* 25: 7–40.

British Columbia. 1994. *BC's Pulp Mills: Effluent Status Report.* Victoria: Province of British Columbia, Ministry of Environment, Lands and Parks.

Burger, Thomas. 1976. *Max Weber's Theory of Concept Formation: History, Laws, and Ideal Types.* Durham, N.C.: Duke University Press.

Cashore, Benjamin, and Ilan Vertinsky. 2000. "Policy Networks and Firm Behaviours: Governance Systems and Firm Responses to External Demands for Sustainable Forest Management." *Policy Sciences* 33: 1–20.

Cebon, Peter. 1993. "The Myth of Best Practices: The Context Dependence of Two High-Performing Waste Reduction Programs." In *Environmental Strategies for Industry,* ed. K. Fischer and J. Schot. Washington, D.C.: Island Press.

Cerin, P., and P. Dobers. 2001. "What Does the Performance of the Dow Jones Sustainability Index Tell Us?" Working Paper, Dept. of Industrial Economics and Management, Royal Institute of Technology, Stockholm.

Chang, I. 1982. "Outliers in Time Series." Ph.D. diss., University of Wisconsin–Madison, Department of Statistics.

Chang, I., G. C. Tiao, and C. Chen. 1988. "Estimation of Time Series Parameters in the Presence of Outliers." *Technometrics* 30: 193–204.

Chen, C. M., M. C. Liu, M. L. Shih, S. C. Yu, C. C. Yeh, S. T. Lee, T. Y. Yang, and S. J. Hung. 2001. "Microsomal Monooxygenase Activity in Tilapia (*Oreochromis mossambicus*) Exposed to a Bleached Kraft Mill Effluent Using Different Exposure Systems." *Chemosphere* 45, 4–5: 581–88.

Chertow, Marian R., and Daniel C. Esty. 1997. *Thinking Ecologically: The Next Generation of Environmental Policy.* New Haven, Conn.: Yale University Press.

Clarke, D. P. 2001. "EPA in the Information Age." *Environmental Forum* 18, 3 (May–June): 22–34.

Coglianese, Cary. 1999. "Policy Implications of Environmental Management Systems." Paper prepared for the Research Summit on Environmental Management Systems sponsored by the U.S. Environmental Protection Agency, the Multi-State Working Group on Environmental Management Systems, and the National Academy of Public Administration, the Council of State Governments, and the Brookings Institution, Washington, D.C., Nov. 2–3, 1999.

Coglianese, Cary, and Jennifer Nash. 2001a. "Environmental Management Systems and the New Policy Agenda." In id., eds., *Regulating from the Inside: Can Environmental Management Systems Achieve Policy Goals?* Washington, D.C.: Resources for the Future.

———. 2001b. "Management-Based Environmental Policy: An Introduction." In id., eds., *Regulating from the Inside: Can Environmental Management Systems Achieve Policy Goals?* Washington, D.C.: Resources for the Future.

———, eds. 2001c. *Regulating from the Inside: Can Environmental Management Systems Achieve Policy Goals?* Washington, D.C.: Resources for the Future.

Cole, Robert E. 1994. "Differing Quality Paradigms and Their Implications for Organizational Learning." In *The Japanese Firm: Sources of Competitive Strength*, ed. Masahiko Aoki and Ronald S. Dore, pp. 66–83. Oxford: Clarendon Press.

Collins, L. 1994. "Environmental Performance and Technological Innovation: The Pulp and Paper Industry as a Case in Point." *Technology in Society* 16, 4: 427–46.

Cordiero, J., and J. Sarkis. 1997. "Environmental Proactivism and Firm Performance: Evidence from Security Analyst Earnings Forecasts." *Business Strategy and the Environment* 6, 2: 104–14.

Coyle, M. 2000. "Citizen Suits OK: High Court Reverses Shift Against Private Environmental Actions." *National Law Journal* 22, 22 (Jan. 24, 2000): A4.

Crow, Patrick. 1992. "Environmental Regulation Vise Squeezing U.S. Refiners." *Oil and Gas Journal* 90, 15: 21–26.

Daft, Richard. 1992. *Organization Theory and Design*. St. Paul, Minn.: West Publishing.

Dasgupta, Susmita, Hemamala Hettige, and David Wheeler. 1997. "What Improves Environmental Performance? Evidence from Mexican Industry." Working Paper 1877. Washington, D.C.: World Bank, Development Research Group.

Davies, J. C., and J. Mazurek. 1996. *Industry Incentives for Environmental Improvement: Evaluation of US Federal Initiatives*. Washington, D.C.: Global Environmental Management Initiative.

Davis, T., and Jay Mazurek. 1996. *Industry Incentives for Environmental Improvement: Evaluation of US Federal Initiatives*. Washington, D.C.: GEMI.

Day, Robert, Alexander Amati, and Brian Neubert. 1997. "The Financial Impact of Environmental Events and Issues in the Forest Products Industry." Report prepared for the Office of Policy Planning and Evaluation, U.S. EPA, Washington, D.C.

Delmas, Magali. 2001. "Stakeholders and Competitive Advantage: The Case of ISO 14001." *Production and Operations Management* 10, 3 (Fall): 343–58.

DiMaggio, Paul J. 1988. "Interest and Agency in Institutional Theory." In *Institutional Patterns and Organizations: Culture and Environment*, ed. Lynne G. Zucker, pp. 3–21. Cambridge, Mass.: Ballinger.

DiMaggio, Paul J., and Walter W. Powell. 1983. "The Iron Cage Revisited: Institutional Isomorphism and Collective Rationality in Organizational Fields." *American Sociological Review*, 48: 147–60.

Doering, B., et al. 1992. *Environmental Regulations and the Pulp and Paper Industry*. Ottawa: National Round Table on the Environment and Economy.

Dube, M. G., and D. L. MacLatchy. 2000. "Endocrine Responses of *Fundulus heteroclitus* to Effluent from a Bleached-Kraft Pulp Mill Before and After Installation of

Reverse Osmosis Treatment of a Waste Stream." *Environmental Toxicology and Chemistry* 19, 11: 2788–96.

Dwyer, John Richard Brooks, and Alan Marco. 2000. "The Air Pollution Permit Process for U.S. and German Automobile Assembly Plants." In *Regulatory Encounters: Multinational Corporations and American Adversarial Legalism*, ed. Robert A. Kagan and Lee Axelrad. Berkeley: University of California Press.

Eamer, R. J. 1998. "Creating Value in the Mature Paper Industry." *TAPPI Journal* 81, 9: 61.

Edelman, Murray. 1964. *The Symbolic Uses of Politics*. Urbana: University of Illinois Press.

Environment Canada. 1975. "Status Report on Abatement of Water Pollution from the Canadian Pulp and Paper Industry—1974." EPS 3-WP-75-6.

———. 1977. "Status Report on Abatement of Water Pollution from the Canadian Pulp and Paper Industry—1976." EPS 3-WP-77-9.

———. 1980. "Status Report on Abatement of Water Pollution from the Canadian Pulp and Paper Industry—1978." EPS 3-WP-80-4E.

———. 1982. "Status Report on Abatement of Water Pollution from the Canadian Pulp and Paper Industry—1980." EPS 3-WP-82-3.

———. 1984. "Status Report on Abatement of Water Pollution from the Canadian Pulp and Paper Industry—1982." EPS 1/PF/1.

Epstein, M., M. Palepup, and G. Krishna. 1999. "What Financial Analysts Want." *Strategic Finance* 80, 10 (Apr.): 48–52.

Epstein, Marc J. 1996. *Measuring Corporate Environmental Performance*. Chicago: Irwin Professional Publishing.

Epstein, Richard A. 1995. "The Permit Power Meets the Constitution." *Iowa Law Review* 81: 407–422.

Estrada, J., K. Tangen, and H. O. Bergeson. 1997. *Environmental Challenges Confronting the Oil Industry*. Colchester, U.K.: John Wiley.

Eto, Komyo. 2000. "Minamata Disease." *Neuropathology*, 20: S14–S19.

Fahey, P. 1992. "Advocacy Group Boycotting of Television Advertisers, and Its Effect on Programming Content." *University of Pennsylvania Law Review* 140: 647–709.

Fischer, Kurt, and Johan Schot, eds. 1993. *Environmental Strategies for Industry: International Perspectives on Research Needs and Policy Implications*. Washington D.C.: Island Press.

Fisse, B., and J. Braithwaite. 1983. *The Impact of Publicity on Corporate Offenders*. Buffalo: State University of New York Press.

Florida, Richard. 1999. "Adoption and Impacts of Environmental Management Systems." Prepared for the Research Summit on Environmental Management Systems sponsored by the U.S. Environmental Protection Agency, the Multi-State Working Group on Environmental Management Systems, the National Academy of Public Administration, and the Brookings Institution, Washington, D.C., Nov. 2–3, 1999.

Florida, Richard, and Derek Davison. 2001. "Why Do Firms Adopt Advanced Environmental Practices (and Do They Make a Difference)?" In *Regulating from the Inside: Can Environmental Management Systems Achieve Policy Goals?* ed. Cary Coglianese and Jennifer Nash. Washington, D.C.: Resources for the Future.

Florida, Richard, M. Atlas, and M. Cline. 1999. "What Makes Companies Green? Organizational Capabilities and the Adoption of Environmental Innovations" Prepared for the Association of American Geographers, 95th Annual Meeting, Hawaii, Mar. 24, 1999.

Foster, Sheila. 1998. "Justice from the Ground Up: Distributive Inequities, Grassroots Resistance, and the Transformative Politics of the Environmental Justice Movement." *California Law Review* 86: 775, 779–88, 793–802, 811–27.

Fowler, R. 1995. "International Environmental Standards for Transnational Corporations." *Environmental Law* 25: 1–30.

Friedman, M. 1991. "Consumer Boycotts: A Conceptual Framework and Research Agenda." *Journal of Social Issues* 47 (1): 149–168.

Fuchs, D. A., and D. A. Mazmanian. 1998. "The Greening of Industry: Needs of the Field." *Business Strategy and the Environment* 7: 193–203.

Fung, A., and D. O'Rourke. 2000. "Reinventing Environmental Regulation from the Grassroots Up: Explaining and Expanding the Success of the Toxics Release Inventory." *Environmental Management* 25, 2 (Feb.): 115–27.

Galbraith, Jay R. 1973. *Designing Complex Organizations.* Reading, Mass.: Addison-Wesley.

Gentry, Bradford S., and Lisa O. Fernandez. N.d. "Valuing the Environment: How Fortune 500 CFOs and Analysts Measure Corporate Performance." Yale Center for Environmental Law and Policy, Working Paper.

Ghobadian, A., H. Viney, J. Lui, and P. James. 1998. "Extending Linear Approaches to Mapping Corporate Environmental Behavior." *Business Strategy and the Environment* 7: 13–23.

Gifford, J., and P. McFarlane. 1990. "The Development of Environmental Control Legislation and Effluent Standards for Australasian Wood Processing Industries." Proceedings of the Third IAWPRC Symposium on Forest Industry Wastewaters, Tampere, Finland.

Gladwin, Thomas. 1993. "The Meaning of Greening: A Plea for Organizational Theory." In *Environmental Strategies for Industry,* ed. Kurt Fischer and Johan Schot. Washington, D.C.: Island Press.

Glaser, Barney G., and Anselm L. Strauss. 1967. *The Discovery of Grounded Theory: Strategies for Qualitative Research*. Chicago: Aldine.

Global Environment Management Initiative [GEMI]. See Davis and Mazurek 1996.

Gouldson, Andrew, and Joseph Murphy. 1998. *Regulatory Realities: The Implementation and Impact of Industrial Environmental Regulation*. London: Earthscan Publications.

Grabosky, Peter, and John Braithwaite. 1986. *Of Manners Gentle: Enforcement Strategies of Australian Business Regulatory Agencies*. Melbourne: Oxford University Press.

Gray, R., D. Walters, J. Bebbington, and I. Thompson. 1995. "The Greening of Enterprise: An Exploration of the (Non) Role of Environmental Accounting and Environmental Accountants in Organizational Change." *Critical Perspectives in Accounting* 6, 3: 211–39.

Gray, Wayne B., and Ronald J. Shadbegian. 1998. "Environmental Regulation, Investment Timing and Technology Choice." *Journal of Industrial Economics* 46, 2: 235–57.

Greening, D., and B. Gray. 1994. "Testing a Model of Organizational Response to Social and Political Issues." *Academy of Management Journal* 37, 3: 467–98.

Greeno, J. L. 1991. Environmental Excellence: Meeting the Challenge." Arthur D. Little, *Prism*, Third Quarter, 13–31.

Greenpeace. 1992. "Greenpeace Accused of Spreading Lies." *The Gazette* (Montreal), Jan 29, p. F1.

Gunningham, Neil. 1987. "Negotiated Non-Compliance: A Case Study of Regulatory Failure." *Law and Policy* 9: 69–87.

———. 1994. "Beyond Compliance: Management of Environmental Risk." In *Environmental Outlook: Law and Policy*, ed. B. Boer, R. Fowler, and N. Gunningham. Sydney: Federation Press.

Gunningham, Neil, and Darren Sinclair. 1999. "Environmental Management Systems, Regulation and the Pulp and Paper Industry: ISO 14001 in Practice." *Environmental and Planning Law Journal* (Australia) 16, 1: 5.

———. 2002. *Leaders and Laggards: Next-Generation Environmental Regulation*. Sheffield, U.K.: Greenleaf Publishing.

Gunningham, Neil, and Peter Grabosky. 1998. *Smart Regulation: Designing Environmental Policy*. New York: Oxford University Press.

Haagen-Smit, A. J. 1958. "Air Conservation." *Science* 128, 3329: 869–78.

Haines, Fiona. 1997. *Corporate Regulation: Beyond "Punish or Persuade."* Oxford: Clarendon Press.

Hajer, Maarten A. 1995. *The Politics of Environmental Discourse: Ecological Modernization and the Policy Process*. New York: Oxford University Press.

Hamilton, J. T. 1993. "Pollution as News: Media and Stock Market Reactions to the TRI Data." *Journal of Environmental Economics and Management* 27, 1: 38–48.

Hannan, Michael T., and John Freeman. 1977. "The Population Ecology of Organizations." *American Journal of Sociology* 82: 929–64.

———. 1984. "Structural Inertia and Organizational Change." *American Sociological Review* 49 (Apr.): 149–64.

Harper, M. C. 1984. "The Consumer's Emerging Right to Boycott: NAACP v. Claiborne Hardware and Its Implications for American Labor Law." *Yale Law Journal* 93, 3: 409–54.

Harrison, Kathryn. 1994. "Passing the Buck: Federalism and Canadian Environmental Policy." Ph.D. diss., Department of Political Science, University of British Columbia.

———. 1995. "Is Cooperation the Answer? Canadian Environmental Enforcement in Comparative Context." *Journal of Policy Analysis and Management* 14: 221–24.

———. 1996. "The Regulator's Dilemma: Regulation of Pulp Mill Effluents in a Federal State," *Canadian Journal of Political Science* 29: 469–96.

———. 1999a. "Environmental Regulation vs. Environmental Information: A View from Canada's National Pollutant Release Inventory." Paper presented at Annual Meeting of Association of Public Policy Analysis and Management, Washington D.C., November.

———. 1999b. "Racing to the Top of the Bottom? Industry Resistance to Eco-labelling of Paper Products in Three Jurisdictions." *Environmental Politics* 8, 4: 110–37.

———. 2002. "Ideas and Environmental Standard Setting: A Comparative Study of Regulation in the Pulp and Paper Industry." *Governance* 15, 1: 65–96.

Hartman, Raymond, Maimil Hug, and David Wheeler. 1997. *Why Paper Mills Clean Up: Determinants of Pollution Abatement in Four Asian Countries.* World Bank Policy Research Paper No. 1710. Washington, D.C.: World Bank.

Hass, J. L. 1996. "Environmental ('Green') Management Typologies: An Evaluation, Operationalization and Empirical Development." *Business Strategy and the Environment* 5: 59–68.

Henriques, I., and P. Sadorsky. 1996. "The Determinants of an Environmentally Responsive Firm: An Empiric Approach." *Journal of Environmental Economics and Management* 30, 3: 386–95.

Hillary, R. 2000. "The Eco-Management and Audit Scheme, ISO 14001 and the Smaller Firm." In *Small and Medium-Sized Enterprises and the Environment,* ed. id. Sheffield, U.K.: Greenleaf Publishing.

Hillmer, S. C., W. R. Bell, and G. C. Tiao. 1983. "Modeling Considerations in the Seasonal Adjustment of Economic Time Series." *Applied Time Series Analysis of Economic Data,* 74–100. Washington, D.C.: U.S. Bureau of the Census.

Himmelberger, James, and Halina Brown. 1995. "Global Corporate Environmentalism: Theoretical Expectations and Empirical Experience." *Business Strategy and the Environment* 4: 192–99.

Hirshhorn, Joel, and Kirsten Oldenburg. 1991. *Prosperity Without Pollution: The Prevention Strategy for Industry and Consumers.* New York: Van Nostrand Reinhold.

Hobbs, J. 2000. "Promoting Cleaner Production in Small and Medium-Sized Enterprises." In *Small and Medium-Sized Enterprises and the Environment,* ed. R. Hillary, p. 150. Sheffield, U.K.: Greenleaf Publishing.

Hoberg, George. 1993. "Environmental Policy: Alternative Styles." In *Governing Canada: State Institutions and Public Policy.* Toronto: HBJ-Holt.

———. 1999. "Sleeping with an Elephant: The American Influence on Canadian Environmental Regulation." In *A Reader in Environmental Law,* ed. B. Hutter, pp. 337–64. New York: Oxford University Press.

Hoffman, Andrew. 1997. *From Heresy to Dogma: An Institutional History of Corporate Environmentalism.* San Francisco: New Lexington Press.

Hunt, C. B., and E. R. Auster. 1990. "Proactive Environmental Management: Avoiding the Toxic Trap." *Sloan Management Review* 31: 7–18.

Joyce, S., and I. Thomson. N.d. "Earning a Social License to Operate: Social Acceptability and Resource Development in Latin America." Cited in *Mining Journal,* June 11, 1999.

Joyner, C. 1984. "The Transnational Boycott as Economic Coercion in International Law: Policy, Place and Practice." *Vanderbilt Journal of Transnational Law* 17, 2: 206–86.

Kagan, Robert A. 1993. "Regulatory Enforcement." In *Handbook of Regulation and Administrative Law,* ed. D. H. Rosenbloom and R. D. Schwartz. New York: Marcel Dekker.

———. 2000. "The Consequences of Adversarial Legalism." In *Regulatory Encounters: Multinational Corporations and American Adversarial Legalism,* ed. Robert A. Kagan and Lee Axelrad. Berkeley: University of California Press.

Kagan, Robert A., and John T. Scholz. 1984. "The Criminology of the Corporation and Regulatory Enforcement Styles." In *Enforcing Regulation,* ed. Keith Hawkins and John M. Thomas. Boston: Kluwer-Nijhoff.

Kagan, Robert A., and Lee Axelrad. 2000. *Regulatory Encounters: Multinational Corporations and Adversarial Legalism.* Berkeley: University of California Press.

Karels, A., and A. Oikari. 2000. "Effects of Pulp and Paper Mill Effluents on the Reproductive and Physiological Status of Perch (*Perca fluviatilis* L.) and Roach (*Ru-*

tilus rutilus L.) During the Spawning Period." *Annales Zoologici Fennici* 37, 2: 65–77.

Karels, A., E. Markkula, and A. Oikari. 2001. "Reproductive, Biochemical, Physiological, and Population Responses in Perch (*Perca fluviatilis* L.) and Roach (*Rutilus rutilus* L.) Downstream of Two Elemental Chlorine-free Pulp and Paper Mills," *Environmental Toxicology and Chemistry* 20, 7: 1517–27.

Karels, A., M. Soimasuo, and A. Oikari. 1999. "Effects of Pulp and Paper Mill Effluents on Reproduction, Bile Conjugates and Liver MFO (Mixed Function Oxygenase) Activity in Fish at Southern Lake Saimaa, Finland." *Water Science and Technology* 40, 11–12: 109–14.

Karkkainen, B. C. 2001. "Information as Environmental Regulation: TRI and Performance Benchmarking, Precursor to a New Paradigm." *Georgetown Law Journal* 89: 257.

Kelman, Steven. 1981. *Regulating America, Regulating Sweden: A Comparative Study of Occupational Safety and Health Policy.* Cambridge, Mass.: MIT Press.

Kenkeremath, Nandan. 1996. "Restoring Reason to Regulation: Applying Scientific Assessment and Cost-Benefit Analysis to Environmental Law." *American Industrial Hygiene Association Journal* 57, 9: 791–93.

Kleindorfer, P., and E. Orts. 1996. "Informational Regulation of Informational Risks." Wharton School, University of Pennsylvania Working Paper.

Knickerbocker, Brad. 1994. "Making Paper Safer for the Environment." *Christian Science Monitor,* Apr. 12.

Konar, Shameek, and Mark Cohen. 1997. "Information as Regulation: The Effect of Community Right-to-Know Laws on Toxic Emissions." *Journal of Environmental Economics and Management* 32: 109.

Kovacs, T. G., P. H. Martel, and R. H. Voss. 2002. "Assessing the Biological Status of Fish in a River Receiving Pulp and Paper Mill Effluents." *Environmental Pollution* 118, 1: 123–40.

KPMG. 1996. *Canadian Environmental Management Survey.* Toronto: KPMG.

Krause, Martine. 2000. "Licensing Biologics in Europe and the United States." In *Regulatory Encounters: Multinational Corporations and American Adversarial Legalism,* ed. Robert A. Kagan and Lee Axelrad, pp. 313–40. Berkeley: University of California Press.

Kubasek, N. 1996. "Following Canada's Lead: Preventing Prosecution for Environmental Crimes." *Business Horizons,* Sept.–Oct., pp. 64–70.

Landy, Marc, and Loren Cass. 1997. "U.S. Environmental Regulation in a More Competitive World." In *Comparative Disadvantages? Social Regulation and the Global Economy,* ed. P. Nivola. Washington, D.C: Brookings Institution.

Lanoie, P., B. Laplante, and M. Roy. 1997. "Can Capital Markets Create Incentives for Pollution Control?" World Bank Policy Research Department.

Larsson, D. G. J., and L. Forlin. 2002. "Male-Biased Sex Ratios of Fish Embryos Near a Pulp Mill: Temporary Recovery After a Short-Term Shutdown." *Environmental Health Perspectives* 110, 8: 739–42.

Magat, Wesley, and W. Kip Viscusi. 1990. "Effectiveness of the EPA's Regulatory Enforcement: The Case of Industrial Effluent Standards." *J. Law and Economics* 33: 331–60.

Mauser, A. 1996. "The Integration Process of Environmental Issues in Company Strategies." *Greening of Industry Conference Proceedings.* Heidelberg, 1996.

McCleary, Richard, and Richard A. Hay. 1980. *Applied Time Series Analysis for the Social Sciences,* Beverly Hills, Calif.: Sage Publications.

McClelland, John D., and John K. Horowitz. 1999. "The Cost of Water Pollution Regulation in the Pulp and Paper Industry." *Land Economics* 75, 2: 220–32.

McGinnis, J. M., and W. H. Foege. 1993. "Review: Actual Causes of Death in the United States." *Journal of the American Medical Association* 270, 18: 2207–12.

Mehta, Alex, and Keith Hawkins. 1998. "Integrated Pollution Control and Its Impact: Perspectives From Industry." *Journal of Environmental Law* 10: 61.

Meidinger, E. 2001. "Environmental Law for Global Civil Society: The Forest Certification Prototype." Paper prepared for Conference on Social and Political Dimensions of Forest Certification, University of Freiburg, Germany, June.

Meyer, John W., and W. Richard Scott, with the assistance of Brian Rowan and Terrence E. Deal. 1983. *Organizational Environments: Ritual and Rationality.* Beverly Hills, Calif.: Sage.

Meyer, John W., and Brian Rowan. 1977. "Institutionalized Organizations: Formal Structure as Myth and Ceremony." *American Journal of Sociology* 83: 340–63.

Mickwitz, Per, and Mikael Hildén. 2001. "The Role of Permit Systems for the Control of Point Source Pollution—Viewed Through the Results of a Multicriteria Evaluation." Paper presented at Evaluation 2001, the Sixth Annual Conference of the American Evaluation Association, St. Louis, November 9, 2001.

Miller, J. L., and A. B. Anderson. 1986. "Updating the Deterrence Doctrine." *Journal of Criminal Law and Criminology* 77: 418.

Mol, Arthur P. J. 1995. *The Refinement of Production: Ecological Modernization Theory and the Chemical Industry.* Utrecht: Van Arkel.

Moore, Walter. 1942. "Field Studies in the Oxygen Requirements of Certain Fresh-Water Fishes." *Ecology* 23, 3: 319-29.

Morag-Levine, Noga. 1994. "Between Choice and Sacrifice: Constructions of Community Consent in Reactive Air Pollution Regulation." *Law and Society Review* 28: 1035–77.

————. 1995. "Chasing the Wind: Reactive Law, Environmental Equity, and Local-ized Air Pollution Regulation" Ph.D. diss., University of California, Berkeley.

Munkittrick, K. R., M. E. McMaster, L. H. McCarthy, M. R. Servos, and G. J. Van Der Kraak. 1998. "An Overview of Recent Studies on the Potential of Pulp-Mill Effluents to Alter Reproductive Parameters in Fish." *Journal of Toxicology and Environmental Health–Part B–Critical Reviews* 1, 4: 347–71.

Murphy, J., and B. Thomas. 1999. "A Role to Play: The Role of Business in Community Development." *Community Quarterly*, no. 50 (Sept.): 5–14.

Nash, Jennifer. 2000. "Voluntary Codes of Practice: Non-Governmental Institutions for Promoting Environmental Management in Firms," National Academy of Sciences/National Research Council Workshop on Education, Information, and Voluntary Measures in Environmental Protection. Washington, D.C., November.

Nash, Jennifer, and John Ehrenfeld. 1999. "Environmental Management Systems and Their Roles in Environmental Policy." Paper prepared for the Research Summit on Environmental Management Systems sponsored by the U.S. Environmental Protection Agency, the Multi-State Working Group on Environmental Management Systems, and the National Academy of Public Administration, the Council of State Governments, and the Brookings Institution, Washington, D.C., Nov. 2–3.

————. 2001. "Factors That Shape EMS Outcomes in Firms." In *Regulating from the Inside: Can Environmental Management Systems Achieve Policy Goals?* ed. Cary Coglianese and Jennifer Nash. Washington, D.C.: Resources for the Future.

Nash, J., K. Nutt, J. Maxwell, and J. Ehrenfeld. 1992. "Polaroid's Environmental Accounting and Reporting System: Benefits and Limitations of a TQEM Tool." *Total Quality Environmental Management*, Aug., 3–15.

National Academy of Public Administration. 2000. *Environment.gov: Transforming Environmental Protection for the Twenty-First Century. A Report.* Washington, D.C.: National Academy of Public Administration.

Nehrt, Chad. 1998. "Maintainability of First Mover Advantages When Environmental Regulations Differ Between Countries." *Academy of Management Review* 23, 1: 77–97.

Newman, J. C. 1993. "Opportunity Knocks and Leaders Answer." *Directors and Boards*, Fall, 32–48.

New Zealand. 2000. Ministry for the Environment. Cabinet Paper on Proposal to Develop a National Environmental Standard to Regulate Dioxins from Industrial Facilities. http://www.mfe.govt.nz/issues/waste/orgamo.htm at 23.07.01.

Norberg-Bohm, Vicki, and Mark Rossi. 1998. "The Power of Incrementalism: Environmental Regulation and Technological Change in Pulp and Paper Bleaching in the US." *Technology Analysis. and Strategic Management* 10: 225–41.

O'Brien, David M. 1981. *The Public's Right to Know: The Supreme Court and the First Amendment*. New York: Praeger.

Organization for Economic Co-Operation and Development. 1999. Working Party on Pollution Prevention and Control. *Environmental Requirements for Industrial Permitting Case Study of the Pulp and Paper Sector Part One [ENV/EPOC/PPC (99)8/FINAL/PART 1]*. Paris: OECD.

———. 2000. Public Management Committee. *Reducing the Risk of Policy Failure: Challenges for Regulatory Compliance*. OECD Working Papers 3, no. 77. Paris: OECD.

Pargal, Sheoli, Hemamala Hettige, Manjula Singh, and David Wheeler. 1997. "Formal and Informal Regulation of Industrial Pollution: Comparative Evidence from Indonesia and the United States." Development Research Group working paper. Washington, D.C.: World Bank.

Parrott, J. L., M. R. van den Heuvel, L. M. Hewitt, M. A. Baker, and K. R. Munkittrick. 2000. "Isolation of MFO Inducers from Tissues of White Suckers Caged in Bleached Kraft Mill Effluent." *Chemosphere* 41, 7: 1083–89.

Pearson, T. H. 1972. "The Effect of Industrial Effluent from Pulp and Paper Mills on the Marine Benthic Environment." *Proceedings of the Royal Society of London, Series B, Biological Sciences* 180, 1061, *A Discussion on Freshwater and Estuarine Studies of the Effects of Industry* (Mar. 21), pp. 469–85.

Peters, Thomas J., and Nancy Austin. 1985. *A Passion for Excellence: The Leadership Difference*. New York: Random House.

Pfeffer, Jeffrey, and Salancik, Gerald R. 1978. *The External Control of Organizations*. New York: Harper & Row.

Porter, Michael. 1988. "How Competitive Forces Shape Strategy." In James Brian Quinn, Henry Mintzberg, and Robert M. James, *The Strategy Process: Concepts, Contexts, and Cases*. Englewood Cliffs, N.J.: Prentice-Hall.

———. 1991. "America's Green Strategy." *Scientific American* 264 (Apr.).

Porter, Michael, and Claas van der Linde. 1995a. "Green and Competitive: Ending the Stalemate." *Harvard Business Review*, Sept.–Oct., 120–34.

———. 1995b. "Toward a New Conception of the Environment-Competitiveness Relationship." *Journal of Economic Perspectives* 9, 4: 119–32.

Powell, Walter W., and Paul DiMaggio, eds. 1991. *The New Institutionalism in Organizational Analysis*, Chicago: University of Chicago Press.

Prakash, Asseem. 2000. *Greening the Firm: The Politics of Corporate Environmentalism*. Cambridge: Cambridge University Press.

Raizada, R. 1998. "Corporate Responses to Government and Environmental Group Actions Designed to Protect the Environment." Ph.D. diss., University of British Columbia.

Rappaport, A., and M. Flaherty. 1991. "Multinational Corporations and the Environment: A Survey of Global Practice." Medford, Mass.: Center for Environmental Management, Tufts University.

Regens, James L., Barry J. Seldon, and Euel Elliott. 1997. "Modeling Compliance to Environmental Regulation: Evidence from Manufacturing Industries." *Journal of Policy Modeling* 19, 6: 683–96.

Reinhardt, Forest L. 2000. *Down to Earth: Applying Business Principles to Environmental Management.* Boston: Harvard Business School Press.

Rest, Kathleen M., and Nicholas Ashford. 1988. "Regulation and Technological Options: The Case of the Occupational Exposure to Formaldehyde." *Harvard Journal of Law and Technology* 1: 63.

Rhone, G. 1996. *Canadian Standards Association Sustainable Forest Management Certification System.* Ottawa: Industry Canada.

Roome, N. 1992. "Developing Environmental Management Strategies," *Business Strategy and the Environment* 1, pt. 1: 11–23.

Russo, Michael V., and Paul A. Fouts. 1997. "A Resource-Based Perspective on Corporate Environmental Performance and Profitability." *Academy of Management Journal* 40, 3: 534–59.

Sabatier, Paul, and Daniel Mazmanian. 1983. *Can Regulation Work? The Implementation of the 1972 California Coastline Initiative.* New York: Plenum Press.

Sanchez, Carol M. 1997. "Environmental Regulation and Firm-Level Innovation: The Moderating Effects of Organizational and Individual-level Variables." *Business and Society* 36, 2 (June): 140–68.

Schaefer A., and B. Harvey. 1988. "Stage Models of Corporate 'Greening': A Critical Evaluation." *Business Strategy and the Environment* 7, 109–23.

Schein, Edgar H. 1985. *Organizational Culture and Leadership.* San Franciso: Jossey-Bass Publishers. 2d ed., 1992.

Schmidheiny, Stephan. 1992. *Changing Course: A Global Business Perspective on Development and the Environment.* Cambridge, Mass.: MIT Press.

Schmidheiny, Stephan, and Federico Zorraquín. 1996. *Financing Change: The Financial Community, Eco-Efficiency, and Sustainable Development.* Cambridge, Mass.: MIT Press.

Scholz, John T. 1984. "Cooperation, Deterrence and the Ecology of Regulatory Enforcement." *Law and Society Review* 18: 601.

Scruggs, Lyle A. 1999. "Institutions and Environmental Performance in Seventeen Western Democracies." *British Journal of Political Science* 29.

Seegert, G., D. Brown, and E. Clem. 1997. "Improvements in the Pigeon River Following Modernization of the Champion International Canton Mill." In *Biological Sciences Symposium Proceedings.* Atlanta, Ga.: TAPPI Press.

Shrivastava, P., and H. Scott. 1992. "Corporate Self-Greenewal: Strategic Responses to Environmentalism." *Business Strategy and Environment* 1, 3.

Sibley, P. K., D. G. Dixon, and D. R. Barton. 2001. "Impact of Bleached Kraft Pulp Mill Effluent on the Nearshore Benthic Community of Jackfish Bay, Lake Superior." *Water Quality Research Journal of Canada* 36, 4: 815–33.

Smart, B., ed. 1992. *Beyond Compliance: A New Industry View of the Environment.* Washington, D.C.: World Resources Institute.

Smith, Maureen. 1997. *The U.S. Paper Industry and Sustainable Production: An Argument for Restructuring.* Cambridge, Mass.: MIT Press.

Smith, N. Craig. 1990. *Morality and the Market: Consumer Pressure for Corporate Accountability.* New York: Routledge.

Sonnenfeld, David A. 1996. "The Ghost of Wesley Vale: Environmentalists' Influence on Innovation Within Australia's Pulp and Paper Industry." *Competition and Change* 1: 379–401.

———. 2000. "Social Movements and Ecological Modernization: The Transformation of Pulp and Paper Manufacturing." Working Paper # 00–6. Berkeley: University of California, Berkeley, Workshop on Environmental Politics.

———. 2002. "Social Movements and Ecological Modernization: The Transformation of Pulp and Paper Manufacturing." *Development and Change* 33: 1–27.

Stanbury, W. T. 1993. *Regulating Water Pollution by the Pulp and Paper Industry in Canada.* Vancouver: University of British Columbia.

Stanley, Elaine. 1999. "Available Environmental Data for Deterrence Research." Presentation by EPA Office of Compliance at Forum on Deterrence of Environmental Violations and Environmental Crimes, National Institute of Justice, Washington, D.C., July 12.

Steger, U. 1993. "How German Companies Are Dealing with Environmental Issues." Chapter 5 in *Environmental Strategies for Industry: International Perspectives on Research Needs and Policy Implications,* ed. Kurt Fischer and Johan Schot. Washington, D.C.: Island Press.

Steinzor, Rena I. 1996. "Regulating Reinvention and Project XL: Does the Emperor Have Any Clothes?" *Environmental Law Reporter: News and Analysis* 26: 10527–28.

———. 1998. "Reinventing Environmental Regulation: The Dangerous Journey from Command to Self-Control." *Harvard Environmental Law Review* 22, 103: 202.

Stewart, Richard B. 2001. "A New Generation of Environmental Regulation." *Capital University Law Review* 29: 21–182.

Stigler, George. 1970. "The Optimum Enforcement of Laws." *Journal of Political Economy* 78: 526.

Suchman, Mark, and Lauren Edelman. 1996. "Legal Rational Myths: The New Institutionalism and the Law and Society Tradition." *Law and Social Inquiry* 21, 4: 903–40.

Sunstein, Cass R. 1991. "Administrative Substance." *Duke Law Journal* 1991: 607–35.

Susskind, Lawrence, and Josua Seconda. 1998. "The Risks and Advantages of Agency Discretion: Evidence from the EPA's Project XL." *UCLA Journal of Environmental Law and Policy* 17: 67–116.

Thompson, Andrew R. 1980. *Environmental Regulation in Canada: An Assessment of the Process.* Vancouver: Westwater Research Center.

Thompson, K. M., and J. D. Graham. 1997. "Producing Paper Without Dioxin Pollution." Chapter 7 in *The Greening of Industry: A Risk Management Approach,* ed. John D. Graham and Jennifer K. Hartwell. Cambridge, Mass.: Harvard University Press.

Thornton, Dorothy. 2001. "The Effect of Management on the Machinery of Environmental Performance." Ph.D. diss., Health Service and Policy Analysis, University of California, Berkeley.

Thurman, David S. 1973. *The Right of Access to Information from the Government.* New York: Oceana Publications.

Tolbert, Pamela S., and Lynne G. Zucker. 1983. "Institutional Sources of Change in the Formal Structure of Organizations: The Diffusion of Civil Service Reform, 1880–1935." *Administrative Science Quarterly* 28: 22–39.

Tsai, S. H. T., and J. Child. 1997. "Strategic Responses of Multinational Corporations to Environmental Demands." *Journal of General Management* 23: 1.

University of North Carolina at Chapel Hill and the Environmental Law Institute. 2000. *Second Public Report on the National EMS Database. National Database on Environmental Systems: The Effects of Environmental Management Systems on the Environmental and Economic Performance of Facilities.* Chapel Hill: University of North Carolina and Environmental Law Institute.

U.S. Congress. Office of Technology Assessment. 1995. *Environmental Policy Tools: A User's Guide.* Washington, D.C.: Office of Technology Assessment.

U.S. Council on Environmental Quality. 1970. *Environmental Quality: The First Annual Report of the Council on Environmental Quality Together with the President's Message to Congress, Transmitted to the Congress, August 1970.* Washington, D.C.: GPO.

———. 1995. *Environmental Quality: 25th Anniversary Report of the Council on Environmental Quality.* Washington D.C.: GPO.

U.S. Dept. of Health and Human Services. CDC [Centers for Disease Control]. 2001. *Morbidity and Mortality Weekly Report* [MMWR] 50, no. 22 (June 8, 2001). Cited as CDC 2001.

U.S. EPA [Environmental Protection Agency]. 1992. *Water Quality Report to Congress: Executive Summary.* http://www.epa.gov/305b.

————. 1995. *Profile of the Pulp and Paper Industry.* Washington, D.C.

————. 2000. *US EPA Performance Track.* http://www.epa.gov/performancetrack/index_bkup71201.htm.

U.S. National Research Council. 1996. Committee on Inland Aquatic Ecosystems. Water Science and Technology Board. Commission on Geosciences, Environment, and Resources. *Freshwater Ecosystems: Revitalizing Educational Programs in Limnology.* Washington, D.C.: National Academy Press.

Verweij, Marco. 2000. "Why Is the River Rhine Cleaner Than the Great Lakes (Despite Looser Regulation)?" *Law and Society Review* 34: 1007.

Victor, Peter A., and Terrence N. Burrell. 1981. *Environmental Protection Regulation: Water Pollution and the Pulp and Paper Industry.* Ottowa: Economic Council of Canada.

Vogel, David. 1986. *National Styles of Regulation: Environmental Policy in Great Britain and the United States.* Ithaca, N.Y.: Cornell University Press.

————. 1995. *Trading Up: Consumer and Environmental Regulation in a Global Economy.* Cambridge, Mass.: Harvard University Press.

Wagner, Wendy E. 2000. "Symposium: Innovations in Environmental Policy: The Triumph of Technology-Based Standards." *University of Illinois Law Review* 2000: 83–113.

Walley, N., and B. Whitehead. 1994. "It's Not Easy Being Green." *Harvard Business Review* 72, 3: 6–52.

Walsh, Mary Williams. 1992. "Canadian Mill's Quandary: Can It Make Money on Pollution-Free Paper?" *Los Angeles Times*, Mar. 8, p. D–3.

Weber, Edward. 1998. *Pluralism by the Rules: Conflict and Cooperation in Environmental Regulation.* Washington, D.C.: Georgetown University Press.

Weber, Max. 1968 [1922]. *Gesammelte Aufsätze zur Wissenschaftslehre.* 3d ed. Tübingen: Mohr.

Weick, Karl E. 1976. "Educational Organizations as Loosely Coupled System." *Administrative Science Quarterly* 21: 1–19.

Whittington, R. 1993. *What is Strategy—And Does It Matter?* London: Routledge.

Wilson, Graham. 1985. *The Politics of Safety and Health.* Oxford: Clarendon Press.

Winsemius, P., and U. Guntram. 1992. "The Environmental Challenge." *Business Horizon*, Mar./Apr., p. 12.

Wisconsin Department of Natural Resources. 2000. *Wisconsin's Green Tier Regulatory Proposal.* http://www.dnr.state.wi.us/org/caer/cea/green-tier/factsheets/concept.htm.

Wokutch, Richard E. 1992. *Worker Protection, Japanese Style: Occupational Safety and Health in the Auto Industry.* Ithaca, N.Y.: ILR Press.

Wokutch, Richard E., and Craig V. Vansandt. 2000. "National Styles of Worker Protection in the United States and Japan: The Case of the Automotive Industry." *Law and Policy* 22: 369–84.

Yosie, T., and T. Herbst. 1997. *The Journey towards Corporate Environmental Excellence: Integrating Business Methods with Environmental Management.* Center for Strategic and International Studies, http://www/csis.org/e4e/yosiepg.html.

Young, J. 1993. "Louisiana-Pacific's Samoa Mill Establishes TCF Pulp Production." *Pulp and Paper* 67: 61–63.

Zucker, Lynne G. 1983. "Organizations as Institutions." In *Research in the Sociology of Organizations*, ed. Samuel B. Bacharach, 2: 1–47. Greenwich, Conn.: JAI Press.

Index

In this index an "f" after a number indicates a separate reference on the next page, and an "ff" indicates separate references on the next two pages. A continuous discussion over two or more pages is indicated by a span of page numbers, e.g., "57–59." *Passim* is used for a cluster of references in close but not consecutive sequence.